D1591872

The Italian
Cookbook

First published by Lorenz Books in 2001

© Anness Publishing Limited 2001

Lorenz Books is an imprint of Anness Publishing Limited
Hermes House, 88–89 Blackfriars Road, London SE1 8HA

Published in the USA by Lorenz Books, Anness Publishing Inc.
27 West 20th Street, New York, NY 10011

www.lorenzbooks.com

All rights reserved. No part of this publication may be reproduced, stored in a
retrieval system, or transmitted in any way or by any means, electronic, mechani-
cal, photocopying, recording or otherwise, without the prior written permission of
the copyright holder.

A CIP catalogue record for this book is available from the British Library.

Publisher: Joanna Lorenz
Managing Editor: Linda Fraser
Editor: Susannah Blake
Jacket and Text Design: Chloë Steers
Typesetting: Jonathan Harley
Illustrations: Angela Wood
Recipes: Alex Barker, Angela Boggiano, Carla Capalbo,
Joanna Farrow, Shirley Gill, Christine Ingram, Sara Lewis,
Jennie Shapter, Kate Whiteman, Jeni Wright

1 3 5 7 9 10 8 6 4 2

NOTES

Bracketed terms are intended for American readers.

For all recipes, quantities are given in both metric and imperial measures and,
where appropriate, measures are also given in standard cups and spoons. Follow
one set, but not a mixture, because they are not interchangeable.

Standard spoon and cup measures are level.
1 tsp = 5ml, 1 tbsp = 15ml, 1 cup = 250ml/8fl oz

Australian standard tablespoons are 20ml. Australian readers should use 3 tsp in
place of 1 tbsp for measuring small quantities of gelatine, flour, salt, etc.

Medium (US large) eggs are used unless otherwise stated.

Contents

INTRODUCTION

U ntil Italy was unified in 1861, each region produced its own characteristic cuisine, relying exclusively on ingredients that could be gathered, cultivated or reared locally. Nowadays, although regional produce can be very easily transported, Italians still prefer to base their cooking on local ingredients, because they regard quality and freshness as more important than diversity and innovation. As a result, the most flavoursome sun-ripened tomatoes, aubergines (eggplant) and (bell) peppers are still found in the south; the freshest fish and shellfish can be found along the coast; and the finest hams come from the area where the pigs are raised. Italian cooking remains distinctly regional. For example, in the dairy-farming north butter is used in place of the olive oil so prevalent in the south; bread and polenta are eaten instead of pasta. The only unifying feature is the insistence on high quality ingredients.

Good food has always been essential to the Italian way of life. The Italian cooking culture is one of the oldest in the world, dating back to the ancient Greeks. The Romans adored good food and often ate and drank to excess. The early Romans were peasant farmers who ate only the simple, rustic foods they could produce, such as grain, cheeses and olives. For them, meat was an unheard-of luxury; animals were bred to work in the fields and were too precious to eat. Trading links with other parts of the world encouraged Roman farmers to cultivate new vegetables and fruits and, of course, vines, while their trade in salt and exotic spices enabled them to preserve and pickle meat, game and fish. Food became a near obsession and ever more elaborate dishes were devised to be served at the decadent banquets for which the Romans were famed. The decline and fall of the Roman Empire led inevitably to a return to simple, basic foods.

For centuries, regional cuisine reverted to its original uncomplicated style. With the Renaissance, however, came great wealth and a new interest in elaborate food and once again rich families strove to outdo each other with lavish banquets. The poor continued to subsist on simple foods, but the wealthier middle classes developed a taste for fine foods and created their own bourgeois dishes. The finer features of Italian cooking even reached the French, when Catherine de Medici went to Paris to marry the future Henri II, taking 50 of her own cooks with her. They introduced new ingredients and cooking techniques to France and in return learnt the art of French cuisine. In those regions of Italy that border France, you can still find reciprocal influences of French classical cooking, but generally speaking Italians do not like elaborately sauced dishes, preferring the natural flavours of their raw ingredients.

The essence of Italian cooking today is simplicity. The Italian way of cooking fish is a good example of this. In coastal areas, freshly caught fish is most often simply chargrilled over hot coals, then served with nothing more than a splash of extra virgin olive oil, a wedge of lemon and freshly ground black pepper. Recipes such as Tuna Carpaccio, in which the fish is so delicious raw that cooking seems unnecessary, and Grilled Salmon with Fennel, where the delicate flavour of fennel is used to complement rather than obscure the fresh taste of the fish, are typically simple, as is squid chargrilled with chillies.

Italians learn to appreciate good food when they are young children, and eating is one of the major pleasures of the day. Witness an Italian family gathered around for Sunday lunch in a local restaurant, and consider how the Italian menu of antipasti followed by pasta, rice or gnocchi, then fish, meat and vegetables served in sequence is devised so that each can be savoured separately – both the food and the occasion are to be enjoyed as long as possible. The first course, or antipasti, is a unique feature. In restaurants, this can be a vast array of different dishes, both hot and cold, from which diners can choose as few or as many as they wish. At home with the family, it is more likely to be a slice or two of salami or prosciutto, with fresh figs or melon if these are in season.

The variety of Italian ingredients available in supermarkets and delicatessens provide the perfect inspiration for any number of delicious meals, from a simple dish of pasta to a full-blown four-course dinner. A plate of antipasti followed by pasta or risotto flavoured with seasonal ingredients, then simply cooked meat or fish, and finally a local cheese and fruit, make a veritable feast. You could prepare a different meal along these lines every day of the year and almost never repeat the same combination.

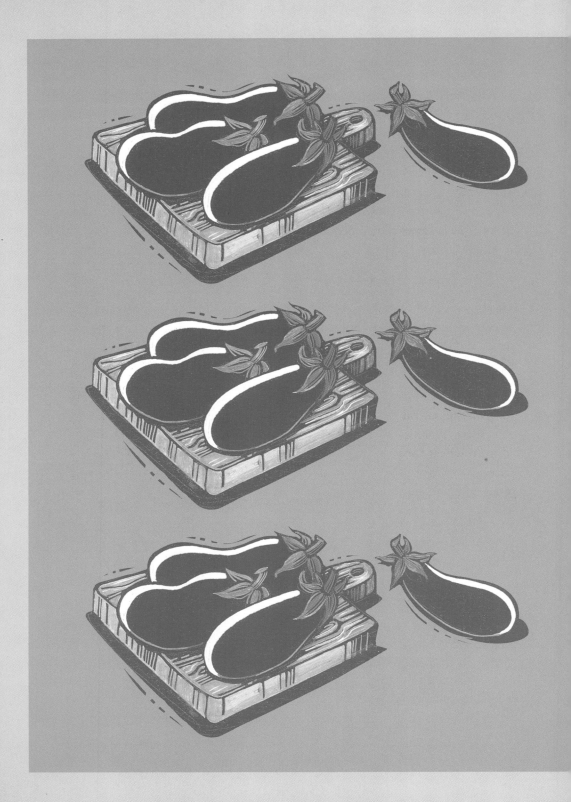

THE ITALIAN KITCHEN

Italian cooking relies on the rich supply of wonderful local ingredients for its delicious freshness and flavour. In the south this means plump, sun-ripened tomatoes and peppers, colourful vegetables and the freshest of fish; the central plains produce succulent peaches, figs and nuts; and, in the north, there is excellent meat and plenty of game. The south produces durum wheat for pasta and the very best olive oil; while the north grows rice for risotto and maize for polenta, and makes good use of butter and cream in its traditional dishes.

PASTA

This wonderfully simple and nutritious staple, which can be fresh or dried, sums up the essence of Italian cooking. In Italy, pasta is an essential part of every full meal and does not constitute a meal on its own. *Il primo*, as the pasta course is known, is eaten between the appetizer and the main course. Sometimes small pasta shapes, known as *pastina*, are served in soup.

The argument about the origins of pasta are not clear. The Chinese claim that they were the first to discover the art of noodle-making and that pasta was brought to Italy by Marco Polo. The Italians, of course, claim it as their own invention and historians believe that the Romans used to eat pasta. The popularity of pasta really spread in the 14th century, when bakeries in southern Italy started to sell it as an alternative to bread.

Pasta became the traditional first course of the south, although in the poorest areas it constituted a full meal. Its popularity filtered up to the north of Italy and by the 19th century huge factories had been set up to mass-produce pasta, which became an integral part of Italian cooking.

Nowadays, dried pasta is usually factory-made. The dough is made from hard durum wheat, which produces an elastic dough that is ideal for shaping into hundreds of different forms, from long, thin spaghetti to elaborate spirals and bow-shaped farfalle. Basic pasta dough is made only from durum wheat and water, although it is sometimes enriched with eggs to make *pasta all'uovo*, which has an attractive yellow tinge, or coloured and flavoured with ingredients such as spinach or squid ink to make *pasta verdi* and *pasta nera*. These traditional flavourings are generally more successful than gimmicky modern creations, such as chocolate flavoured pasta. Dried pasta has a nutty flavour and should retain a good firm texture when cooked. It is generally served with thinner-textured, robust sauces.

Fresh pasta is usually made by hand, using superfine plain (all-purpose) white flour enriched with eggs. Unlike dried pasta dough, it can be easily kneaded and is very malleable. Fresh pasta is often filled with meat, fish, vegetables or cheese to make ravioli, tortelli or cappelletti, or layered with meat or vegetables and creamy bechamel sauce to make lasagne.

Commercially made fresh pasta is made with durum wheat, water and eggs. The dough is harder than that used for hand-made pasta, but it can be easily kneaded by machine. The flavour and texture of all fresh pasta is very delicate, so it is best suited to more creamy sauces.

Buying and Storing

Always buy dried pasta made from Italian durum wheat. Even after the packet has been opened, dried pasta can be stored almost indefinitely in an airtight container. Hand-made fresh pasta will keep only for a couple of days, but it freezes well. Machine-made fresh pasta is pasteurized and vacuum-packed, so it can be stored in the refrigerator for up to two weeks and can be frozen for up to six months. When buying coloured and flavoured pasta, such as *pasta verdi*, make sure that it has been made with natural ingredients.

Pasta Varieties

The shape of pasta can be divided roughly into four categories: long, flat, short and filled. The best-known long strand pasta is spaghetti, which takes its name from the word *spago*, meaning string. Spaghetti originated in Naples and was the first pasta to be sold in supermarkets outside Italy. It is still very popular, but today other varieties are also readily available: spaghettini is a slightly thinner version, and linguine is flatter. Bucatini are thicker and hollow. The thinnest pasta strands are vermicelli, which are made from plain and egg varieties and go well with light sauces, particularly the tomato and seafood sauces for which Naples is famous, and capelli d'angelo, meaning angel's hair, which is a very fine pasta that is used in broths and soups, and is often popular with children.

Spaghetti also comes in different types, lengths, flavours and colours, including whole-wheat, spinach and chilli.

The other type of long pasta is the wider ribbon pasta. The most common is tagliatelli, which takes its name from *tagliare* (to cut). Tagliatelli originated in Bologna and is made both with and without egg, and sometimes with spinach. Dried tagliatelli is usually sold folded into nests, which unravel during cooking. A mixture of white and green noodles is known as paglia e fieno (straw and hay). Tagliatelli is usually about 1 cm/1/2 in wide, but there are finer versions called tagliatellina, tagliarini and tagliolini.

Pappardelle are the widest ribbon pasta and are often served with hare sauce. Fettucine is the thinner, Roman version of tagliatelli. Trenette are from Liguria and are traditionally served with pesto sauce.

In Italy, flat fresh pasta is often called maccheroni – not to be confused with the short tubes. One of the most familiar varieties is lasagne, which comes in sheets designed to be baked between layers of sauce in the oven. Dried lasagne is sold flat-packed in boxes, and there are three main types: plain, spinach and whole-wheat. The shape varies from narrow rectangles to squares, and the sheets may be flat or wavy.

Cannelloni are large, fat tubes rolled around a filling. In Italy, they are traditionally made from sheets of fresh lasagne, but ready-made dried tubes are more convenient and easier to use.

As for short pasta shapes, the list is almost endless. They tend to have wonderfully descriptive names, such as, orecchiette (little ears), penne (quills) and cappellacci, (little hats). New varieties are constantly coming on the market and they come in a wide range of different colours and flavours. Red, white and green pasta shapes are often packed together and labelled tricolore.

There are many types of filled pasta, the only difference being their shape and size. Ravioli are square, tortelli are usually round, while tortellini are ring-shaped. Fillings include meat, pumpkin, ricotta and spinach, seafood, chicken and rabbit.

Choosing Pasta Sauces

The variety and range of sauces that can be served with pasta are seemingly endless. They vary from minimalist sauces, such as garlic and olive oil, to light vegetable sauces shellfish sauces, robust meat sauces, and rich and creamy sauces containing eggs, cheese and nuts.

When choosing the appropriate pasta shape for a sauce, there are no hard and fast rules. Some regional dishes are always made with the same pasta shape, such as fettucine all'Alfredo, tagliatelle Bolognese and penne all'arrabbiata, and it is rare to see them served with anything other than the named pasta. These classic dishes are few and far between however and, with the increasing number of different pasta shapes on the market it can sometimes be difficult to know which shapes and which sauces will go well together.

Long, thin pasta is best served with either a thin, clinging sauce, or one that is smooth and thick. If too thin and watery, the sauce will simply run off the long strands; if too chunky or heavy, it will fall to the bottom of the bowl, leaving the pasta at the top. Clinging sauces made with olive oil, butter, cream, eggs, finely grated cheese and chopped fresh herbs are good with long pasta. When ingredients such as vegetables, fish and meat are added to a smooth thick sauce, they should be very finely chopped.

Short pasta shapes with wide openings, such as conchiglie, penne and rigatoni, will trap meaty or spicy sauces, as will spirals and curls. Egg pasta has different properties from plain pasta and goes especially well with the rich creamy and meaty sauces that are popular in northern Italy. Fresh home-made egg pasta absorbs butter and cream and makes the sauce stick to it. Almost any pasta is suitable for the classic Italian tomato sauce.

Cooking and Serving Pasta

Properly cooked pasta should be al dente, meaning firm to the tooth. Accurate timing is essential: always go by the time given on the packet or, with fresh home-made pasta, by the time given in the recipe. As a general guide, very thin fresh noodles will take 2–3 minutes; thicker noodles and pasta shapes 3–4 minutes; stuffed fresh pasta 5–7 minutes; and dried pasta will vary from 8–20 minutes.

Before starting to cook, check the recipe to see whether the pasta or the sauce needs the longest cooking time. A sauce can often be made ahead of time and reheated, but the timing of the pasta is crucial. Allow 75–115g/3–4 oz of pasta per person.

1 Bring a large pan of water to the boil. Add a teaspoon of salt, then the pasta. Return to the boil and start timing. Reduce the heat and simmer over a medium to high heat for the required cooking time.

2 Do not break up long pasta strands. Stand them in the pan: as they heat they will become pliable and slip into the water. Stir frequently during cooking with a wooden fork or spoon.

3 When the pasta is cooked, drain well. Shake and stir with a wooden fork or spoon so that any trapped water can drain out. Tip the pasta into a warmed serving dish. Stir in the sauce, or serve separately, according to the recipe.

Gnocchi

These mouthwatering little dumplings fall into a slightly different category from pasta. They are made with a variety of ingredients, including semolina, polenta, potatoes or a mixture of potato and flour. They may be shaped like elongated shells, ovals, cylinders or flat discs. However they are made, gnocchi should always be extremely light and almost melt in the mouth.

In the past, gnocchi and pasta were made from the same mixture of durum wheat and water. In some parts of Italy, this original flour and water dough is still used.

Traditional Mantuan gnocchi, which date back to the 15th or 16th century, are made from pumpkin. The pumpkin gives them a pretty golden colour, and they are served simply with a little butter and grated cheese.

Today, gnocchi are mostly made of potato flour, but there are several regional variations. In Rome they are made from a boiled potato and egg mixture and cut into flat rounds. In Sicily they are made from a simple flour and water dough, and are pressed against a textured surface.

Culinary Uses

Gnocchi can be served like pasta, either as a first course, in clear soup or broth, or occasionally as an accompaniment to the main course. Almost any pasta sauce can be served with gnocchi; they are good with a creamy Gorgonzola sauce or fresh tomato sauce, or can be served simply, drizzled with a little olive oil and sprinkled with freshly grated Parmesan.

Buying and Storing

Gnocchi are sold either in vacuum-sealed packages in shops and supermarkets, or loose on delicatessen counters. These shop-bought gnocchi are usually cylindrical with a ridged surface, as though rolled with the tines of a fork. They tend to be very filling, so a fairly small portion is enough for a first course; allow about 115g/4oz per serving.

Ready-made gnocchi can be stored in a plastic bag in the refrigerator for 2–3 days. Home-made gnocchi dough will also keep for a couple of days before cooking.

COOKING GNOCCHI

Gnocchi are usually poached in lightly salted, barely simmering water. However, exceptions, such as gnocchi alla romana, are baked in the oven.

1 Drop the gnocchi into a large pan of salted boiling water in batches and cook for 2–3 minutes; when they rise to the surface, they are done.

2 Scoop out the cooked gnocchi with a slotted spoon and transfer to a plate: keep them warm while you cook the rest.

3 Drizzle the gnocchi with olive oil or pour the sauce of your choice over the gnocchi and serve immediately.

RICE, GRAINS & PULSES

Almost as important as pasta in Italian cooking are rice, polenta and pulses, which all appear as first courses in various guises. Italy has always relied heavily on these protein-rich ingredients when luxuries like meat were in short supply, and a host of delicious recipes were developed using these modest foods – from rich and creamy risottos to wholesome bean salads.

RICE

The Saracens introduced rice to Italy in the 11th century, but it only became popular in the 16th century, when it began to be cultivated on a large scale in the Po Valley. Traditionally, rice has played a much greater part in the cooking of northern Italy than in the south, particularly in the Veneto.

Today, Italy produces a huge quantity and variety of rice. Most is still grown in the Po Valley in Piedmont, where conditions are perfect for cultivating the short-grain Carnaroli, Arborio and Vialone Nano rice, which make the best risotto. Italian rice is classified by size, ranging from the shortest, roundest ordinario, which is used for puddings, to semifino, used in soups and salads, then fino and the longer grains of the finest risotto rice, superfino. Superfino rice swells to at least three times its original size during cooking, producing a firm *al dente* texture and a rich, creamy smoothness.

Culinary Uses

Rice is the key ingredient in risotto and is often used in soups; it makes an excellent addition to minestrone. Baked rice dishes are also popular. Cooked rice is layered with meatballs, vegetables or poultry and cheese, then topped with breadcrumbs and baked. The Italians never serve main dishes on a bed of rice, but prefer to serve plain boiled rice on its own with plenty of butter and cheese stirred in.

Buying and Storing

For use in Italian cooking, buy superfino. Shorter grain semifino is best for soups, and ordinario for puddings. Once opened, reseal the packet tightly; it can be stored in a dry place for several months.

FARRO

This is the Tuscan name for spelt, a hard brown wheat with pointed grains, which is very little used in other parts of Italy. Farro is much harder than other wheat, but it can be grown even in poor soil. In Tuscany it is used to make *gran farro*, a nourishing soup that is served instead of pasta.

Culinary Uses

Farro is used mainly as an ingredient for soup, but in remoter country areas of Italy it is sometimes used to make bread. Farro is a very hard grain and needs to be boiled for up to 3 hours to make it digestible before adding to other recipes. It can also be cooked simply and served with olive oil and freshly ground black pepper.

POLENTA

For centuries, this grainy yellow cornmeal, which is made from ground maize (corn) and cooked into a kind of porrige, has been a staple in the north of Italy, particularly around Friuli and the Veneto.

The Romans made a savoury porridge made from farro, which they called *puls*, and the tradition continued in northern Italy, where gruels were prepared from local cereals, such as buckwheat, barley and oats. Maize was only introduced into Italy from the New World in the 17th century; soon it was being grown in all the north-eastern regions, where cornmeal overtook all other types of grain in popularity, because it combined so well with the local dairy products, such as butter and cheese.

Traditionally, polenta was cooked in a *polaio*, a special copper pot that was hung in the fireplace; here, it was stirred for at least an hour, to be served for breakfast, lunch or dinner – and sometimes all three.

Polenta is often branded according to the type of maize from which it is made. Granturco and fioretto are the most common types. In Italy, polenta is available ground to various degrees of coarseness to suit different dishes, but there are two main types – coarse and fine. Coarse polenta has a more interesting texture but takes longer to cook than the finer variety.

Culinary Uses

Polenta is extraordinarily versatile and can be used for any number of recipes, from rustic meals to highly sophisticated dishes. Although it is most often served as a first course, it can also be used as a vegetable dish or main course and even made into biscuits (cookies), cakes and breads.

Plain boiled polenta can be served on its own, or enriched with butter and cheese to make a very satisfying dish. It goes wonderfully well with all meats, sausages and game, helping to cut the richness and mop up the sauce. It can be left to cool and set, cut into squares, then fried, grilled (broiled) or baked and served with a topping or filling of meat, cheese, vegetables and mushrooms. Fried or grilled polenta form the basis of crostini, which are served as an antipasti.

Buying and Storing

It is possible to buy quick-cooking polenta, which can be prepared in only 5 minutes. However, if you can spare the 20 minutes or so that it takes to cook traditional polenta, it is best to buy this for its superior texture and flavour. Whether you choose coarse or fine meal is a matter of personal preference; for soft polenta or sweet dishes, fine-ground is better, while coarse-ground meal is better for frying. After the packet has been opened, any leftover polenta can be stored in an airtight container for at least a month.

COOKING POLENTA

Polenta needs to be stirred continuously while cooking. However, it is well worth the effort as the final result is delicious. For four people, you will need about 330g/11oz/2⅔ cups polenta.

1 Bring 2 litres/3½ pints/8½ cups water to the boil in a large heavy pan. Turn the heat down to medium to high and add a teaspoon of salt. Using a long-handled wooden spoon, stir the water with one hand while you add the polenta in a slow steady stream with the other.

2 When all the polenta has been added to the pan, cook, stirring continuously, for 20–25 minutes, breaking up any lumps and scraping the polenta away from the bottom and sides of the pan.

PULSES

Many pulses were brought to Italy from the Middle East, but some, such as broad (fava) beans, were indigenous. Since Roman times, they have played an important part in the Italian diet and beans make an essential addition to many traditional Italian dishes. Pulses were a staple food for the Greeks and Romans, and several recipes for bean stews still survive from that time. They were also used as ritual offerings to the dead at Roman funerals.

HARICOT BEANS

These beans have always been a popular peasant food in Italy, but during the Renaissance Catherine de Medici tried to refine Italian cuisine and beans fell out of favour with the nobility and sophisticated urban dwellers. However, thanks to their nutritious and economical qualities, they have once again become an important part of Italian cooking.

Haricot beans are eaten all over Italy but are particularly associated with Tuscan cooking; indeed, the Tuscans are sometimes nicknamed the bean-eaters. The most popular varieties include the red-and-cream speckled borlotti, pale green flageolet, the small white cannellini and navy, and the larger black-eyed beans.

Culinary Uses

Haricot beans can be made into any number of nutritious soups and stews, or served as the basis of a substantial salad. Cooked beans can be combined with garlic, fresh sage and tomatoes and simmered for 15–20 minutes until tender and fragrant and are delicious served with chunky country sausage, such as cotechino and zampone. Small, white cannellini beans are often served as a side dish simply dressed with extra virgin olive oil.

COOKING DRIED BEANS

Dried beans should be soaked in a large bowl of cold water for at least 8 hours before cooking.

1 *Place the soaked beans in a large pan of cold water and bring to a rapid boil. Continue to boil rapidly for 10 minutes. Reduce the heat and simmer gently for 1–2 hours, depending on the size and freshness of the beans.*

2 *To flavour beans, add whatever herbs or spices you wish to the cooking liquid, but do not add salt or acidic ingredients, such as tomatoes or vinegar, until the beans are cooked or they will toughen and remain hard.*

To make a hearty stew, after the initial boiling (step 1), place the beans in an ovenproof dish with pancetta, garlic and herbs, pour over water to cover and cook in a low oven for 1–2 hours.

Buying and Storing

During the summer and early autumn in Italy, you may find fresh haricot beans, sometimes still in the pod. Borlotti come in a speckled pod and cannellini in a slim yellowish pod. Allow at least 300g/11oz per serving. Most haricot beans, however, are sold dried. Try to buy these from a shop with a quick turnover, or they may become wizened and very hard. Prepacked beans will have a "best before" date on the packet. Loose beans will keep for several weeks in a cool dry place, but are at their best soon after purchase.

Canned beans make a good substitute, but you cannot control the texture and they are sometimes too mushy – which is fine for recipes that call for puréed beans but less good for dishes such as stews.

BROAD/FAVA BEANS

These pale green, rather flat beans are at their best when eaten fresh from the fat green pod in late spring and early summer. At this time of year, they are very small and tender with a bittersweet flavour. Later in the season, they tend to be tougher and should be cooked and skinned: hold the hot beans under cold running water and the skin will slip off quite easily. Dried broad beans, which are tan in colour, should be soaked, and the skins removed before cooking. They will need to be boiled in unsalted water for about 45 minutes.

Culinary Uses

Broad beans are particularly popular in the area around Rome, where they are eaten raw with prosciutto, salami or Pecorino. Cooked beans have a milder flavour than raw and are excellent with ham and pancetta. They are particularly good puréed or mashed and flavoured with salty prosciutto. Dried beans are a popular ingredient in chunky soups and stews.

CHICKPEAS

These round golden pulses are slightly larger than the average pea and are shaped rather like hazelnuts and have a distinctive, nutty flavour and firm texture. They are the oldest of all known pulses and, though not indigenous to Italy, have become very popular in Italian country cooking. They are always sold either dried or canned.

Buying and Storing

Fresh broad beans in the pod tend to be very heavy so, when buying, allow about 350g/12oz per person. Try to choose pods that are not bulging with beans as this indicates age and the beans will be tough. Fresh and dried broad beans can be stored in the same way as haricot beans.

Culinary Uses

Chickpeas are cooked and used in the same way as dried beans and are an essential ingredient of *tuoni e lampo* (thunder and lightning), a sustaining dish of chickpeas and pasta served with tomato sauce and Parmesan cheese. They are a very popular ingredient in hearty soups and stews. They can also be served cold as a salad, dressed with lemon juice, chopped fresh herbs and extra virgin olive oil, to make a substantial salad. Dried chickpeas can be very hard, so it is best to soak them in cold water for at least 12 hours, then cook them in unsalted boiling water 1–2 hours until tender.

LENTILS

Although lentils grow in pods, they are always sold podded and dried. Italian lentils are the small brown variety, which are grown in the area around Umbria; they do not break up during cooking and are often mixed with small pasta shapes or rice for a contrast of flavours and textures.

Culinary Uses

Lentils make the perfect bed for cooked sausage, such as zampone or cotechino, and are delicious served cold as a salad, dressed with extra virgin olive oil. They absorb the flavours of whatever aromatics they are cooked with and are particularly good when herbs or spices are added to their cooking liquid. The ultimate Italian pulse feast is Umbrian *imbrecciata*, a hearty and sustaining soup made with lentils, haricot beans and chickpeas.

CHEESES

Italy produces a huge variety of cheeses, ranging from fresh, mild creations such as mozzarella to aged, hard cheeses with a very mature flavour such as Parmesan. All types of milk are used, including sheep's, goat's and buffalo's and some cheeses are made from a mixture of milks. Many Italian cheeses are suitable for cooking but they are also eaten after the main course.

Fresh, rindless cheeses were first introduced to Italy by the ancient Greeks, who taught the Etruscans their cheese-making skills. They in turn refined the craft, developing the first long-matured cheeses with hard rinds, which could last for many months and would travel. Today's Parmesan and Pecorino cheeses are probably very similar to those matured, hard cheeses that were produced 2,500 years ago.

In ancient days, the milk was left to curdle naturally before being made into cheese. The Romans discovered that rennet would speed up this process. Originally, they probably used rennet made from wild artichokes, a method that is still used in remoter parts of Italy, but later they began to use animal rennet. The process used to make farmhouse cheeses today has changed very little since Roman times.

Italian cheeses can be divided into four categories: hard, semi-soft, soft and fresh. Some cheeses have a very high fat content while others are low in fat, making them suitable for dieters. Many Italian cheeses are eaten at different stages of maturity; a cheese that has been matured for about a year is known as *vecchio*; after 18 months, it becomes *stravecchio*. These older cheeses tend to have a very powerful flavour. Most Italian cheeses can be eaten both on their own and used as an ingredient for cooking, though very strong, mature cheeses are often best kept for cooking.

HARD CHEESES

There are a wonderful array of Italian hard cheeses available. Many people think that they are purely for use in cooking, but they can be equally enjoyed on their own with fresh figs, wafer thin slices of prosciutto or a glass of Barolo.

PARMESAN

This strongly flavoured, golden cheese has a rich sharp taste. It is by far the best-known and most important of the Italian hard cheeses and is used extensively in the Italian kitchen. There are two basic types, Parmigiano Reggiano and Grana Padano, but the former is infinitely superior both in flavour and texture.

Parmigiano Reggiano is said to be one of the finest cheeses in the world and can be made only in a strictly defined zone, which lies between Parma, Modena, Reggio-Emilia, Bologna and Mantua. The farmers of this area claim that Parmigiano Reggiano has been made there for over 2,000 years. The milk comes only from local cows, which graze on the area's rich pastureland.

It takes about 600 litres/132 gallons of milk to make one 30–35kg/66–77lb wheel of Parmigiano Reggiano. First, the milk is partially skimmed and some of the whey from the previous day's cheese-making is added. The mixture is then carefully heated before rennet is added to encourage the milk to curdle.

The curds are poured into wheel-shaped forms and the cheese is then aged for a minimum of two years; a really fine Parmesan may be aged for up to seven years. During this time, the cheese is nurtured like fine wine, until it becomes a pale golden staw colour with a slightly granular flaky texture that melts in the mouth and a nutty, mildly salty flavour. Authentic Parmigiano Reggiano has the word "Reggiano" branded all over the rind so that even the smallest piece of cheese can be easily identified.

Grana Padano is similar to Parmigiano Reggiano, but is inferior in flavour and texture. Although it is made in the same way, the milk used comes from other regions and the cheese is matured for no more than 18 months, so it does not have the wonderful crumbly texture of Reggiano and its flavour is sharper and saltier. It has a grainy texture – hence the name *grana* – and is suitable for grating and cooking in the same way as Parmigiano Reggiano. It can also be enjoyed on its own.

Culinary Uses

A really good Parmigiano Reggiano can be eaten on its own, cut into chunks or slivers; it is delicious served with ripe pears and a good red wine. But Parmesan, both Reggiano and Grana, really comes into its own when used for cooking. Unlike other cheeses, it does not become stringy or rubbery when exposed to heat, so it can be grated over any number of hot dishes, from pasta, polenta and risotto to minestrone, layered with aubergines (eggplant) or truffles and baked in the oven, or added to rich, creamy sauces.

Fresh Parmesan slivers are excellent with asparagus or in a crisp salad. Don't throw away the rind from Parmesan; use it to add extra flavour to soups and vegetable stocks.

Buying and Storing

If possible, buy Parmigiano Reggiano, which is easily recognizable by the imprint "Reggiano" in pinpricks on the rind. Whether you buy Reggiano or Grana, always buy it in a piece cut from a whole wheel and grate it freshly when you need it; if possible, avoid pre-packed pieces and never buy ready-grated Parmesan, which is tasteless. Tightly wrapped in foil, a hunk of Parmesan can be stored in the refrigerator for at least a month.

ASIAGO

This cheese from the Veneto region develops different characteristics as it ages. The large round cheeses have reddish-brown rinds and weigh 10–12kg/22–26½lb each. They are made from partially skimmed cow's milk and have a fat content of 30 per cent. Asiago starts life as a pale straw-coloured dessert cheese, pitted with tiny holes, with a mild, almost bland flavour. After six months, the semi-matured cheese, asiago da taglio, develops a more piquant, saltier flavour, but can still be eaten on its own. Once it has been allowed to mature for 12–18 months, the cheese becomes grainy and sharp-tasting, and is really only suitable for grating and cooking.

DOC CHEESES
Italy operates a system known as DOC (Denominazione di Origine Controllata), which protects certain indiginous cheeses. DOC cheeses are produced to agreed standards and within determined areas. So far, 26 cheese have been given DOC classification, and more will surely follow.

PROVOLONE

This southern cheese is straw-white in colour and has a smooth, supple texture and an oval or cylindrical shape. Provolone comes in many different sizes and can often be found hanging from the ceiling in Italian delicatessens. It can be made from different types of milk and rennet; the strongest versions use goat rennet, which gives them a distinctively spicy flavour. In the south, buffalo milk is often used, and the cheeses are sometimes smoked.

There are variations of Provolone, which include Caciocavallo, a smooth smoky cheese made from a mixture of cow's and goat's or sheep's milk. It takes its name from the way the oval cheeses are tied up in pairs and hung up to dry over a wooden pole, as though on horseback. In Calabria, a version called Burrino is made enclosing a lump of unsalted butter in the centre of the cheese.

Culinary Uses

Milder, fresh Provolone can be eaten on its own or in a sandwich with mortadella or ham. Once it becomes strong, it should only be used for cooking and can be used in the same way as Parmigiano Reggiano.

Buying and Storing

Enclosed in their wax rinds, Provolone and similar cheeses will keep for several months. Once they have been opened, they should be eaten within a week.

PECORINO

All Italian cheeses made from sheep's milk are known as Pecorino, but they vary greatly in texture and flavour, from soft and mild to dry and strong. The best-known hard Pecorino cheeses are Sardo from Sardinia and Romano from Lazio, which is probably the oldest Italian cheese, dating back to Roman times. Then, as now, the cheeses were shaped and laid on *canestri*, rush mats, to be air-dried. Sicilian Pecorino is still called Canestro.

Sardo and Romano are both medium-fat and salty with a sharp flavour, which becomes sharper as the cheese ages. The milder Sardo is usually aged for only a few weeks; the Romano for up to 18 months. Hard Pecorino is a pale, creamy colour with a firm granular texture with tiny holes like Parmesan. Pecorino Pepato from Sicily is studded with whole black peppercorns.

Fresh Pecorino comes from Tuscany and is sometimes known as Caciotta. This semi-hard cheese has a delicious mild, creamy flavour, but is difficult to find outside Italy, as it keeps for only a short time.

Culinary Uses

Hard Pecorino can be grated and used like Parmesan. It has a slightly more pungent flavour than Parmesan, which is well suited to spicy pasta sauces but it is too strong for more delicate dishes, such as risotto or mild and creamy chicken dishes. Caciotta can be cut into cubes and marinated in olive oil for about 2 hours, then served with a grinding of black pepper to make a delicious and unusual antipasti.

Buying and Storing

Fresh or semi-hard Pecorino should be eaten the day you buy it, but well-matured Pecorino will keep in the refrigerator for several weeks wrapped tightly in foil.

Semi-hard Cheeses

There are many Italian semi-hard cheeses, which tend to have a firm yet springy texture and a mild yet full-bodied flavour.

Bel Paese

This cheese, poetically named beautiful country, is a baby among Italian cheeses, having been created by the Galbani family from Lombardy early last century. It is made from cow's milk, and contains more than 50 per cent fat, which makes it very creamy. It is the colour of buttermilk, with a very mild flavour, and is wrapped in pale yellow wax to preserve its freshness. A whole Bel Paese weighs about 2kg/4½lb, but it is often sold ready-packed in wedges.

Culinary Uses

Bel Paese can be eaten on its own; its mild creaminess makes it popular with almost everyone. It is also excellent for cooking, with a good melting quality, and can be used as a substitute for mozzarella, but will not add much flavour to a dish.

Buying and Storing

Like most cheeses, it is best to buy a wedge of Bel Paese cut from a whole cheese as pre-packed pieces tend to be rather soggy and tasteless. Use freshly cut cheese as soon as possible after purchase, although wrapped in foil or clear film (plastic wrap) it can be stored in the refrigerator for 2–3 days.

Fontina

The only genuine Fontina comes from the Val d'Aosta in the Italian Alps. It is made from the unpasteurized milk of Valdostana cows and has a fat content of 45 per cent. Although, nowadays, Fontina is produced on a large scale, the methods are strictly controlled and the cows are grazed only on alpine grass and herbs. Because the cheese is matured for only about four months, it has a mild, almost sweet, nutty flavour and a creamy texture, with tiny holes. Matured Fontina develops a much fuller flavour and is best used for cooking. A whole Fontina weighs about 15–20kg/33–44lb; the cheese is pale golden and the soft rind is orangey-brown. The rind of authentic Fontina has the words "Fontina dal Val d'Aosta" inscribed in white writing.

Culinary Uses

Fontina is delicious eaten on its own and, because it melts beautifully and does not become stringy, it can be used instead of mozzarella in a wide variety of dishes. It is also perfect for making *fonduta*, the Italian equivalent of a Swiss cheese fondue.

Taleggio

This square, creamy cheese from Lombardy has a fat content of almost 50 per cent. It has an edible rind and a mild, salty-sweet flavour that can become pungent if it is left to age for too long; it reaches maturity after only six weeks. The cheeses are dipped in brine for about 14 hours before maturing, which gives them a salty tang. Each cheese weighs about 2kg/4½lb.

Culinary Uses

Taleggio is perfect eaten on its own as a cheese course. Like Fontina and many other semi-hard cheeses, it melts into a velvety smoothness when cooked and does not become stringy, so it can be used in any dish that needs a good melting consistency.

Buying and Storing

Both Fontina and Taleggio should be eaten as soon as possible after purchase. If necessary, they can be tightly wrapped in waxed paper or clear film (plastic wrap) and kept in the refrigerator for 1–2 days.

Soft Cheeses

These soft and creamy cheeses can vary in taste from mild to quite pungent, depending on type and maturity.

Stracchino

Traditionally, this cheese was made in the winter months when the cows were tired from their long trek down from the mountains to their winter quarters on the plain of Lombardy – *stracchino* comes from the Lombardian dialect meaning tired. The cheese is made from very creamy milk and matured for only about ten days, and never longer than two months. It is smooth and rindless with a fat content of about 50 per cent. It is similar to Taleggio. Fresh stracchino is known as crescenza.

Culinary Uses

Stracchino should be eaten as a dessert cheese and is not suitable for cooking. On Christmas Eve in Lombardy, Robiola, a square stracchino with a reddish rind, is served as a special delicacy with a spicy candied fruit relish.

Gorgonzola

This cheese has been made in the village of Gorgonzola since the 1st century AD, when the cheeses were matured in the chilly caves of the Valsassina. Originally, it was made only in Gorgonzola but is now produced all over Lombardy. It is made from alternate layers of hot and cold curds, which creates air pockets between the layers in which mould will grow. The best cheeses are left until mould forms naturally but, often, copper wires are inserted into the cheese to encourage the growth. The cheeses are matured for three to five months.

Gorgonzola is a very rich, creamy cheese, the colour of buttermilk, with greenish-blue veining and a fat content of 48 per cent. Its

> **Serving Gorgonzola**
> *It is best to scrape off the rind before serving Gorgonzola. Like many blue cheeses, it is wrapped in foil to prevent it from drying out. As the cheese ferments, the natural bacteria in the cheese produce moisture, which gathers on the rind, making it unpleasant to eat.*

flavour can range from very mild (*dolce*) to extremely powerful (*piccante*), depending on maturity. The best-known mild version is Dolcelatte, which is exceptionally creamy with a sharp flavour.

Culinary Uses

Although it is usually eaten as a cheese course, Gorgonzola is also used in cooking, particularly in creamy sauces or as a filling for pancakes and ravioli.

Buying and Storing

Supermarkets sell vacuum-packed portions of Gorgonzola, which are acceptable but not nearly as good as a wedge cut from a whole, foil-wrapped cheese. Wrapped in clear film (plastic wrap), the cheese will keep for several days in the refrigerator.

Caprini

These little disc-shaped goat's cheeses come from southern Italy. They have a pungent flavour, which becomes even stronger as the cheeses mature. Fresh Caprini do not travel well, but they are available bottled in olive oil flavoured with herbs and chillies.

Culinary Uses

Fresh goat's cheeses can be fried and served warm with salad leaves as an appetizer, or crumbled over pizzas to make an unusual topping. Bottled Caprini should be drained and eaten as a cheese course.

Fresh Cheeses

These soft, creamy curd cheeses usually have a very mild, milky flavour and a high moisture content, making them low in fat.

Mozzarella

The best mozzarella is made in the area around Naples, using water buffalo's milk. It has a moist, springy texture and a milky flavour. The cheeses are made by the *pasta filata* method, where the curds are cut into strips, then covered with boiling water. As they rise to the surface, they are torn into shreds and scrunched into egg-shaped balls each weighing about 200g/7oz. These are placed in light brine for 12 hours, then packed in their own whey inside a paper or polythene wrapping to keep them fresh.

Culinary Uses

Fresh mozzarella is delicious served in salads, particularly with fresh tomatoes and basil, and is perfect for topping pizzas. Smoked mozzarella is good in sandwiches or as part of antipasti.

Buying and Storing

For salads, buy buffalo's milk mozzarella. Cow's milk mozzarella is adequate for cooking. Unopened mozzarella can be kept in the refrigerator for several days but once opened it should be eaten immediately.

Ricotta

This soft white cheese derives its name (recooked) from the process of reheating the leftover whey from hard cheeses and adding fresh milk. Ricotta has a solid yet granular consistency and a fat content of 20 per cent. Traditionally, the freshly made cheeses are left to drain in little baskets. Commercially produced ricotta is made from cow's milk, but in rural areas sheep's or goat's milk is sometimes used.

Culinary Uses

Ricotta is widely used in Italian cooking for both savoury and sweet dishes. It has very little flavour, so makes a perfect vehicle for flavourings such as herbs, nutmeg or honey.

Buying and Storing

Fresh ricotta should be eaten the day it is bought, but pre-packed ricotta can be stored for a much longer time.

Mascarpone

This delicately flavoured triple cream cheese from Lombardy contains 90 per cent fat and is too rich to be eaten on its own. It can be used in much the same way as whipped or clotted cream and has a similar texture. Mascarpone is made from the cream of curdled cow's milk and is mildly acidulated.

Culinary Uses

In Italy, mascarpone is most commonly used in desserts but can also be used for savoury dishes. It makes wonderfully creamy sauces for pasta and combines well with walnuts and globe artichokes.

Buying and Storing

In Italy, delicatessens serve mascarpone by the *etto* (about 100g/3½oz) from large earthenware bowls, but outside Italy it is sold in 250g/9oz or 500g/1¼lb plastic tubs. Pre-packed cheese can be stored for a week in the refrigerator; fresh mascarpone should be eaten immediately.

CURED MEATS & SAUSAGES

Italy is famous for its cured meats and sausages and they play an important part in the country's cuisine. Every region has its own special cured meats, hams and sausages, each differing as widely in appearance, taste and texture as the regions themselves. Prosciutto crudo and salami appear in every guise. They can be served as an appetizer or added to other dishes to give extra flavour.

Traditionally, most rural families kept a pig and cured every part of it, from snout to tail, to provide food throughout the year. In any Italian larder, a range of home-cured hams, sausages and bacon would be found hanging from the ceiling. Today, hundreds of varieties of cured meats and sausages are commercially produced, many still using the traditional methods.

CURED MEATS
Most cured meats are preserved with salt and air-dried and, throughout Italy, you can find regional variations on the same theme.

PROSCIUTTO
The most famous of these salted, air-dried hams (prosciutto crudo) is prosciutto di Parma. It comes from the area around Parma, where Parmesan cheese is made. The pigs are fed partly on whey left over from the cheese-making, which gives their flesh a very mild and sweet flavour. Because they are reared in sheds and never allowed to roam outdoors, they tend to be rather fatty. Parma hams are made from the pig's hindquarters, which are salted and air-dried for at least a year, and sometimes up to two.

San Daniele hams come from the Friuli region. Many regard them as superior even to Parma ham. San Daniele pigs are kept outside, so their flesh is much leaner than Parma pigs, and their diet of acorns gives it

a distinctive flavour. San Daniele ham is produced in smaller quantities than Parma ham, which makes it even more expensive.

Italy also produces a range of cooked hams (prosciutto cotto), which are usually boiled and flavoured with herbs and spices.

Culinary Uses
Wafer-thin slices of prosciutto crudo are delicious served with melon or fresh figs or, when these are out of season, with little cubes of unsalted butter. If you serve bread with this ham, choose an unsalted variety, such as pane toscano, to counterbalance the salty-sweetness of the ham. Prosciutto crudo can be rolled up with thin slices of veal and fresh sage leaves and pan-fried in butter and white wine or Marsala, finely chopped and added to risotto and pasta sauces, or used as a filling for ravioli.

Prosciutto cotto is sometimes served as an antipasti with raw ham, but it is more often eaten in sandwiches and snacks.

Buying and Storing
The best part of any ham comes from the centre. Avoid buying the end pieces, which tend to be very salty and rather chewy. Because prosciutto crudo should be very thinly sliced, buy only what you need at any one time as it tends to dry out very quickly. Ideally, it should be eaten on the day it is bought, although it can be stored in the refrigerator for up to three days.

PANCETTA, LARDO AND SPECK

These Italian bacons are made from pork belly, which is cured in salt and spices. Pancetta and lardo resemble unsmoked bacon in taste and texture. Pancetta is rolled up into a sausage shape, while lardo is flat. Speck is a fatty bacon, which is smoke-cured over beechwood with herbs and spices, then air-dried.

Culinary Uses

Pancetta and lardo can be eaten raw as an antipasti but they are usually cut into strips, cooked like bacon and added to dishes. Speck is too fatty to be eaten raw and is generally added to soups, stews and sauces.

Buying and Storing

Italian bacon is sold in the piece. Wrapped in clear film (plastic wrap), it will keep in the refrigerator for up to one month.

BRESAOLA

This dark red, cured raw beef is a speciality of Valtellina in Lombardy. It can be made from any cut. It is cured in salt, then air-driedbefore being pressed.

Culinary Uses

Bresaola is often served as an antipasti, sliced very thinly and simply dressed with olive oil and lemon juice.

Buying and Storing

Try to buy bresaola made from beef fillet. Use it as soon as possible after slicing or it will dry out and develop a sharp flavour.

SAUSAGES

Most Italian sausages are made with pork and are cured and ready to eat. Venison and wild boar sausages are popular in country areas. Today, sausages are generally factory-produced, but many towns in Italy still have *salumerie*, which sell home-made sausages. Fresh sausages are made from pork and tend to contain a high proportion of fat.

SALAMI

There are dozens of types of salami with different textures and flavours. They are made from pork, but vary according to the kind of meat used, the proportion of lean meat to fat, how finely it is minced, the seasonings and the period of drying.

Salame di Felino is a soft, coarse-cut sausage. It has a high proportion of lean pork to fat and is flavoured with pepper-corns, garlic and the local white wine.

Salame Fiorentina is a large, coarse-cut pork sausage from Tuscany. It is often flavoured with fennel seeds and pepper.

Salame Milano is a deep red sausage made from equal quantities of finely minced pork, fat and beef, seasoned with pepper, garlic and white wine. It is speckled with grains of fat that resemble rice.

Salame Sardo is a fiery red salami from Sardinia. This rustic sausage is flavoured with red (bell) pepper.

Salame Ungharese is made from finely minced pork or a mixture of pork and beef, and is flavoured with paprika, pepper, garlic and white wine.

Buying and Storing

Salami can be bought ready-sliced and vacuum-packed, but the slices taste better if they are freshly cut from a whole salami. Freshly cut salami is best eaten the same day. However, it can be stored for 3–4 days in the refrigerator.

MORTADELLA

This is the most famous cured sausage from Bologna and is also the largest, often having a diameter of up to 45cm/18in. It is considered to be the finest Italian pork sausage, with its wonderfully smooth texture, although it has a rather bland flavour. Apart from its huge size, mortadella is distinctive for its delicate, pale pink colour studded with cubes of creamy white fat, peppercorns and, sometimes, pale green pistachios or olives.

Culinary Uses

Mortadella is usually thinly sliced and eaten cold, either in a sandwich or as part of a plate of assorted cold meats as an antipasti. It can also be cut into cubes and stirred into risotto or pasta sauces just before the end of cooking, or finely chopped to make an excellent stuffing for poultry or filled pasta.

Buying

Authentic Bolognese mortadella is made only from pure pork, but cheaper varieties may contain all sorts of other ingredients, such as beef, tripe, pig's head, soya flour and artificial colourings. Beware of mortadella that looks too violently pink and, if you are buying it sliced and pre-packed, check the ingredients on the packet before you buy.

COPPA

This salted and dried sausage comes from Lombardy and Emilia Romagna. It is made from neck or shoulder of pork, and the casing is made from natural skin. Coppa is unsmoked and is very hard. It has a rectangular shape and a deep red colour.

Culinary Uses

Coppa is highly esteemed and is quite expensive. It is always eaten raw and can be served as part of an antipasti.

ZAMPONE

This speciality sausage from Modena is a pig's trotter stuffed with minced pork shoulder and other cuts, including skin. The sausage retains the shape of the trotter and the filling has a creamy texture. Each zampone weighs up to 2kg/4½lbs.

Culinary Uses

Zampone is traditionally soaked and simmered for a long time, then sliced into rings and served with lentils or mashed potatoes. It is also often served as part of *bollito misto*, the traditional Italian dish of mixed boiled meats.

LUGANEGA

This spiced, fresh pork sausage is a speciality of northern Italy and often contains Parmesan cheese. It is sold in a long rope, which is coiled up like a snake, by whatever length you require.

COTECHINO

This large, fresh pork sausage is a speciality of Emilia Romagna, Lombardy and the Veneto. It is lightly spiced, then salted.

Culinary Uses

Luganega can be grilled (broiled) or pan-fried with white wine. Cotechino is boiled and served hot. Luganega and cotechino are both usually served with lentils, cannellini beans or mashed potatoes.

Meat, Poultry & Game

Until recently, meat did not figure largely in Italian cooking, which relied heavily on the peasant staples of pasta, bread, vegetables and, in coastal areas, fish. As the country became more prosperous, however, more people added meat to their daily menu and now animals are farmed all over Italy to provide lamb, beef, veal, pork and kid.

MEAT

The area around Rome is famous for its lamb, and spit-roasted suckling lamb and kid are popular specialities of the region. Superb beef cattle are bred in Tuscany. Beef from other regions comes from working cattle that have reached the end of their useful lives, and is best used for slow-cooked stews. Veal is popular throughout Italy and the best meat comes from the milk-fed calves reared in Piedmont. Many peasant families still own a pig and pork is very popular.

Italians never waste any edible part of their meat, so offal of all kinds is used in many dishes. In Tuscany a variety of offal ranging from brains to sweetbreads and lungs may be served, while the Milanese version also includes cockscombs.

LAMB

Southern Italy is the main producer of lamb. They are slaughtered at different ages, resulting in distinctive flavours and texture. The youngest lamb is *abbacchio*, which is month-old milk-fed lamb from Lazio, whose pale pinkish flesh is meltingly tender. It is usually spit-roasted whole. Spring lamb, aged about four months, is often sold as *abbacchio*. It has darker flesh, which is also very tender and can be used for roasting or grilling (broiling). *Agnello* is older lamb; it has a slightly stronger flavour and is suitable for roasting or stewing.

Culinary Uses

Lamb is cooked in many ways, from roast leg of lamb to fried breaded cutlets and chops. Roast lamb is the traditional Easter dish. It is served in large chunks, rather than thin slices, which should be so tender they fall off the bone.

Buying

Italian lamb tends to be seasonal. *Abbacchio* should have very pale flesh, almost like veal. A milk-fed lamb will be not much bigger than a rabbit. Spring lamb should have pinkish flesh and very little fat. Mature lamb should have dark red flesh with a layer of creamy fat on the outside.

BEEF

The quality of Italian beef tends to have a poor reputation. In agricultural areas, particularly the south, where cattle are working animals, beef can be stringy and tough. This type of beef is only suitable for long, slow cooking. In Tuscany, however, superb beef cattle from Val di Chiana produce meat that can rival any other world-renowned beef.

Culinary Uses

Thick-cut T-bone steaks from Val di Chiana cattle are grilled over wood fires until well-browned on the outside and very rare inside. Rump or fillet steaks are also cooked very rare and sliced on the bias. A modern creation is carpaccio, wafer-thin slices of raw beef marinated in olive oil and aromatics and served as an antipasti. Thinly sliced topside is rolled around a stuffing to make *involtini* (beef olives). A favourite Italian family dish is *bollito misto*, a mixture of boiled meats and offal, which includes beef. Leftover boiled beef can be sliced and made into a salad.

VEAL

This is the most popular meat in Italy and appears in literally hundreds of recipes and traditional dishes. Like lamb, calves are slaughtered at different ages to produce different qualities of meat. The best and most expensive veal comes from Piedmont and Lombardy where the calves are fed only on milk and are slaughtered at just a few weeks old. This produces very tender, pale meat with no fat. Older calves, up to nine months old, still have tender flesh, but it is darker in colour than milk-fed veal. Veal from bullocks aged between one and three years, which have never worked in the fields, is still quite tender and is lighter in colour than beef.

COOKING VEAL

To cook veal escalopes, pound lightly, dust with flour, then fry in melted butter for just a few moments on each side. Mix the pan juices with lemon, white wine or Marsala and pour over the fried veal.

To stuff veal escalopes, roll very thin escalopes around a filling and braise in tomato sauce, or roll around Fontina cheese and fry in butter.

To cook veal cutlets, coat with egg and breadcrumbs and fry until golden, or season with herbs and gently cook with white wine.

Culinary Uses

Young, milk-fed veal is ideal for escalopes, which need very little cooking. Veal from very young, milk-fed calves can be served as chops, cutlets or a rolled roast. An unusual combination that works wonderfully well is *vitello tonnato*, cold roast veal thinly sliced and coated in a rich tuna sauce. Veal from bullocks should be treated in the same way as tender beef. It can be grilled (broiled), roasted or casseroled, but it is not suitable for escalopes. Loin of veal is usually boned and roasted with herbs, or braised in milk. Less tender cuts, such as shoulder and breast, are casseroled or braised. The shin (shank) is cut into *osso buco*, complete with bone marrow, and braised with white wine and tomatoes until meltingly tender.

Buying

Young veal should have very pale, slightly rosy fine-grained flesh with no trace of fat. Older veal should be pinker than young veal, but paler than beef, with only a faint marbling of fat. It should feel firm, not flabby. Escalopes should be cut only from very young veal and should be sliced across the grain so that they keep their shape and do not shrivel during cooking. If you are buying boned veal, ask the butcher for the bones as they make wonderful stock, which can be used in soups and stews.

PORK

Although much Italian pork is made into sausages, salami and hams, fresh meat is also enjoyed throughout Italy. It is often cooked with local herbs such as fennel, rosemary and sage. Different regions eat different parts of the pig. For example, Tuscany is famous for its *arista di maialle alla fiorentina* of pork roasted with rosemary, while in Naples the snout is considered a great delicacy.

Culinary Uses

Pork chops or cutlets can be grilled (broiled) or braised with fresh herbs or globe artichokes. Pork loin is deliciously tender braised in milk, which produces a rich, creamy gravy, or it can be roasted with rosemary or sage.

WILD BOAR

These animals are the ancestors of the domestic pig and used to roam in large numbers in the forests of Tuscany and Sardinia. However, they are becoming increasingly rare due to overhunting. Baby wild boar are an enchanting sight, with light brown fur striped with horizontal black bands. The adults have coarse brown coats and fierce-looking tusks. The flesh of a young boar is as pale and tender as pork; older animals have very dark flesh, which is tougher but full of flavour.

Culinary Uses

Haunches of wild boar are made into hams, which are displayed in butchers' shops. Young animals can be cooked in the same way as pork. Older boar should be marinated for at least 24 hours to tenderize the meat before roasting or casseroling. The classic Italian sweet and sour sauce, *agrodolce*, which is sharpened with red wine vinegar, complements the gamey flavour of wild boar perfectly.

OFFAL

There is a huge variety of offal available in Italy. Liver is a particular favourite; the finest is tender calf's liver, which is regarded as a luxury. Chicken livers are popular for topping crostini or for pasta sauces, and pork liver is a Tuscan speciality. Butchers often sell pig's liver ready-wrapped in natural caul, which keeps the liver tender as it cooks. Lamb's and calf's kidneys, brains and sweetbreads are specialities of northern Italy. They are alike in texture and flavour, but sweetbreads are creamier and more delicate. Every region has its own recipes for tripe, which almost always comes from veal calves. All parts of a veal calf are considered great delicacies. The head is used in *bollito misto* (mixed boiled meats), and the trotters give substance to soups and stews. Oxtail comes from older beef cattle.

Culinary Uses

Most offal is improved by soaking in milk before cooking. Some offal, such as liver and brains, require very little cooking to preserve their delicate texture. In Venice, thinly sliced calf's liver is cooked with onions and is often served with grilled polenta. The Milanese version is coated in egg and breadcrumbs and fried in butter. The simplest way to cook liver is to sauté it quickly in butter with fresh sage. Brains and sweetbreads can be blanched, then quickly fried in butter, or pounded to a paste and made into croquettes. Kidneys should be sautéed in butter, or braised with wine and onions or Marsala.

Pre-prepared (dressed) tripe should be blanched for 30 minutes before cooking. Tripe can be cooked in fresh tomato sauce flavoured with herbs. In Parma, it is usually fried in butter and topped with a little Parmesan cheese, while in Bologna, eggs are added to the mixture.

POULTRY AND GAME

These are widely enjoyed in Italian cooking. Chicken, guinea fowl and turkey appear in a huge variety of simple and delicious dishes, usually filleted for quick cooking. Duck and goose make their appearance, too, often cooked with sharp fruits to counteract the richness of the meat. Many recipes use wild duck. Hunting is a commonly enjoyed activity in Italy, making game a popular ingredient.

GUINEA FOWL

These birds are very decorative with grey-and-white spotted plumage. They originally came from West Africa but are now farmed all over Europe, so that, although they are technically game, they are classified as poultry. They taste similar to chicken, but have a firmer texture and robust flavour.

Guinea fowl are only about the size of a small spring chicken, although their abundant plumage tends to make them appear larger. One bird will only feed about three people.

Culinary Uses

Guinea fowl are hugely popular in Italy, where they are served in much the same way as chicken. Guinea hens are usually more tender than the male of the species. Their flesh is firmer than that of chicken, so it is best to cover the breasts with bacon before roasting and baste frequently during cooking. They are often stuffed with vegetables to keep the flesh moist. Guinea fowl breasts are sometimes sautéed and served with the pan juices mixed with balsamic vinegar, or with a sauce of cream and Marsala. The birds can be roasted or pot-roasted whole, or cut into serving pieces and casseroled with herbs or mushrooms. A popular autumn dish in Tuscany is guinea fowl braised with sweet chestnuts.

QUAIL

These small, migratory birds, which belong to the partridge family, are found in Italy throughout the summer months. Wild quails have the reputation of being so stupid that they never run away from hunters, but stay rooted to the spot as sitting targets. As a result, they have become very rare, and most of the birds now available are farmed. They are very small – you need two to serve one person – and have a delicate, subtly gamey flavour. Farmed quails have less flavour than the wild birds and benefit from added flavourings, such as grapes.

Culinary Uses

Quail are usually browned in butter until golden all over, then roasted in a hot oven for about 15 minutes. They are often served with a light sauce containing peeled grapes or raisins soaked in Grappa, a pungent, clear brandy. They are sometimes wrapped in vine leaves before roasting, which helps to keep their flesh moist and tender, and imparts a wonderful flavour.

PHEASANT

Occasionally you may still catch a glimpse of a pheasant with its beautiful plumage and long tail feathers in the Italian countryside. Cock pheasants have bright, iridescent blue and green feathers, while hen pheasants are browner and less dramatic-looking.

Pheasant farming is still unknown in Italy and wild pheasants are something of a rarity, so they are regarded as a luxury. They are not hung, but are eaten almost as soon as they are shot, so their flavour is less gamey than in some other countries. Although pheasants are expensive, they are meaty birds for their size, so a cock pheasant will feed three to four people and a hen pheasant two to three.

Culinary Uses

Hen pheasants are smaller than cocks, but their meat is juicier and the flavour is finer. Young hen pheasants can be roasted with or without a stuffing, but cock birds are more suitable for casseroling. Pheasant breast tends to be dry so, unless the bird is very young, it is best to wrap the breast in streaky (fatty) bacon before roasting. Alternatively, thickly smear the pheasant with butter before roasting. Placing a good knob of butter inside the cavity will also keep the flesh moist. For special occasions, pheasant are often stuffed with candied fruits or pomegranate seeds and nuts. Roast pheasant is often served with a risotto.

Pheasant can also be pot-roasted or casseroled with wine and herbs. If you are serving cock birds, it is worth removing the lower part of the legs after cooking, as they contain hard sinews that are not pleasant to eat. Pheasant breasts can be sautéed and served with a wine or balsamic vinegar sauce, but they can sometimes be rather dry.

PIGEON

Wood pigeons have dark, gamey flesh and a robust flavour, which the Italians love. They are generally too tough to roast, but they make great casseroles. Domestic pigeons are also reared for food and you will often see large dovecotes in farmyards. Domestic birds are less likely to be tough than wild ones, but their flavour is less robust.

Culinary Uses

Wild pigeons can be tough so, unless they are young, they are usually best cooked slowly in a casserole or stew. In Tuscany, they are braised with fresh tomatoes and olives; the classic Venetian pigeon dish stews them with pancetta, ox tongue and fresh green peas. To roast wild pigeons, they should be marinated in a red wine marinade for three days before cooking, stuffed with a moist vegetable stuffing, wrapped in streaky (fatty) bacon, and basted frequently with the marinade during cooking.

RABBIT AND HARE

Farmed and wild rabbits are often used in place of chicken or veal in Italian cooking. The meat is very pale and lean and the taste is somewhere between that of chicken and veal. Wild rabbit has a stronger flavour, which combines well with robust flavours; farmed rabbit is very tender and delicate.

Hare cannot be farmed, so the animals available are always wild. A hare weighs about twice as much as a rabbit – about 2kg/4½lb. The flesh is a rich, dark brown and has a strong gamey flavour that is very similar to wild rabbit.

Culinary Uses

Farmed rabbit can be used in place of chicken or turkey in most recipes. Wild rabbit can be stewed or braised in white wine or Marsala, or with aubergines (eggplant), bacon and tomatoes. It can be roasted with root vegetables or fresh herbs. In Sicily, rabbit is often cooked with sultanas (golden raisins) and pine nuts in a sweet and sour sauce.

Hare is often casseroled in red wine or Marsala, cooked in a sweet and sour sauce or made into a rich sauce for pappardelle or other wide noodles. Both rabbit and hare are often served with polenta or fried bread.

FISH & SHELLFISH

Italy's coastal waters once teemed with a huge variety of fish and shellfish. Sadly, pollution and over-fishing have taken their toll, and there is no longer the abundance of seafood there once was, but what remains is of excellent quality. A visit to an Italian fish market will reveal fish and shellfish of every description, many unknown outside Italy.

FISH

It is impossible to give a complete list of all the fish that you will find in Italy. Popular favourites are monkfish, dentex – a white-fleshed fish that can only be found in Italy – sole and even non-indigenous fish such as salmon. Freshwater fish, such as trout, perch, carp and eels, abound in the lakes and rivers and are eaten with gusto. Eels are regarded as a particular delicacy and can be cooked in many ways, from grilling (broiling) and baking to stewing and frying.

Some fish are dried, salted or preserved in oil. The most popular is tuna, which is packed in olive oil and sold by weight from huge cans. Salted dried cod is creamed to a rich paste or made into soups and stews. Tiny, strong-tasting anchovies are salted, or packed in olive oil, or preserved in a sweet and sour marinade. Sardines are also very popular and are good in pasta sauces.

PREPARING FISH

Fish should usually be gutted and hard scales removed before cooking.

1 To gut fish, carefully slit open the belly with a knife, pull out the guts with your fingers and wash the cavity in cold water.

2 To scale, hold the fish by the tail and carefully remove the scales with a blunt knife or de-scaler, working from the tail towards the head.

CHOOSING FRESH FISH

If you buy fish in an Italian early morning market it is usually guaranteed to be ultra-fresh, but in fishmongers and restaurants you may need to check more carefully. Fish should have bright, slightly bulging eyes and shiny, faintly slimy skin. Open up the gills to check that they are clear red or dark pink and prod the fish lightly to check that the flesh is springy. All fish should have only a faint, pleasant smell; you can tell a stale fish a by its disagreeable odour.

SARDINES

Fresh sardines probably take their name from Sardinia, where they were once abundant. These small, silvery fish are still found in Mediterranean waters, where they grow to about 13cm/5in. They are at their best in spring. Allow about four larger sardines or six smaller fish per serving and eat when extremely fresh.

Culinary Uses

Sardines can be grilled (broiled), cooked on a barbecue, or baked. Their oily flesh combines well with spices and piquant ingredients such as capers and olives. In Sicily, they are stuffed with breadcrumbs, pine nuts, sultanas and anchovies and fried, then finished in the oven. Sardines can also be deep-fried, either plain or stuffed with a mixture of mushrooms, fresh herbs and cheese or with chopped spinach and cream.

RED MULLET

These small Mediterranean fish rarely weigh more than 1kg/2¼lb. They have rose-coloured skin and a faint golden streak along their sides. Their flesh is succulent with a distinctive, almost prawn-like flavour. The liver of red mullet is regarded as a great delicacy and is not removed when cooking; it imparts a gamey flavour. These fish are extremely perishable and should be eaten the day they are bought. The skin should always be very bright; dullness is a sure sign that the fish is not fresh.

Culinary Uses

Red mullet goes well with Mediterranean flavours, such as olive oil, olives, herbs, garlic, saffron and tomatoes. It can be baked in greaseproof (waxed) paper with herbs, or grilled (broiled). It is also delicious baked on a bed of sautéed mushrooms and onions mixed with breadcrumbs.

SEA BASS

The silvery sea bass, which come from Mediterranean waters, are as beautiful to look at as to eat, although they have a rapacious nature. They are highly prized for their delicate white flesh and lack of small bones. They are usually sold whole and rarely weigh more than 1kg/2¼lb.

Culinary Uses

Sea bass has rather soft flesh, so it is best grilled (broiled), cooked on a barbecue or pan-fried and dressed with a drizzle of olive oil. It can be stuffed with sprigs of fresh herbs, such as fennel, or laid on a layer of rich tomato sauce and sprinkled with seasoned breadcrumbs, and baked in the oven. Sea bass can also be poached or baked, but do keep the scales on when cooking in this way as they help to hold the fragile flesh together.

GILT-HEAD SEA BREAM

This Mediterranean fish takes its name from the crescent-shaped golden mark on its domed head and the gold spots on each cheek. It has beautiful silvery scales and slightly coarse but delicious flaky white flesh. They are quite large and one fish will serve two people. It is best simply grilled (broiled), wrapped in greaseproof (waxed) paper and baked, or cooked on a barbecue.

SWORDFISH

In Italy, you will occasionally find a whole swordfish on the fishmonger's slab. These very large Mediterranean fish, which can grow up to 5m/16½ft long, are immediately recognizable by their long sword-like upper jaw. Because of their huge size, they are usually sold cut into steaks. Their firm, close-grained, almost meaty flesh has given them the nickname steak of the sea.

Culinary Uses

Swordfish tends to be dry, so it should always be marinated in oil, lemon juice or wine and herbs before cooking. It is excellent grilled (broiled) or cooked on a barbecue, or part-cooked in butter or olive oil, then baked in a sauce. It has a firm texture, making it ideal for kebabs. It is plentiful in the waters around Sicily, where it is cooked with traditional Mediterranean ingredients such as olives, tomatoes and capers. It is also delicious sliced wafer-thin, marinated in olive oil, lemon juice and herbs and served raw.

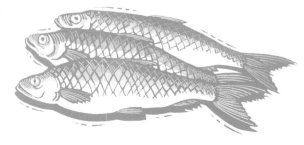

SHELLFISH

Italian coastal waters are host to a huge variety of shellfish and crustaceans, many with wonderfully exotic names, such as *datteri di mare* (sea dates), which are a kind of mussel, and *fragolino di mare* (sea strawberry), which is a tiny octopus that turns bright pink when cooked. Almost all shellfish is considered edible, from clams to razor-shells, sea snails and small scallops. Shrimps and prawns come in all sizes and colours, from vibrant red to pale grey, while crustaceans range from blue-black lobsters to bright orange crawfish.

SQUID AND CUTTLEFISH

Despite their appearance, squid and cuttlefish are actually molluscs, whose shell is located inside the body. They are indistinguishable in taste, but cuttlefish have a larger head and a wider body with stubbier tentacles. Once the bone has been removed, cuttlefish are very tender. The shell of a squid is nothing more than a long, thin, transparent quill. Both squid and cuttlefish have ten tentacles. Squid and cuttlefish are immensely popular in Italy, cut into rings and served as part of either a seafood salad or mixed fried fish. Their black ink is used to flavour and colour risotto and fresh pasta.

Culinary Uses

Small squid and cuttlefish should be cooked briefly, just until they turn opaque, or they will become rubbery and tough. Larger specimens need long, slow cooking to make them tender. They can be stuffed with minced fish or meat, anchovies and seasoned breadcrumbs or rice; baked with tomatoes and wine sauce until tender; cut into rings and fried in a light batter; or simply dusted with seasoned flour and deep-fried. Both squid and cuttlefish are also delicious stewed in their own ink.

PREPARING SQUID

To clean squid, hold the body in one hand and the head in the other, and pull away the head gently but firmly. The entrails will come away. Cut off the tentacles and remove the dark ink sac from the head. Pull out the transparent quill and rinse the body. Peel off the purplish membrane. Unless the squid are tiny enough to serve whole, cut the body into 5mm/¼in rings and the tentacles into manageable pieces.

OCTOPUS

These look and taste similar to squid but are much larger and have only eight tentacles. Their ink sac is located in their liver, and the ink has a strong, pungent taste.

Culinary Uses

Very small octopuses can be cooked in the same ways as squid and cuttlefish. Larger specimens must be pounded to tenderize them before long, slow cooking.

MUSSELS

These shellfish have a smooth texture and sweet flavour. Mussels are usually farmed and, in Italy, are sold by the litre. Allow 550ml/18 fl oz/2½ cups mussels per serving.

Culinary Uses

Mussels are usually steamed open and can be served with a garlicky tomato sauce, or baked with garlic butter or breadcrumbs. They make a good addition to pasta dishes.

PREPARING MUSSELS

Scrape away the beard protruding from the shell and scrub the shells in cold water. Give any open mussels a sharp tap with the back of a knife and discard any that do not close, as they are probably dead.

CLAMS

There are almost as many different types of clam as there are regions in Italy, ranging from tiny smooth-shelled *arselle* or *vongole* to long thin razor shells and the large Venus clams with beautiful ridged shells called *tartufi di mare* (sea truffles). All have a sweet flavour and a slightly chewy texture. Because they vary so much in size, it is best to ask the fishmonger how many clams you will need for a particular dish.

Culinary Uses

Clams can be served raw like oysters, or steamed open in the same way as mussels. The cooking time depends on the size of the clams; tiny specimens take only a minute or two. Large clams can be pan-fried, stuffed and grilled (broiled) or baked.

PREPARING CLAMS

Clams tend to be rather gritty. To allow them to disgorge any sand and grit, place them in a large bowl and cover with fresh cold water. Leave to stand for at least an hour. To open large clams, prise them open with an oyster knife, or spread them out on a baking sheet and place them in a medium oven for a few minutes until they open.

SHRIMPS, PRAWNS AND SCAMPI

In the coastal waters around Italy, there are many varieties of shrimps and prawns, which are known collectively as shrimp in the United States. The smallest are the *gamberetti*, small pink or brown shrimp that are usually boiled and served simply dressed with olive oil and lemon juice as part of an antipasti. Next in size come the *gamberelli*, pink prawns with a delicate flavour. These are the prawns that are most commonly used in mixed fried seafood. *Gamberi rossi* are the larger variety of prawn, which turn bright red when they are

cooked. They are highly prized for their fine, strong flavour, and are eaten plainly cooked and dipped into mayonnaise. Best, and most expensive of all, are *gamberoni*, large succulent prawns from the Adriatic, which have a superb flavour and texture. Similar to these is the *cicala*, which resembles a small, flat lobster.

Culinary Uses

Shrimp and prawns can be used in a large number of recipes. Peeled prawns and scampi (extra large shrimp) can be pan-fried in olive oil flavoured with garlic and/or chilli, parsley and capers; or coated in batter or egg and breadcrumbs and deep-fried. Small shrimp are served as antipasti, either on their own, or as a stuffing for tomatoes. They can be added to risotto and pasta dishes or seafood sauces. They go well with spicy tomato sauce or mushrooms, and can be used to make seafood casseroles. Large prawns and scampi can be skewered or split and grilled (broiled), or boiled and served with lemon wedges or mayonnaise.

Buying

Almost all the shrimps and prawns you buy in Italy are uncooked. They should have bright shells that feel firm; if they look limp or smell of ammonia, do not buy them.

VEGETABLES

Fresh, locally grown vegetables have always played a very important role in Italian cooking, particularly in the south of the country, where meat was traditionally considered a luxury that few could afford. They are often served as dishes in their own right but are also an essential ingredient in many other dishes, from stews and casseroles to pasta sauces and fillings.

One of the great joys of Italy is shopping at the markets, which offer a great range of seasonal vegetables, from asparagus and beans from the north to aubergines (eggplant), (bell) peppers and courgettes (zucchini) from Calabria and Sicily. Italians almost never buy imported or out-of-season vegetables, but prefer to purchase fresh seasonal produce bursting with flavour.

ASPARAGUS
This attractive, long-stemmed vegetable has been grown commercially in north-eastern Italy for over 300 years and is highly prized as a luxury vegetable. It has a short growing season from April to early June. Both green and white asparagus are cultivated in Italy: the green variety is grown above ground, while the fat white spears with their pale yellow tips are grown under mounds of soil to protect them from the light, and harvested almost as soon as the tips appear above the soil to retain their pale colour.

Culinary Uses
In spring, Italians enjoy young asparagus spears simply boiled, steamed or roasted in olive oil and served as a first course with butter and freshly grated Parmesan. For an extra treat, they add a fried egg and dip the asparagus tips into the creamy yolk. When served as an accompaniment, asparagus can be crisply fried in egg and breadcrumbs. The tips are also good added to risotto.

Buying and Storing
Asparagus starts to lose its flavour as soon as it has been cut, so only buy the freshest spears. The tips should be firm and tight, not drooping and open. The stalks should be straight and fresh-looking, not yellowed, wizened or woody at the base. Asparagus can be stored in the vegetable drawer of the refrigerator for 2–3 days.

COOKING ASPARAGUS
Freshly cut asparagus needs no trimming. Cut off at least 2cm/³⁄₄in from the bottom of bought spears until the end looks moist. Peel the lower half of thick stalks.

To boil, stand the asparagus upright in a deep pan of boiling water and cook for 5–8 minutes, until tender but still al dente.

To microwave, wash the asparagus and lay them in a dish in a single layer. Cover tightly with microwave clear film (plastic wrap) and cook on full power for about 5 minutes per 500g/1¼lb, until tender.

To roast, heat olive oil in a roasting pan, turn the asparagus in the oil, then cook in a hot oven for 5–10 minutes.

To fry, roll the asparagus in beaten egg and then fine dried breadcrumbs. Fry, a few at a time, in very hot olive oil until crisp and golden. Drain on kitchen paper and sprinkle with salt.

GLOBE ARTICHOKES

Artichokes are cultivated throughout Italy and are a particular speciality of Roman cooking. The artichoke itself is actually the flower bud of the large, silvery-leaved plant. There are many different varieties, from tiny purple plants with tapered leaves to large bright or pale green globes.

Culinary Uses

Tiny artichokes can be quartered and eaten raw or braised with olive oil, parsley and garlic. Large specimens can be served boiled with a dressing to dip the leaves into, or stuffed with savoury fillings. They can also be cut into wedges, battered and deep-fried.

Buying and Storing

Artichokes are available almost all year round, but they are at their best in summer. Whichever variety you are buying, look for artichokes with tightly packed, stiff leaves – as open leaves indicate they are too mature – and a very fresh colour. When an artichoke is old, the tips of the leaves will turn brown. If possible, buy artichokes that are still attached to their stems; they will keep fresher and the peeled, cooked stems are often as delicious as the artichoke itself.

Artichokes will keep fresh for several days if you stand them in a jug (pitcher) of water like a bunch of flowers. If they have no stalks, wrap them tightly in clear film (plastic wrap) and store in the vegetable drawer of the refrigerator for 1–2 days.

CARDOONS

These vegetables are related to artichokes, but only the leaf-stalks are eaten. They are a very popular winter vegetable in Italy and are commercially grown in mounds of soil to keep them creamy white, but in the wild the stalks are pale green and hairy and they can grow to an enormous size.

COOKING GLOBE ARTICHOKES

To prepare artichokes, snap off the stalk and pull off the tough outer leaves. Place the artichokes in a bowl of water mixed with lemon juice, until ready to cook.

1 Bring a large pan of water to the boil. Add the artichokes, return to the boil and simmer for about 30 minutes, until the outer leaves can be pulled off easily.

2 Drain the artichokes upside-down, then pull out the centre leaves and scoop out the inedible hairy choke with a spoon.

To make stuffed artichokes, *remove the choke before cooking and fill the cavity with stuffing. Braise in olive oil and water, or invert in an ovenproof dish, pour over olive oil and water, cover with foil and bake at 190°C/375°F/Gas 5 for 1 hour.*

Culinary Uses

The tough outer stalks of cardoons are always discarded, then the stalks are cut into lengths and the hearts into wedges. They can be eaten raw as a salad and are good fried, puréed or boiled and served with butter or baked with a creamy sauce.

Buying and Storing

Cardoons bought in the market will have been trimmed of their outer stalks and are sold with a crown of leaves, rather like large heads of celery. Wrapped in a plastic bag, they can be stored in the vegetable drawer of the refrigerator for 2–3 days.

CABBAGE

This is an essential ingredient of many hearty Italian soups. Three main types are used: curly-leaved Savoy cabbage, which is used in Milanese dishes, round white or red cabbage and the speciality of Tuscany, cavolo nero, a tall leafy cabbage whose name means black cabbage, but which is actually dark, purplish green.

Culinary Uses

Italians rarely eat cabbage as a vegetable, but prefer to add it, shredded, to hearty winter soups, such as minestrone, or to blanch, stuff and braise the whole outer leaves and serve as a main course.

The simplest way to cook cabbage is to shred it, then toss it in butter or olive oil until just tender. Winter cabbages are good shredded and braised with pancetta and garlic, while red cabbage can be spiced with apples, cinnamon and cloves and stewed in a little white wine.

Buying and Storing

Cabbage heads should be solid and firm, with fresh, un-yellowed leaves. It is best to buy them complete with their outer leaves; not only are these tasty for cooking, but they protect the hearts and give a good indication of the freshness of the cabbages. A cabbage can be stored in the vegetable drawer of the refrigerator for up to a week.

ONIONS

These play an essential role in Italian cooking. Many different varieties are grown, including mild yellow onions, the very strongly flavoured white onions and their baby version, which is used for pickling and sweet-and-sour onions. The best-known Italian onions are the vibrant deep red variety, which are delicious raw or cooked and are particularly good in salads.

Culinary Uses

The best Italian onions are grown in Piedmont, so many classic Piedmontese recipes include these versatile bulbs. Large onions can be stuffed with Fontina cheese or minced meat and herbs and baked. Baby white onions are traditionally cooked in a sweet-and-sour sauce of sugar and wine vinegar, and served cold as an antipasti or hot as an accompaniment.

Onions are also an essential ingredient in many traditional Italian dishes and a huge number of recipes begin with chopping and sautéeing onions. For most cooked dishes, onions are sliced or chopped and are usually sweated gently in olive oil to produce a mellow flavour. Onions are rarely browned in Italian cooking, as this can produce a bitter taste. Raw onion, particularly mild red onion, is often sliced into very thin rings and added to salads.

Buying and Storing

You will often find fresh young onions in Italian markets. These are sold in bunches like large, bulbous spring onions, complete with their leaves. They have a mild flavour and can be used for pickling or in salads. They can be stored in the refrigerator for 3–4 days. Older onions should feel firm when squeezed and not be sprouting green leaves. Stored in a dry, airy place, they will keep for many weeks.

FENNEL

This vegetable was originally used as a medicinal remedy for various conditions, including flatulence, but it has become one of the most important of all Italian vegetables. Bulb or Florence fennel, so-called to distinguish it from the feathery green herb, resembles a fat white celery root – both in appearance and texture – and has a delicate but distinctive flavour of aniseed and a very crisp, refreshing texture.

Culinary Uses

Fennel is delicious cut vertically into thin slices and eaten raw, dressed with a vinaigrette, or as part of a mixed salad. In southern Italy, raw fennel is served with cheese as a dessert instead of fruit and is an excellent aid to digesting a meal.

When cooked, fennel's aniseed flavour becomes more subtle and the texture resembles cooked celery. For cooked fennel recipes, the bulb is usually quartered, blanched in a large pan of salted boiling water until just tender, then sautéed in butter, baked with grated Parmesan cheese, or braised. Braised fennel is particularly good with white fish.

Buying and Storing

Fennel is available all year round. If possible, buy it with its topknot of feathery green fronds, which you can chop and use as a herb or garnish in any dish where you would use dill. The bulbs should feel firm and the outer layers should be crisp and white, not wizened and yellowish. It should have a delicate, very fresh scent of aniseed and the crisp texture of green celery. Whole fennel bulbs can be stored in the refrigerator for up to a week. Once cut, they should be used immediately, or the cut surfaces will discolour and the texture will soften. Allow a whole bulb per serving.

AUBERGINES/EGGPLANT

This purple vegetable plays an important part in the cooking of southern Italy and Sicily, possibly because its dense, satisfying texture makes a good substitute for meat. You will find many different aubergines in Italian markets, the two main types being the familiar deep purple elongated variety and the rotund paler mauve type, which has a thinner skin.

Culinary Uses

Aubergines are very versatile and can add a wonderful depth of flavour to any dish in which they appear. They are good grilled (broiled), stewed, sautéed, stuffed and baked, and can be enjoyed on their own or with other ingredients. Their rich colour enhances the appearance of many dishes.

PREPARING AND COOKING AUBERGINES

Some people believe that aubergines should always be sliced and salted for about 30 minutes before cooking to draw out the bitter juices; others deem this unnecessary. However, salting does stop the aubergine soaking up large quantities of oil during cooking.

The simplest way to cook aubergines is to slice them and fry them in a generous quantity of very hot olive oil. For a more substantial dish, coat them in light batter, then fine dry breadcrumbs, and deep-fry until golden brown.

Buying and Storing

Choose aubergines with glossy skins that feel quite firm when gently pressed. They should feel heavy for their size; a light aubergine will probably be spongy inside and contain a lot of seeds. They can be stored in the refrigerator for up to a week.

PEPPERS

Called bell peppers in the US, these are generically known as capsicums. Although they come in a range of different colours – green (these are unripe red peppers), red, yellow, orange and even purplish-black – all peppers have a sweet flavour and crunchy texture and are interchangeable in recipes.

Culinary Uses

Each region of Italy has its own specialities using peppers. They can be used raw or lightly roasted or grilled (broiled) in salads or as an antipasti and can be cooked in a variety of ways – roasted and dressed with olive oil or vinaigrette dressing and capers, stewed, or stuffed and baked.

COOKING PEPPERS

To grill (broil) peppers, place them under a very hot grill or hold them over a gas flame and turn until the skin blackens and blisters. Put them in a plastic bag, seal and leave until the peppers are cool enough to handle, then peel off the skin.

To stuff peppers, halve them lengthways, cut away the calyx and stem and pull out the core, seeds and white membranes. Fill with stuffing and arrange in a shallow ovenproof dish. Drizzle over some extra virgin olive oil and pour in enough water to come about 2cm/¾in up the sides of the peppers. Bake at 200°C/400°F/Gas 6 for about 1 hour.

Buying and Storing

Choose firm peppers with unwrinkled, shiny skins. The skin of green peppers may be mottled with patches of orange or red; this indicates that the pepper is ripening, and as long as the pepper is unblemished, there is no reason not to buy it. Peppers can be stored in the refrigerator for up to two weeks.

TOMATOES

It is impossible to imagine Italian cooking without tomatoes, which seem to be a vital ingredient in almost every recipe. Italians grow an enormous variety of tomatoes, from plum tomatoes to ridged, pumpkin-shaped, green-tinged salad tomatoes, bright red fruits bursting with aroma and flavour, and tiny cherry tomatoes.

Culinary Uses

Tomatoes are used in many, many ways. They can be eaten raw, sliced and served with a drizzle of olive oil and some torn basil leaves and make the perfect partner for white mozzarella and green basil to make up the colours of the Italian flag. Raw ripe tomatoes can be chopped with herbs and garlic to make a fresh-tasting pasta sauce, or made into a topping for Bruschetta. Tomatoes can be grilled, fried, baked, stuffed, stewed and made into sauces and soups. They add colour and flavour to almost any savoury dish.

Buying and Storing

Try to buy tomatoes loose so that you can smell them. Ripe tomatoes should have a wonderful aroma. They are at their best in summer, when they have ripened naturally in the sun. Choose tomatoes according to how you wish to prepare them. Salad tomatoes should be very firm and easy to slice. The best tomatoes for cooking are the plum tomatoes, which hold their shape.

Always try to buy vine-ripened tomatoes as tomatoes will only ripen properly if left on the vine. If you can find only unripe tomatoes, you can ripen them by putting them in a brown paper bag with a ripe tomato or leaving them in a fruit bowl with a banana; the gases the fruits give off will ripen the tomatoes, but they cannot improve the flavour.

Spinach, Swiss Chard and Spinach Beet

Spinach and its close relatives Swiss chard and spinach beet, are dark green leafy vegetables, rich in minerals and vitamins. Unlike many other vegetables, they are often served in Italy as an accompaniment to a main course, although they appear in numerous composite dishes as well. Curly-leaf spinach is a summer variety with very dark green leaves. Winter spinach has flat, smooth leaves, but tastes very similar. Usually, only the leaves are eaten and the stalks are discarded. Spinach has a delicate, melting quality and should be cooked only very briefly or it will become watery.

The coarser Swiss chard has a less pronounced flavour than spinach. The leaves have broad, creamy or pale green midribs, and both the leaves and stalks are eaten, but are cooked in different ways. Swiss chard is available all year round, but is popular in autumn and winter, when more delicate spinach is not available.

Spinach beet has a much smaller stalk and more closely resembles spinach. The stalks are usually left attached to the leaves for cooking. Its coarser texture makes it more suitable than spinach for recipes that require more than the briefest cooking.

Culinary Uses

Tender young spinach leaves can be eaten raw in salads or cooked and served cold with a dressing of olive oil and lemon. Spinach, spinach beet and Swiss chard leaves can be cooked and served as a vegetable dish. They are delicious sautéed in butter with chopped garlic, with only the water that clings to their leaves after washing. They can also be stewed in a large covered pan until wilted, then tossed in olive oil or butter and seasoned with freshly grated nutmeg. Swiss chard stems tend to be stringy so are usually snapped to remove the stringy parts, then cut into lengths and blanched in salted water or vegetable stock before being baked in a sauce, sautéed in butter or used as a stuffing.

Cooked spinach is used to make gnocchi and is often combined with ricotta to make fillings for pasta and pancakes. Florentine-style recipes usually contain spinach, and it is a classic partner for eggs, fish, poultry and white meats. Spinach, spinach beet and Swiss chard are all used in savoury tarts, and they make excellent soups and soufflés.

Buying and Storing

Spinach, Swiss chard and spinach beet should look very fresh and green, with no signs of wilting. The leaves should be unblemished and the stalks crisp. For use in salads, buy very young spinach with small, delicate leaves. Spinach and spinach beets contain a very high proportion of water and wilt down to about half their weight during cooking, so always buy at least 250g/9oz per serving. Balls of ready-cooked spinach beet are often sold in Italian delicatessens. Loose spinach will not keep well so should be used as soon as possible. Packed loosely in a plastic bag, it can be stored in the refrigerator for a couple of days. Unopened bags of pre-packed spinach can be stored for up to a week.

SQUASH AND COURGETTES/ZUCCHINI

All members of the squash family are widely used in northern Italian cooking. Squash and courgettes both have large, open, deep-yellow flowers, which are considered a great delicacy. Squash come in a variety of shapes and sizes, from huge orange pumpkins to small, pale, pear-shaped butternut squash and green, ridged acorn squash. They all have dense, sweet-tasting flesh. Courgettes have a shiny, green, edible skin and a sweet, delicate flavour. In Italy, tiny specimens are often sold with their flowers still attached.

Culinary Uses

The pumpkin is the symbol of Mantua and recipes from this region use the flesh in a multitude of ways, from pumpkin-filled tortelli to risotto, soups and sweet dessert tarts. Before using in this way, pumpkin and squash should be peeled and seeded, blanched in boiling salted water, then sweated in butter until soft. Pumpkin flowers can be coated in batter and deep-fried, stuffed with a filling of ricotta, or chopped and added to risotto for extra colour and flavour.

Courgettes are best sautéed in butter or olive oil flavoured with plenty of chopped garlic and parsley or dipped in batter and deep-fried. The flowers can be prepared in the same way. They are also good made into fritters, or served with a creamy white sauce seasoned with Parmesan cheese or nutmeg. Courgettes combine well with other Mediterranean vegetables, such as tomatoes and aubergines. They can be served cold as part of an antipasti, either dressed in a mint-flavoured vinaigrette or tomato sauce. Large courgettes can be halved, stuffed with a meat or vegetable filling and baked in the oven. Young courgettes are delicious eaten raw in a salad, either thinly sliced or grated.

PREPARING SQUASH, PUMPKINS AND COURGETTES

Squash and pumpkins should be peeled and the seeds and fibrous parts removed. Cut the flesh into chunks or slices. The skin of large pumpkins may be too hard to peel; if so, break open the pumpkin with a hammer or drop it on the floor, discard the seeds, then scoop out the flesh with a large spoon.

Courgettes do not need to be peeled. Top and tail, then slice, dice, cut into batons or grate as appropriate. Courgette flowers may contain small insects, so wash them briefly under cold running water and gently pat dry with kitchen paper. Cut off all but 2.5cm/1in of the stems.

Buying and Storing

Courgettes are available almost all year round, but are at their best in spring and summer when they are still small. The smaller courgettes are, the better they taste. They should have smooth, glossy, green, unblemished skins and feel firm and heavy for their size. Larger specimens are ideal for stuffing. If you can find courgettes in markets, go for tiny ones, which still have their flowers attached. Allow about 250g/9oz courgettes per serving. Courgettes can be stored in the vegetable drawer of the refrigerator for up to a week.

Squash should feel firm and heavy for their size. All whole squashes keep well, but once they are cut open, they should be wrapped in clear film (plastic wrap) and stored in the refrigerator for up to 3 days.

Squash or courgette flowers are not commonly available so it is easiest to grow them yourself. They should be cooked straight away, as they are extremely perishable and will wilt quickly.

SALAD LEAVES

In high season, you will find dozens of different salad leaves in an Italian market, ranging from round garden lettuces to bitter dark green leaves and purple radicchio. Salads are served after the main course, dressed with olive oil and vinegar.

DANDELION

These leaves have a peppery taste and long, green indented leaves. They can be picked from the wild before the plant has flowered, but only the young leaves should be eaten. Cultivated dandelion leaves are more tender than wild leaves but have less flavour.

Culinary Uses

Young dandelion leaves are usually served raw in salads together with other leaves. They can also be cooked like spinach.

RADICCHIO

The most familiar round type of radicchio has purplish-red leaves with pronounced cream-coloured veins. It has a bitter taste.

Culinary Uses

Radicchio is good, used in small quantities, in salads. It can also be quartered and grilled with olive oil, or stuffed with a mixture of breadcrumbs, anchovies, capers and olives and baked.

Buying and Storing

Radicchio leaves should be fresh-looking with no trace of brown. They can be stored in the refrigerator for up to a week.

ROCKET/ARUGULA

These dark green leaves have a peppery flavour. Home-grown rocket has a better flavour than the immature leaves found in supermarkets. It should be picked as soon as the leaves are fully grown.

Culinary Uses

Rocket adds zest to any green salad or can be eaten on its own with a simple dressing of olive oil and lemon juice or balsamic vinegar. It can be added to pasta sauces and risotto, or cooked like spinach.

Buying and Storing

In Italy, rocket is always sold in small bunches. The leaves should look very fresh with no sign of wilting. Wrap it in damp newspaper or damp kitchen paper and store in the refrigerator for 1–2 days.

LAMB'S LETTUCE

This delicate salad plant is also know as cornsalad or mâche. It has tender, rounded leaves bunched together in a rosette shape. It has a delicate but distinctive flavour.

Culinary Uses

Lamb's lettuce is usually served by itself or in a mixed green salad, but it can also be cooked in the same way as spinach.

Buying and Storing

Lamb's lettuce should look fresh and green, with no withered or drooping leaves. The smaller and rounder the leaves, the better the flavour. It can be stored in the salad drawer of the refrigerator for 2–3 days.

MUSHROOMS

Italians have always been passionate collectors of edible wild mushrooms; in spring and autumn, the woods and fields are alive with fungi hunters in search of these flavourful delicacies. Button (white) mushrooms are rarely eaten in Italy, even when fresh wild varieties are out of season: Italians prefer to use dried or preserved wild fungi with their robust, earthy taste.

The Greeks and Romans greatly enjoyed mushrooms and the Romans succeeded in cultivating several different types. However, cultivation on a large scale really only began in the 17th century, when a French botanist discovered how to grow mushrooms in compost all year round.

STORING, PREPARING AND COOKING FRESH MUSHROOMS

Mushrooms should always be stored in a paper bag rather than in plastic as the plastic will cause them to sweat and become slimy. They can be stored in a paper bag in the refrigerator for 1–2 days.

Cut off the earthy base of the stalk and brush the caps with a soft brush or wipe them clean with a slightly damp cloth.

With few exceptions, wild mushrooms should be sliced and sautéed to destroy any mild toxins they may contain.

PORCINI

These mushrooms, which are also known as ceps, are highly esteemed and Italians consider them to be the king of mushrooms. In autumn, porcini are found in woodlands, where they can grow to an enormous size – up to 25cm/10in. They have a fine flavour and meaty texture. Porcini tend to be expensive and they are most often dried, which intensifies their flavour.

Culinary Uses

Young porcini can be thinly sliced and eaten raw, dressed with olive oil. Larger caps are delicious brushed with olive oil and grilled (broiled). The stalks have a good flavour; chop them and cook with the caps, or use for sauces, stocks and soups. They also add flavour to field and wild mushrooms.

Storing

Fresh porcini can be kept in the refrigerator for 1–2 days. Dried mushrooms will keep in an airtight container for at least a year. Small porcini in perfect condition can be frozen whole. Large or blemished ones should be sliced and sautéed in butter, then drained and frozen. Do not defrost before use, or they will become mushy – simply cook from frozen. Frozen mushrooms will only keep for about one month.

TRUFFLES

These fungi grow about 20cm/8in under the ground, usually near oak trees. They are in season from October to late December. Their knobbly, round shape conceals a pungent, earthy and delicious aroma and flavour. There are two main varieties, black and white. The more highly prized black truffles grow mostly in the Périgord region of France, but they are also found in Tuscany and Piedmont. The more common Piedmont truffle is the white variety, which has a more delicate flavour.

No one has yet succeeded in cultivating truffles, so they remain rare and expensive. They are sniffed out by trained pigs or dogs. Truffles must be left to mature to develop their full flavour, so truffle-hunters often recover small truffles that the animals have unearthed until they reach full maturity.

History

Truffles have been eaten since ancient times. They were favoured by the Egyptians, the Greeks and Romans believed they had aphrodisiac properties, and during the Middle Ages they were thought to be manifestations of the devil. Louis XIV of France subscribed to the earlier theory and, from his reign, truffles were consumed by all those rich enough to afford them.

Culinary Uses

Truffles can be eaten raw or cooked. White Piedmont truffles are usually served raw, shaved very thinly over fresh pasta or eggs. They can be heated very briefly in butter and seasoned with salt, white pepper and nutmeg. Black or white truffles are delicious with all poultry and white meat. A few slivers of truffle will add a touch of luxury to almost any savoury sauce. A classic Italian truffle dish, which is a speciality of the Marches and Abruzzi, consists of sheets of fresh pasta layered with butter, cream, slivers of truffle, ham and chicken livers.

Buying and Storing

If you are lucky enough to find a fresh truffle, use it as soon as possible, as the flavour is volatile. Brush off the earth from the skin and peel the truffle, keeping the peelings to use in a sauce. To give whole fresh eggs the most wonderful flavour, put them in a bowl with the truffle, cover and leave overnight; the eggs will absorb the superb musty aroma of the truffle.

Canned or bottled truffles are more commonly available than fresh. Whole ones are extremely expensive, but cheaper pieces and even peelings are available. The most economical way to enjoy the flavour of truffles is to buy Italian oil scented with white truffles. A drop or two of the oil will transform a dish into something really special, and will enhance the flavour of sauces, pasta and salads.

Caesar's Mushrooms

These large mushrooms with an orangey-yellow cap have an excellent flavour. They can be found in Italy, but are rare elsewhere.

Culinary Uses

Caesar's mushrooms are one of the few wild mushrooms that can be eaten raw. They can be thinly sliced and eaten raw and are very good combined with hazelnuts.

Honey Fungus

These small golden mushrooms are a parasitic fungus that destroys the trees on whose roots it grows. The caps are good to eat (the stalks should be discarded).

Culinary Uses

In their raw state, honey fungus are mildly toxic, but they are good blanched in hot oil or boiling water, then stewed in butter with a little garlic, seasoning and parsley. They make an excellent filling for a frittata.

FRUIT & NUTS

Italy produces an abundance of soft, stone and citrus fruits, all bursting with flavour and often available fresh from the tree. There are apples and pears from the northern regions; nuts, peaches, plums and figs from the central plains; while the south and Sicily produce almost every kind of fruit – grapes, cherries, oranges and lemons – as well as pistachio nuts and almonds.

After a full meal of antipasti, pasta and a main course, it is hardly surprising that Italian desserts very often consist of nothing more than a bowl of seasonal fresh fruit served on its own or made into a refreshing fruit salad. Soft fruits form the basis of ice creams, sorbets, granita and milkshakes, while nuts and winter fruits, which are often dried or candied, are baked into delicious tarts and pastries.

FIGS

These soft-textured fruits were said to grow in the Garden of Eden, where Adam and Eve used the leaves to cover their nakedness. In fact, they probably originated in Asia Minor, although the oldest fig tree in the world is reputed to be growing in a garden in Palermo in Sicily. The Greeks and Romans are said to have enjoyed figs; over two dozen types of figs are thought to have been known to the Romans.

Today, figs are grown all over Italy, but the most luscious fruits of all are said to be grown in Sicily's hot climate, which is perfect for fig-growing. During the summer months you will often find Italian farmers at the roadside selling punnets of ripe figs from their own trees. There are two types of Italian figs, green and purple. Both have thin, edible skins and very sweet, succulent, red flesh. They are in season from July to October and are best eaten off the tree when perfectly ripe.

Culinary Uses

Fresh figs are delicious served on their own, but are also good with nuts such as walnuts, pistachios and almonds. They can be served raw with prosciutto or salami as an antipasti, or stuffed with raspberry coulis or mascarpone as a dessert. Poached in water, sugar syrup or red wine flavoured with a cinnamon stick, vanilla pod or nutmeg, they make a great accompaniment to duck, game or lamb. Fresh figs are wonderful rolled in sugar, then baked until caramelized and served as a dessert. Barely ripe figs make excellent jam.

PREPARING FIGS

Wash the figs briefly and gently pat dry. To serve as an antipasti or dessert, cut the figs downwards from the stalk end into quarters, leaving them attached at the base. Squeeze the base gently to open the fig out like a flower.

Buying and Storing

Ripe figs are extremely delicate and do not travel well, so it is hard to find imported fruit at a perfect stage of maturity. In season in Italy, however, you can find local figs that are just ripe for eating; they should be soft and yielding, but not squashy. Under-ripe figs can be kept at room temperature for a few days until the skin softens, but they will never develop the fine flavour of figs that have been ripened on the tree.

MELON

Many different varieties of sweet, aromatic melons are grown in Italy, and each has its own regional name. Napoletana melons have a smooth pale green rind and delicately scented orange flesh. Cantaloupe melons have a rough skin that is marked into segments and highly scented deep yellow flesh. There is a very similar Tuscan melon, which has a grey-green rind and orange, scented flesh. Green watermelons with refreshing bright pink or red flesh and edible brown seeds are grown in Tuscany. They can be round or sausage-shaped.

Culinary Uses

Italians often eat melon as a starter, usually accompanied by wafer-thin prosciutto or cured meats. Melons and watermelons are sometimes served as a dessert fruit on their own, but more often appear in a fruit salad.

Buying and Storing

The best way to tell whether a melon is ripe is to smell it; it should have a mild, sweet scent. If it smells highly perfumed and musky, it will be over-ripe. The fruit should feel quite heavy for its size and the skin should not be bruised or damaged. Gently press the rind with your thumbs at the stalk end; it should give a little. Melons will ripen quickly at room temperature and should be eaten within two or three days. Wrap cut melon tightly in clear film (plastic wrap) and store in the refrigerator.

GRAPES

Wild grapes grew in the Caucasus in the Stone Age, and early man soon discovered how to cultivate vineyards and make wine. The Greeks and Romans found that drying grapes produced sweet raisins; the Gauls invented the wooden wine cask that helped wine production become a major industry.

Italy is the world's largest producer of grapes of all kinds. Almost every rural property boasts an expanse of vineyards, some producing wine-making grapes intended only for home consumption. Others produce grapes for the enormous Italian wine-making industry. Apulia, Abruzzo and Sicily produce sweet dessert grapes on a vast commercial scale, from large luscious Italia, with their fine muscat flavour, to Cardinal, named for its deep red colour, purple Alphonse Lavallé, and various small seedless varieties.

Culinary Uses

Dessert grapes are best eaten on their own or as an accompaniment to cheese, but they can be used in pastries or cooked with quails or other poultry. Grapes used for cooking are usually peeled and seeded.

PEELING AND SEEDING GRAPES

Grapes used for cooking should be peeled and seeded. Put the grapes in a heatproof bowl, pour over boiling water and leave to stand for 10–20 seconds, depending on the ripeness of the grapes. Drain, then peel off the skin. Halve the grapes and lift out any pips with the tip of a knife.

Buying and Storing

Choosing white, black or red grapes is a matter of preference; beneath the skin, the flesh is always pale green and juicy. Buy bunches of grapes with fruit that is of equal size and not too densely packed on the stalk. The skin should have a delicate bloom and be firm to the touch. The flesh should be firm and very juicy and refreshing. Grapes should be washed immediately after purchase, then placed in a bowl and kept in the refrigerator for up to three days. Storing grapes in a plastic bag causes them to become over-ripe very quickly.

MORELLO CHERRIES
Although Italy does produce sweet dessert cherries, it is best known for the bitter Morello variety, which are preserved in syrup or brandy, or made into ice cream and Maraschino liqueur. These cherries are small, with dark red skins and firm flesh.

Culinary Uses
Morello cherries can be poached in syrup and served whole, or puréed and made into a rich cherry syrup. They make good jam. Bottled cherries in vinegar can be used in sauces for meat, duck and game.

Buying and Storing
Choose shiny, firm cherries with smooth, unblemished skins. Store in a plastic bag in the refrigerator for up to a week.

PEACHES AND NECTARINES
Velvet-skinned peaches have sweet, juicy flesh and are grown in southern and central Italy. The most common variety is the yellow peach, which has succulent, yellow flesh. White peaches have juicy, pink-tinted flesh and are full of flavour. Nectarines have smooth plum-like skins and taste similar to peaches. They also come in yellow and white varieties.

Culinary Uses
Peaches and nectarines can be served as a dessert fruit, but are good macerated in fortified wine or spirits or poached in wine. They go well with almonds and raspberries and can be made into drinks and ice creams.

STONING A PEACH OR NECTARINE
Slice through the seam line all around the fruit. Twist the two halves in opposite directions to separate, then lever out the stone with the point of a knife.

Buying and Storing
Peaches are in season from June to September. Make sure they are ripe, but not too soft, with unwrinkled and unblemished skins. Do not keep peaches and nectarines for more than a few days. Store ripe fruit in the refrigerator; under-ripe fruit will ripen in a few days if kept in a brown paper bag at room temperature.

LEMONS
These tart yellow fruits originated in India or Malaysia and were brought by the Assyrians to Greece, which in turn took them to Italy. The Greeks and Romans appreciated their culinary qualities. Later seafarers ate them to protect against scurvy.

Today, lemons are grown all over Italy, even in the northern regions. Lake Garda actually has a town called Limone, named for its abundance of lemon trees. The most famous Italian lemons come from the area around Amalfi coast, where they grow to an extraordinary size and have such a sweet flavour that they can almost be eaten as a dessert fruit. Their aromatic flavour enhances almost any dish.

Culinary Uses
Lemons are extraordinarily versatile. Their juice is an antioxidant, which prevents discoloration when applied to other fruits and vegetables. As an ingredient, lemon juice is used for dressings and for flavouring drinks and sauces. A squeeze of lemon juice complements mildly flavoured foods, such as fish, poultry and veal. Its acidity also helps to bring out the flavour of other fruits. The rind makes a wonderfully aromatic flavouring for cakes and pastries, and is an essential ingredient of gremolata, a topping of grated rind, garlic and parsley for osso buco. Quartered lemons are always served with mixed fried fish and other fried foods.

PREPARING LEMONS

Before squeezing a lemon, *warm it gently as this will increase the amount of lemon juice that you can obtain. Put the lemon in a heatproof bowl, pour over boiling water and leave to stand for 5 minutes. Alternatively, microwave the lemon on full power for 30 seconds.*

For sweet dishes, *rub a sugar lump over the skin of the lemon to absorb the oil. Use the sugar as part of the recipe.*

To prepare grated lemon rind, *wash and dry unwaxed lemons. Grate the rind or peel it off with a zester, taking care not to include any white pith.*

Buying and Storing

Depending on the variety, lemons may have thick indented skin, or be perfectly smooth. Their appearance does not affect the flavour, but they should feel heavy for their size. If you intend to use the zest, buy unwaxed lemons. Lemons can be stored in the refrigerator for up to two weeks.

ORANGES

These fruits originated in China, but bitter oranges may have been known in Ancient Greece; the mythical golden apples of the Hesperides are said to have been Seville oranges, although this seems historically far-fetched. They were certainly brought to Italy by Arab traders during the Roman Empire and over the centuries became a symbol of wealth and opulence – so much so that the Medici family incorporated them into their coat of arms as five golden balls. Sweet oranges did not arrive in Italy until the 17th century.

Today, many varieties of oranges are grown in southern Italy and Sicily. The best-known Sicilian oranges are the small blood oranges with their bright ruby-red flesh. Other types of sweet oranges include seedless navels and seeded late oranges, which have paler flesh and are available in the winter. Bitter oranges are also grown; these rough-skinned varieties are made into preserves, candied peel and orange liqueur.

Culinary Uses

A favourite Sicilian recipe is a salad of thinly sliced oranges and red onion rings dressed with black olives and their oil. Oranges also combine well with crunchy raw fennel and chicory. They can be sliced and served coated with caramel, or simply macerated in a little lemon juice with a sliver of lemon peel for a refreshing dessert. They can be squeezed for juice, or made into sorbet and granita. Bitter oranges combine well with white fish, calf's liver, duck or game, and add zest to a tomato sauce.

Buying and Storing

Oranges are available all year round, but are at their best in winter. They should have unblemished shiny skins and feel heavy for their size (this indicates that they contain plenty of juice and that the flesh is not dry). Oranges will keep at room temperature for a week and for at least two weeks in the refrigerator. Bring them back to room temperature before eating them.

Nuts

Many different nuts are grown in Italy – chestnuts and hazelnuts in the north, pine nuts in the coastal regions, and almonds, pistachios and walnuts in the south. They are used in a wide variety of savoury dishes, cakes and pastries, or served as a dessert with a glass of sweet white wine.

Almonds

Two varieties of almonds are grown in central and southern Italy. Sweet almonds are eaten as a dessert or used in cooking and baking, while bitter almonds are used to flavour liqueurs, such as amaretto, and bittersweet confections, such as amaretti. These almonds are not edible in their raw state and are poisonous if consumed in large quantities. Both sweet and bitter almonds have a velvety, pale green outer casing; the hard, light brown shell within encloses one or two oval nuts.

Culinary Uses

Early in the season, towards the end of May, sweet almonds can be eaten raw as a dessert. They have a delicious flavour and the brown skin is still soft. Later, dried sweet almonds are blanched, slivered or ground to be used for cakes, pastries and all sorts of confectionery. They can be devilled or salted as an appetizing snack. Toasted almonds are the classic garnish for trout, and also go well with chicken or rabbit. Dried bitter almonds are used in small quantities to add a more intense flavour to biscuits and cakes.

Blanching Almonds
Place the shelled almonds in a strainer and plunge into boiling water for just a few seconds. As soon as the skin begins to loosen, transfer to a bowl of cold water and slip off the skins. Dry thoroughly.

Buying and Storing

Fresh almonds in the shell can be difficult to crack, so you may prefer to buy shelled nuts. They should look plump and the skins should not feel too dry. Pre-blanched almonds can be a disappointment; buy the nuts with their skins on and blanch them yourself. Store shelled almonds in an airtight container for about a month.

Hazelnuts

Fresh hazelnuts are harvested in August and September and are sold in their frilled green husks. The small round nuts have a sweet, milky flavour. In Italy, they are generally dried and used in confectionery and cakes.

Culinary Uses

Hazelnuts are used in confectionery, cakes and biscuits (cookies). They are also good in stuffings for poultry and game.

Buying and Storing

If hazelnuts are sold in their green husks, you can be sure they are fresh. Otherwise, look for shiny shells that are unblemished and not too thick; cracked shells will cause the nut to dry out. Shelled nuts can be kept in an airtight container for about a month.

Walnuts

These nuts grow throughout central and southern Italy. The kernels are convoluted in shape and grow inside a pale brown, indented shell enclosed by a smooth green fleshy husk. Fresh walnuts have a delicious milky sweetness and a soft texture, which hardens as the nuts mature.

Culinary Uses

Fresh walnuts are eaten from the shell, as a dessert. Ground or chopped walnuts are used in cakes, desserts and pasta sauces. Halved nuts are used for decoration.

Buying and Storing

Fresh "wet" walnuts are available from late September to late October. Dried walnuts should not have cracked or broken shells. They will keep for at least two months.

PISTACHIO NUTS

These small, bright green nuts are grown in southern Italy, particularly Sicily. They have a yellowish-red skin, which is enclosed in a smooth, pale shell. Pistachios have a sweet, delicate flavour, which makes them ideal for desserts, but they are also used to stud mortadella and other pale, cooked meats.

Culinary Uses

Pistachio nuts can be eaten raw or roasted and salted. Their colour enhances most white meats and poultry. They make deliciously rich ice cream.

Buying and Storing

If possible, try to buy pistachio nuts still in their shells: they will keep for well over a month. Shelled, blanched pistachio nuts are also available and can be stored in an airtight container for up to two weeks.

CHESTNUTS

Sweet chestnuts are a mainstay of Tuscan and Sardinian cooking. Most varieties contain two or three separate nuts inside the spiky green husk, but commercially grown varieties contain a single, large nut, which is easier to peel and better for serving whole. Chestnuts have shiny, rich reddish-brown shells with a wrinkled, thin skin beneath. They cannot be eaten raw.

Culinary Uses

Peeled chestnuts can be boiled, poached in red wine or milk or fried in butter as a garnish. They make hearty soups, or can be puréed into sauces for game.

PEELING CHESTNUTS

Slit the domed side of the chestnuts with a sharp knife, then drop them into a pan of boiling water and cook for 5 minutes. As soon as the chestnuts are cool enough to handle, peel off the shell and skin. Alternatively, shell the raw chestnuts and drop them into a pan of boiling water. Cook for 20 minutes, drain, then skin.

Buying and Storing

Look for large, shiny specimens that feel heavy for their size and do not rattle. They can be stored in a cool place for two weeks.

PINE NUTS

These small, oblong, cream-coloured nuts are the seeds of the stone pine trees found on the Italian coast. The seeds grow inside a husk between the scales of the pine cones. The soft-textured kernels have an oily, resinous flavour. They can be eaten raw, but are usually toasted to bring out the flavour.

Culinary Uses

Pine nuts are used in both sweet and savoury dishes, and are best known as an ingredient of pesto. They go well with meat and game, and make delicious tarts.

Buying and Storing

Pine nuts are always sold out of the husk. They go rancid quickly, so buy only as much as you need. Store them in an airtight container in the refrigerator for a week.

HERBS, SPICES & AROMATICS

The wonderful flavour of herbs, spices and aromatics adds depth to the simple ingredients used in Italian cooking. It is hard to imagine roast chicken or veal without rosemary or sage, tomatoes without basil, or calf's liver without a few drops of balsamic vinegar. Many wild herbs grow in the Italian countryside and these are often incorporated into traditional Italian recipes.

HERBS

These are used widely in Italian cooking. Always try to use fresh herbs as they have an infinitely superior flavour to the dried varieties, which have a stronger and often quite different taste and lack the subtlety of fresh herbs. They can be used fresh in salads, or added to soups and stews, and meat and fish dishes, or sprinkled over pizzas to give extra flavour.

BASIL

This pungent, sweet herb, with its intense aroma, is associated with Italian cooking more than any other herb. There are over 50 varieties of this annual herb, but the one most commonly used in Italian cooking is sweet basil, which has broad green leaves and a wonderfully spicy aroma.

Culinary Uses

Basil has a volatile flavour that can be lost easily, so it is best added to dishes at the end of cooking. It can be used in any dish that contains tomatoes and is delicious sprinkled on to a pizza. It adds a pungent, sweet note to almost all salads and is particularly good with white fish and seafood. It makes an excellent flavouring for omelettes and is often added to minestrone. The most famous of all basil dishes is pesto, the fragrant Genoese sauce made by pounding together fresh basil, garlic, Parmesan, pine nuts and olive oil.

Buying and Storing

In sunny climates, basil grows outdoors all through the summer. In other places it is available cut or growing in pots all year round, so there really is no reason to use dried basil. Look for sweet basil with bright green leaves – the larger the better. If you have grown your own and have a glut, you can freeze basil leaves, but they lose their fresh texture and darken in colour. Alternatively, put a bunch of basil in a jar and top up with olive oil for a fragrant flavoured oil for dressings. To store fresh cut basil, wrap it in damp kitchen paper and keep in the vegetable drawer of the refrigerator for up to two days.

MARJORAM AND OREGANO

These two highly aromatic herbs are closely related – oregano is the wild variety. Marjoram has a much milder flavour than oregano and is commonly used in northern Italy, while oregano is exclusively used in the cooking of the south. Drying greatly intensifies the flavour of both herbs so, when dried, they should be used sparingly.

Culinary Uses

Marjoram is used to flavour meat, poultry, vegetables and soups; its aromatic flavour goes particularly well with carrots and cucumber. Oregano is used to flavour many tomato-based dishes and pizzas, but should always be used in moderation.

Buying and Storing

Marjoram and oregano are in season all through the summer, but cut fresh herbs are available in supermarkets throughout the year. The leaves dry out quickly, so store them in plastic bags in the refrigerator; they will keep for up to a week. Dried marjoram and oregano should be stored in small airtight jars away from the light.

SAGE

Bitter, aromatic sage grows throughout the Italian countryside. There are several types, including common garden sage, with furry silvery-grey leaves and spiky purple flowers, and clary sage, with hairy curly leaves, which is used to flavour dry vermouth.

Culinary Uses

Used sparingly, sage combines well with almost all meat and vegetable dishes and is often used in minestrone. It has a particular affinity with veal. In Tuscany, white haricot beans are often flavoured with sage.

Buying and Storing

Fresh sage is very easy to grow on a sunny windowsill. It is available, both fresh and dried, from supermarkets all year round. Dried sage is very strongly flavoured, so should be used in tiny quantities. Fresh sage can be stored in a plastic bag in the refrigerator for up to a week.

ROSEMARY

This delicious, spiky green herb has a very strong, aromatic flavour, which intensifies when it is dried.

Culinary Uses

Rosemary combines extremely well with roast or grilled (broiled) lamb, veal and chicken. A few needles will enhance the flavour of baked fish or any tomato dish,

and it adds a wonderful flavour to roast potatoes and onions. Dried rosemary can be substituted for fresh; it is extremely pungent, so should be used very sparingly.

Buying and Storing

Evergreen rosemary bushes, with their attractive blue flowers, grow wild all over Italy. Rosemary is available fresh and dried from supermarkets all year round. Fresh rosemary can be stored in a plastic bag in the refrigerator for up to a week.

PARSLEY

Italian parsley is the flat leaf variety, which has a more robust flavour than curly parsley. It is used to flavour many dishes.

Culinary Uses

Parsley adds colour and flavour to sauces, soups and risottoes. The stalks can be used to add flavour to stocks, soups and stews. Chopped parsley leaves can be sprinkled over cooked savoury dishes as a garnish.

Buying and Storing

Parsley is available all year round, so it should never be necessary to use the dried variety. A large bunch of parsley will keep for up to a week in the refrigerator if washed and wrapped in damp kitchen paper. Chopped parsley freezes well and can be added to cooked dishes straight from the freezer.

SPICES AND AROMATICS

Since Roman times spices and aromatics have played an important part in the Italian cuisine. Dishes are often richly flavoured with spices and aromatics, such as fresh and dried chillies, ground black pepper, saffron, coriander seeds and nutmeg. Hot peppery chillies are very popular in southern Italian cooking, while pungent garlic is used to flavour dishes throughout the country.

SAFFRON

This spice originated in Asia Minor, where it was used by ancient civilizations as a flavouring, as a dye, in perfumery and for medicinal purposes. Arab traders brought the spice to the Mediterranean region in the 10th century; for centuries it was so highly prized that stealing or adulterating it was punishable by death. Nowadays, the best saffron is cultivated in Spain, but it is also grown in Italy.

Saffron consists of the dried stigmas of the saffron crocus. It takes about 80,000 crocuses to produce about 500g/1¼lb of spice and these have to be hand-picked, so it is hardly surprising that saffron is one of the world's most expensive spices. Saffron threads are a vivid orangey-red colour and have a pungent aroma. They are also sold ground into powder. Saffron has a highly aromatic flavour and will impart a rich golden colour to dishes.

Culinary Uses

In Italy, saffron is used mainly to flavour and colour risotto, such as the classic Risotto alla Milanese. It makes an excellent addition to sauces for fish and poultry and is sometimes used to flavour biscuits (cookies), cakes and breads. Saffron has a strong, spicy, slightly bitter taste and only a small amount is needed to give colour and flavour to a dish.

COOKING WITH SAFFRON

Saffron strands should never be added directly to a dish, but should first be infused in hot water to extract the colour and flavour. Place the threads in a small bowl with a little hot water and leave to infuse for at least 5 minutes, then blend the soaking water together with the threads into the dish to bring out the flavour. Saffron should never be fried in oil or butter as this will ruin the flavour.

Buying and Storing

Saffron threads are sold in small boxes or jars containing only a few grams. The wiry threads should be a deep orangey-red in colour. Powdered saffron is convenient to use but the quality tends to be less reliable. Stored in small, airtight containers, saffron will keep for several months.

RED CHILLIES

In summer, bunches of tiny, fresh, red chillies can be bought in Italian markets. Fresh and dried chillies are popular in Italian cooking, particularly in the south. Flakes of spicy, dried red chillies are added to many southern Italian dishes, such as penne all'arrabiata and devilled chicken. As a rule, the smaller the chilli, the hotter it tends to be, so larger dried varieties are generally milder.

Culinary Uses

Fresh red chillies can be used to spice up dishes, preserved in extra virgin olive oil to make a spicy dressing for salads or to drizzle over a pizza, or hung up to dry and crumbled into dishes. A small pinch of dried chilli flakes adds bite to stews and sauces, and goes particularly well with tomatoes. Dried chilli flakes also go wonderfully with very simple pasta dishes, such as Spaghetti with Garlic and Oil. For a really hot pizza, crumble a few flakes of dried chilli over the top. They can be extremely fiery and should be used very sparingly. Always wash your hands immediately after handling chillies.

Buying and Storing
When buying fresh chillies, look for bright, firm, unwrinkled specimens. They can be stored in the refrigerator in a plastic bag for 1–2 weeks. Whole dried chillies should be hung up in bunches and crumbled directly into dishes. Crushed chilli flakes can be bought in jars. Dried chillies can last for years, but they will lose their flavour over a period of time, so only buy small quantities.

GARLIC
This pungent plant is a member of the lily family. The bulb is a collection of cloves held together by a papery white or purplish skin. When crushed or chopped it releases a pungent, slightly acrid oil with a very distinctive flavour and smell. As a general rule, the larger and less dried the clove, the milder and less pungent the flavour will be. Freshly picked garlic is milder than older garlic, and the large, mauve-tinged variety has a more delicate flavour than the smaller white variety.

Culinary Uses
Garlic finds its way into many Italian dishes and should be used in small quantities, unless roasting whole garlic cloves, so as not to flavour food too agressively. It will enliven almost any sauce, soup or stew. It can be roasted with lamb and potatoes, or baked in its skin for a mellower flavour. Blanched, crushed garlic will aromatize olive oil to make an excellent dressing for salads or to use in cooking where only a hint of garlic flavour is required. Raw garlic can be rubbed on toasted ciabatta.

PREPARING GARLIC
The taste of garlic varies depending on how it is prepared. The finer you chop or crush it, the stronger the flavour will be.

1 Place the garlic clove on a board and press down gently with the flat blade of a knife to break the skin. Peel off the papery skin, cut the clove in half and remove any green shoot in the centre with the point of a knife.

2 For a mild flavour, thinly slice the garlic, across the clove, or chop roughly. For a stronger flavour, cut the clove in half lengthways, then chop finely. For a very strong flavour, crush the garlic in mortar with a pestle with a little salt, or press through a garlic crusher.

Buying and Storing
Garlic sold loose by the head or kilo is usually fresher and better than pre-packaged varieties. The heads should feel firm and the skin should not be too papery. Do not buy garlic that is sprouting green shoots; the cloves will be soft and of no culinary value.

Stored in a cool dry place, garlic will keep for many months. If possible, hang the heads in bunches to keep them aerated. Once garlic has become soft or wizened, it is useless, so throw it away.

BOTTLED & PRESERVED FOODS

O ne of the great joys of Italian food is that you can create a delicious meal almost instantly using ingredients from your store cupboard (pantry). Rice and pasta can be combined with any number of bottled or preserved foods to make a speedy and nutritious meal. Unopened jars and cans last for months, if not years, so it is worth keeping a selection in your store cupboard.

OLIVE OIL

Unlike other oils, which are extracted from the seeds or dried fruits of plants, olive oil is pressed from the pulp of ripe olives, which gives it an inimitable richness and flavour. Different regions produce distinctively different olive oils: Tuscan oil is pungent and peppery; Ligurian oil is lighter and sweeter; while the oils from the southern Italy and Sicily are powerful and nutty.

Extra virgin olive oil is the best and is strictly controlled and regulated like wine. It is made simply by pressing the olives to extract the oil, with no further processing. Extra virgin olive oil must have an acidity level of less than 1 per cent. The distinctive fruity flavour makes it ideal for dressings.

Virgin olive oil is pressed in the same way, but has a higher acidity level and a less refined flavour. It too can be used as a condiment, but is also suitable for cooking. Unclassified olive oil is refined, then blended with virgin oil to add flavour. It has an undistinguished taste, which makes it unsuitable for use as a condiment, but it is ideal for cooking.

Culinary Uses

Olive oil can be heated to very high temperatures without burning or smoking, which makes it ideal for frying, sauce-making and other cooking. Extra virgin olive oil should be saved for dressing fish, vegetables and salads.

Buying and Storing

The best olive oil comes from Lucca in Tuscany and is very expensive. It is made with slightly under-ripe olives, which give it a luminous green colour. If your budget does not stretch to this, buy the best extra virgin oil you can afford to use on its own or as a flavouring or in dressings. Experiment with small bottles of different extra virgin oils to see which you prefer. For cooking, pure olive oil is perfectly acceptable. Once opened, olive oil should be kept in a cool place away from the light. The best oil will soon lose its flavour, so use it within six months.

VINEGAR

Like all wine-making countries, Italy produces red and white wine vinegar as a by-product. The best vinegar is made from good wines, which are fermented in oak casks to give a depth of flavour. Good vinegar should be aromatic, with no trace of bitterness, and should be transparent, not cloudy. White wine vinegar is pale golden with a pinkish tinge; red wine vinegar ranges from deep pink to dark red.

Balsamic Vinegar has an extremely mellow, sweet flavour. It is made in the area around Modena; the boiled and concentrated juice of local grapes is aged in a series of barrels of decreasing size and different woods over a very long period – sometimes as long as 50 years – which gives it a slightly syrupy texture and a rich, deep mahogany colour. Like Parmigiano Reggiano and Parma ham, the production of genuine balsamic vinegar is strictly controlled by law; it must have been aged in the wood for at least 12 years.

Culinary Uses

Red and white wine vinegars are principally used to make salad dressings and marinades, or to preserve vegetables. They can be used to add sharpness to sauces. Good balsamic vinegar is also used as a dressing, sometimes on its own and it can be used to finish a delicate sauce for white fish, poultry or calf's liver. A few drops sprinkled over ripe strawberries will enhance their flavour.

Buying and Storing

Price is usually an indication of quality where vinegar is concerned, so always buy the best you can afford. Genuine balsamic vinegar must be labelled "*aceto balsamico tradizionale di Modena*". Proper balsamic vinegar is expensive, but the flavour is so concentrated that a little goes a long way, and it is worth paying more for the genuine article. It can be stored in a cool, dark place for many months.

PURÉED TOMATOES

Rich red passata is simply ripe tomatoes pressed through a strainer to obtain the tomato pulp. It makes a convenient short-cut wherever tomato pulp is required and is popular with Italian cooks for making instant tomato sauces. Passata can be perfectly smooth or slightly chunky. The chunky variety, which is called sugocasa, is sold in tall jars; the smoothest type is available in jars or cartons. Concentrated tomato purée (paste) is available either in small cans or tubes.

Culinary Uses

Passata can be used as a basis for soups and sauces, and as a substitute for fresh tomatoes in any recipe where the tomatoes need to be cooked for a long time, such as stews and casseroles. Concentrated tomato purée can be added to soups, stews and sauces to add extra flavour. It is usually extremely strong and should only be used in small quantities.

PESTO

Although nothing is as good as home-made pesto, there are some excellent bottled varieties of this fragrant sauce. Green pesto is made with basil, pine nuts, Parmesan or Pecorino cheese and extra virgin olive oil, but there is also a red version made with sweet red (bell) peppers or sun-dried tomatoes. Green pesto is sometimes made with other soft-leafed herbs, such as parley, and peppery rocket (arugula).

Culinary Uses

Pesto can be used as an instant dressing for any type of pasta or potato gnocchi. It gives a lift to risotto and tomato sauces, and is delicious stirred into minestrone or tomato-based soups. A spoonful of pesto will add a new dimension to bottled mayonnaise.

OLIVE PASTE

Black, and sometimes green, olives are pounded to a paste with salt and olive oil and packed in small jars. It tends to be very salty and rich, so a little goes a long way.

Culinary Uses

Olive paste can be spread very thinly over pizza bases, or scraped on to toasted croûtons and topped with tomatoes or mushrooms to make crostini. Mixed with olive oil and a little lemon juice, it makes a delicious dip for raw vegetables.

OLIVES

A wide variety of olives is cultivated all over Italy. Most are destined to be pressed into oil but some are kept as table olives to be salted, pickled or marinated. There are two main types of olive: immature green olives and mature black olives; both are inedible in their raw state.

Green olives are the unripe fruit, which are picked in October or November. They have a sharper flavour and crunchier texture than black olives, which continue to ripen on the tree and are not harvested until December. Among the best Italian table olives are the small, shiny black Gaeta olives from Liguria. Wrinkled black olives from Lazio have a strong, salty flavour, while Sardinian olives are semi-ripened and are brown or purplish in colour. The largest olives come from Apulia and Sicily, where giant green specimens are grown. These are sometimes pitted and stuffed with pimiento, anchovies or almonds. Cured olives can be flavoured with all sorts of aromatics, such as garlic, herbs, lemon rind and chillies.

Culinary Uses

Olives can be served on their own or as a garnish or topping for pizza. They are used as an ingredient in many Italian recipes and combine well with fresh Mediterranean ingredients, such as tomatoes, aubergines (eggplant), anchovies and capers and are used in sauces for rabbit, chicken and firm-fleshed fish. Made into a paste with red wine vinegar, garlic and olive oil, they make an excellent topping for crostini.

Buying and Storing

Cured olives vary enormously in flavour so, when buying loose olives, always ask to taste one before making your selection. Loose olives can be stored in an airtight container in the refrigerator for a week.

CAPERS

These are the immature flower buds of a wild Mediterranean shrub. They are picked before the bud begins to open, then pickled in white wine vinegar or preserved in brine, which gives them a piquant, peppery flavour. Sicilian capers are packed in salt, which should be rinsed off before using the capers. Caper berries look like large, fat capers on a long stalk, but they are actually the fruit of the caper shrub. Pickled caper berries can be served as a cocktail snack or used to flavour salads.

Culinary Uses

Capers are mainly used as a condiment or garnish, but they also add a piquant flavour to fish dishes, salads, pizzas and sauces. They have a strong, piquant flavour, so need only be used sparingly.

Buying and Storing

Choosing pickled or brined capers is a matter of taste. Large capers are usually cheaper than small ones; there is no difference in flavour, but small capers make a more attractive garnish and are more highly esteemed. Salt-packed capers are sold loose and in jars. Loose capers berries should be used immediately. Bottled capers should be kept in the refrigerator once opened. Make sure capers left in the jar are covered with the preserving liquid.

SUN-DRIED TOMATOES

Drying tomatoes intensifies their flavour and produces an extremely sweet and pungent taste. If you are lucky, you may still find, in markets in southern Italy, locally grown tomatoes that have been spread out to dry in the sun, but the commercially produced varieties are actually air-dried by machine. These red, wrinkled tomatoes are available dry in packets or preserved in olive oil. Dried tomatoes are brick-red in colour and have a chewy texture. They can be eaten on their own as a snack, but for cooking they should be soaked in hot water until soft; the tomato-flavoured soaking water can be used for a soup or sauce. Bottled sun-dried tomatoes are sold in chunky pieces or sometimes as a paste.

Culinary Uses

Sun-dried tomatoes add piquancy to soups, sauces and vegetable dishes. They make an excellent antipasti combined with sliced fresh tomatoes, mozzarella and basil or with other preserved vegetables. They go well with fresh Mediterranean vegetables and add a extra flavour to egg dishes, such as frittata. Use the oil in which the tomatoes are preserved for salad dressings or for sweating vegetables for a soup or sauce.

DRYING TOMATOES

Home-dried tomatoes are very easy to make and can be preserved in olive oil for up to 6 months.

1 Wash and seed the tomatoes and dry with kitchen paper. Cut in half, place cut-sides down on wire racks on a baking sheet and dry in the oven for 6–8 hours at 120°C/250°F/Gas ½. Set aside to cool.

2 Put the dried tomatoes in clean, lidded jars, top up with olive oil and seal tightly.

VEGETABLES PRESERVED IN OIL

Italians produce a wide variety of vegetables preserved in olive or sunflower oil. The choicest are often grilled (broiled) before being packed in olive oil – tiny artichokes, button (white) and wild mushrooms, red and yellow (bell) peppers and aubergines (eggplant). You will sometimes find large bulbous jars containing layers of different vegetables in oil, which are packed by hand.

Culinary Uses

Oil-preserved vegetables combined with a selection of cured meats makes a wonderful antipasti. They can be chopped or sliced and used to dress hot or cold pasta, or stirred into rice for a cold salad. They make a delicious topping for crostini or pizza.

PICKLED VEGETABLES

Mixed pickled vegetables are sold packed in vinegar and oil. Single varieties are available, but a mixture is more colourful.

Culinary Uses

Pickled vegetables can be served with salami and ham as an antipasti, or drained and mixed with raw vegetables and mayonnaise to make a piquant Russian salad. They go well with plain cold roast meats or poultry.

MUSTARD FRUIT CHUTNEY

This sweet, crystallized fruit preserve with its piquant undertone of mustard was first produced over 100 years ago in Cremona and Venice. Its vibrant appearance comes from the assortment of candied fruits from which it is made – cherries, pears, melons, figs, apricots and clementines, infused in mustard seed oil. It is traditionally served with Italian sausages, such as cotechino, or roast and boiled beef, veal and pork. For an unusual and delicious dessert, serve the chutney as a topping for mascarpone.

Anchovy Fillets

These are available preserved in either salt or oil. The salted fillets have a superior flavour, but they are are only available in catering cans to be sold in delicatessens. You can buy these, soak them for at least 30 minutes to draw out the salt, then dry them thoroughly and pack them in olive oil, but it is more practical to buy ready canned or bottled anchovies.

Culinary Uses

Anchovies can be chopped and added to tomato sauces and salad dressings. They can be stirred into a fish risotto, or mixed with tomatoes and capers and used for topping pizzas or crostini. They are best of all cooked with garlic and olive oil and made into a hot dip for raw vegetables.

Bottled Clams

These shelled shellfish are sold packed in brine in glass jars. They need no further cooking and can be simply heated through and tossed into hot pasta, risotto or tomato sauce. If you have time, drain the clams and reduce the juice in which they are packed with finely chopped garlic and a few dried chilli flakes to make a more intense sauce.

Salt Cod

Air-drying is the oldest known method of preserving fish. Before the days of deep-freezing, dried fish was invaluable for people who wished to observe meatless days, but who lived far from the sea, because the salting and drying process ensures that it remains edible for many months. The most popular dried fish in Italy is salt cod, which is traditionally eaten on Good Friday. It looks rather unappealing, like a flat, greyish board, but once it has been soaked and reconstituted it is absolutely delicious.

Culinary Uses

Before using salted dried cod, it must be soaked under cold running water for at least 8 hours. In Venice, salt cod is beaten with olive oil, garlic, cream and parsley and served on fried polenta. In Florence, the fish is cut into chunks, coated with flour and fried with tomatoes and onions. Salt cod goes well with all kinds of Mediterranean flavours and can be stewed or baked with red (bell) peppers, potatoes, fennel or celery, capers and olives.

Bottarga

This pressed, salted and dried roe of the grey mullet or tuna is a speciality of Sardinia, Sicily and the Veneto. It is usually packed in a sausage shape inside a skin that should be removed before preparing. Wrapped in clear film (plastic wrap), it will keep for several months.

Culinary Uses

Bottarga can be served as an antipasti thinly sliced and dressed with a little olive oil and lemon juice. In Sicily, it is served with fried aubergine (eggplant) and celery salad. It is delicious grated over hot pasta with a knob of butter and chopped fresh parsley or a pinch of dried chilli flakes.

BREADS

No Italian meal is ever served without bread to accompany the food. Indeed, it often constitutes one of the dishes in a meal – for example, bruschetta or pizza. In Tuscany, bread plays a more important part in the food of the region than pasta. A favourite antipasti is toasted bread rubbed with garlic, anointed with plenty of olive oil and sprinkled with coarse salt

Italians buy or make fresh bread every day, but stale or leftover loaves are never wasted. Instead they are made into breadcrumbs and used for thickening sauces and stews, or for stuffings, salads or wonderfully sustaining soups.

There are hundreds of different types of Italian bread with many regional variations to suit the local food. Traditional Tuscan country bread is made without salt, since it is designed to be served with salty cured meats, such as prosciutto and salami. Southern Italian breads often contain olive oil, which goes well very well with fresh tomatoes. Wholemeal (whole-wheat) bread is traditionally baked in a wood oven.

The texture and flavour of the bread depends on the type of flour used and the amount of seasoning, but nearly all Italian breads are firm-textured with substantial crusts. You will never find flabby, soft white sandwich loaves in an Italian bakery, although the traditional white bread rolls can sometimes resemble cotton wool inside.

CIABATTA

These flattish, slipper-shaped loaves with squared or rounded ends are made using olive oil and are often flavoured with fresh or dried herbs, olives or sun-dried tomatoes. They have an airy texture inside, full of large holes, and a pale, crisp crust. Ciabatta is delicious served warm and is excellent split lengthways and filled for sandwiches.

FOCACCIA

This dimpled flat bread is similar to pizza dough. Focaccia is traditionally oiled and baked in a wood oven. A whole focaccia from a bakery weighs several kilos and is sold by weight, cut into manageable pieces. A variety of ingredients can be worked into the dough or served as a topping – onions, pancetta, herbs, cheese or olives.

Focaccine are small versions, which are split and served with fillings. In Apulia, focaccia that is topped with fennel, chicory, anchovies, olives and capers, is traditionally served on Good Friday.

GRISSINI

These crisp, golden bread sticks originated in Turin, but are now found in almost every Italian restaurant, packed in long, narrow envelopes. They range in size from very thin matchsticks to hefty, knobbly, home-baked batons. Italian bakers often use up any leftover dough to make grissini, which are sold loose by weight. They can be rolled in sesame or poppy seeds, which gives them extra flavour and a wonderful texture.

BISCUITS & CAKES

In Italy, a hostess will often buy a cake or dessert to serve at the end of a meal, rather than make it herself. Pastry shops and bakeries sell a wide variety of traditional tarts, spiced yeast cakes and biscuits (cookies) to be enjoyed with coffee or a glass of sweet dessert wine or a liqueur. Some of these, such as panettone, are reserved for special occasions such as Christmas and Easter.

AMARETTI
These delicious little biscuits are made from ground almonds, egg whites and sugar. They have a distinctive flavour, which comes from the addition of bitter almonds. They originated in Venice during the Renaissance. They come in dozens of different forms, from the famous crunchy sugar-encrusted biscuits wrapped in pairs in twists of crisp white paper to soft-centred macaroons wrapped in brightly coloured foil. Amaretti are delicious dipped into hot coffee. They can also be crumbled to make a stuffing for baked peaches or apricots.

CANTUCCI
These hard, high-baked, lozenge-shaped biscuits from Tuscany are designed to be dipped into espresso coffee or vin santo. When moistened, they become soft and crumbly. They are usually lightly flavoured with aniseed or vanilla and studded with almonds or other nuts.

CRUMIRI
These sweet elbow-shaped biscuits are a speciality of Piedmont. The rich golden dough is made with polenta and honey and is piped through a fluted nozzle to give a ridged texture. Although the biscuits seem hard on the outside, the polenta flour gives them a pleasantly crunchy texture. They are good teatime biscuits and are also excellent dipped in hot coffee.

SAVOIARDI
These soft-textured biscuits come from the Savoy region of Piedmont. They are plumper and wider than sponge fingers and have a softer texture. They are good dipped into tea or coffee, and are traditionally served with Zabaglione; but they are best of all used as a base for tiramisu, the rich Italian coffee and mascarpone dessert.

PANFORTE
This flat, disk-shaped cake resembles Christmas pudding in flavour. It is rich, dark and spiced, and full of dried fruit and toasted nuts. It is a speciality of Siena and is sold in a colourful glossy wrapping, often depicting Sienese scenes. It is very rich, so can only be eaten in small quantities, which is just as well as it tends to be expensive.

PANETTONE
This light-textured, spiced yeast bread is packed with sultanas and candied fruit. Originally a speciality of Milan, it is now sold all over Italy as a Christmas delicacy and is traditionally given as a gift. Panettone can vary in size from small to enormous. They are sometimes sold in pastel-coloured dome-shaped boxes, which are often hung from the ceiling of local bakeries and delicatessens and look very festive. At Easter, they are baked into the shape of a lamb or a dove. Panettone is sliced into wedges and eaten like cake.

APERITIFS, WINES & LIQUEURS

B ehind every bar in Italy are displayed row upon row of bottles containing dozens of different aperitifs, wines and liqueurs, many of them never found outside Italy. Many are made from local ingredients, such as herbs, nuts, lemons, artichokes or regional wines. They may be consumed at any time of day, from early in the morning in an espresso to late at night after a meal.

Aperitifs are usually served before a meal to stimulate the appetite and cleanse the palate. Liqueurs, which are very sweet and highly flavoured, are usually served after the meal as digestifs.

AMARO

This very bitter aperitif is flavoured with gentian, herbs and orange peel and contains quinine and iron. Marginally less bitter than straight amaro are the wine-based amari, such as Campari. Others, such as Fernet-Branca are served as a pick-me-up and cure for stomach upsets and to aid digestion.

Amaro is reputed to have digestive and tonic properties and to cure hangovers. It is also thought to have aphrodisiac qualities.

CAMPARI

This bright crimson, wine-based aperitif has a bitter, astringent flavour. It was first produced in the 19th century by the Campari brothers from Milan, and has been produced by the same family ever since. The neat bitters are an essential ingredient of many cocktails. Campari is sold ready-mixed with soda water.

CYNAR

This dark brown, intensely bitter aperitif is made from globe artichokes and is too bitter to swallow on its own. It is usually served as a long drink with ice and soda water. It is thought to be good for the liver.

PUNT E MES

The name of this intensely bitter, red aperitif means point and a half. It is said to have been created by the Carpano distillery when customers ordered their drinks to be mixed according to their own specification. It is usually drunk on its own, but can be served with ice and soda water.

VERMOUTH

Both white and red versions of this fortified wine are made from white wine and flavoured with spices and aromatic herbal extracts. Originally, it was made as a medicinal drink. The first vermouth was made in Turin in the 18th century, and vermouth is still produced there today.

Red vermouths, such as Cinzano and sweet Martini, are sweetened with sugar and tinted with caramel to give them a deep red colour. These sweet red varieties are generically called Italian vermouth. Dry vermouth is white and contains less sugar. It is known as French, but is also produced in Italy by companies such as Martini and Rossi. Other well-known brands include Riccadonna, Cinzano and Gancia.

Culinary Uses

Although the Italians tend to use white wine rather than vermouth in their cooking, dry white vermouth can be substituted in sauces and veal, rabbit or poultry dishes. It adds a touch of dryness and intensity.

Marsala

This rich brown, fortified wine is very useful in cooking for both sweet and savoury dishes. It has a sweet, musky flavour and an alcoholic content of about 18 per cent. It is made in the west of Sicily, near the town from which it takes its name. The best Marsala has been matured for at least five years to give an intense flavour and colour.

Although sweet Marsala is better known, dry varieties are also produced; their flavour is reminiscent of medium sherry. The sweetest version is an intensely rich and sticky dessert wine enriched with egg yolks, which can only be drunk in tiny quantities.

Dry Marsala is generally served as an aperitif, while the sweet version is usually served after a meal, often with little biscuits to dip into the wine. Unlike sherry, sweet Marsala does not deteriorate once the bottle is opened, so it makes a very useful store cupboard (pantry) standby.

Marsala Classification

This fortified wine is classified by age – Fine *is one year old,* Superiore *two,* Superiore Riserva *four,* Stravecchio *ten – and by sweetness. Dry Marsala is labelled* secco, *medium-dry* semi-secco *and the sweetest* dolce.

Culinary Uses

Sweet Marsala is probably best known as an essential ingredient of zabaglione, a light frothy dessert made from whisked egg yolks, sugar and Marsala. It is, however, also used in trifle and many other desserts. Dry Marsala is widely used in Italian cooking, particularly with veal and chicken livers. A few spoonfuls of Marsala added to the pan in which veal or poultry has been sautéed will make a delicious syrupy sauce. It adds extra flavour to wild mushrooms or a mushroom risotto.

Vin Santo

This Tuscan dessert wine, whose name means holy wine, is made from semi-dried grapes that have been hung in the warmest part of the winery to lose their moisture. It has a long, slow fermentation, followed by many years ageing to produce a luscious, syrupy golden wine. Although it is not a fortified wine, Vin Santo's intense flavour has some similarity to sherry and it is drunk in much the same way. Vin santo can be dry or sweet, but the sweet version is more common. It is generally served with a plate of the hard, nutty biscuits (cookies), cantucci or biscotti. These are dipped into the wine to become deliciously soft and make a wonderful dessert.

Grappa

This pungent, colourless brandy has a high alcohol content – about 40 per cent – and is distilled from the pressed skins and pips of the grapes left after wine-making. At its crudest, grappa tastes of raw spirit, but after maturing the taste becomes more refined.

Grappa is made in many regions, usually from local grapes, which lend each variety its characteristic flavour. On the whole, you get what you pay for; cheap grappa is fiery and pungent, while expensive, well-matured varieties can be very smooth. The very best grappa often comes in exquisite hand-blown bottles. The spirit can be flavoured with various aromatics, including rose petals and lemon peel.

Culinary Uses

Grappa is not extensively used in Italian cooking, except with braised kid in *capretto alla piemontese*. It can also be used for flambéeing and for preserving soft fruits. The spirit takes on the sweet flavour of the fruits and can be drunk as a digestif after the fruits have been eaten.

Amaretto

The taste of this sweet liqueur is rather like a liquid marzipan. It is made from apricot kernels steeped in brandy and is flavoured with almonds and aromatic extracts. Of the several brands that are produced, the best is Disaronno Amaretto, which comes in a distinctive squarish rippled, heavy glass bottle with a large, square, black cap.

Serving Amaretto

Although very sweet, almond-flavoured Disaronno Amaretto is quite complex enough to be enjoyed on its own. It tastes best chilled. To make a very refreshing drink, serve poured over crushed ice.

Culinary Uses

The distinctive almond flavour of amaretto enhances many desserts, such as fruit salad, trifle and fruit tarts, and whipped cream.

Galliano

This bright yellow liqueur from Lombardy comes in a distinctive tall, conical bottle. It is flavoured with spices and herbs from the Alpine slopes to the north of Italy and tastes a little like a bittersweet Chartreuse. It is occasionally drunk on its own as a digestif, but is best known as an ingredient for several cocktails such as Harvey Wallbanger or Golden Cadillac.

Liquore al Limone or Cedro

This sweet, golden-yellow liqueur is made from the peel of lemons that grow in such profusion all around the Amalfi coast in southern Italy. Almost every delicatessen in the region sells a home-made version of this opaque yellow drink, whose sweetness is tempered by the tangy citrus fruit. It should be served ice-cold straight from the refrigerator or freezer and makes a refreshing aperitif or digestif.

Maraschino

Made from fermented bitter Maraschino cherries, this sweet, colourless cherry liqueur is famous all over the world. It can be drunk on its own as a digestif, but is more commonly used for flavouring cocktails or sweet dishes.

Nocino

Sticky and dark brown, this liqueur from Emilia-Romagna is made from unripe green walnuts steeped in spirit. It has an aromatic but bittersweet flavour.

Sambuca

This is a colourless liqueur with a strong taste of aniseed, although it is actually distilled from witch elder. Traditionally it is served in a schooner-shaped glass, flambéed and with a coffee bean floating on top. The coffee bean is crunched as the Sambuca is drunk, so that its bitterness counteracts the intense sweetness of the liqueur. This method of serving sambuca is known as with the fly in Italy,

Strega

Made from herbs and flowers, this bright yellow liqueur is rather like a Chartreuse. It is a digestif with a bittersweet flavour, which is often an acquired taste.

ANTIPASTI

In Italian, *antipasto* means before the meal, and no Italian meal would be complete without it. Traditionally, antipasti consisted of a selection of marinated vegetables, served with salami or thin slices of prosciutto. The key to great antipasti is always freshness, good quality ingredients and taste. This chapter offers a wonderful collection of tempting antipasti. Master the simple classics, such as Bruschetta with Tomatoes and Olive Oil, Roasted Pepper Salad with Pine Nuts, and Mozzarella, Tomato and Basil Salad, or try your hand at more sophisticated antipasti, such as Grilled Vegetable Terrine, and Sautéed Mussels with Garlic.

ROASTED PEPPER SALAD WITH PINE NUTS

This wonderful salad combines sweet roasted peppers with sun-dried tomatoes, anchovies, capers and a sprinkling of pine nuts. For the best result, make the salad a few hours before serving to allow the flavours to infuse.

SERVES 4

INGREDIENTS
1 red (bell) pepper
1 yellow (bell) pepper
4 sun-dried tomatoes in oil, drained
4 ripe plum tomatoes, sliced
2 canned anchovies, drained and chopped
15ml/1 tbsp drained bottled capers
15ml/1 tbsp pine nuts
1 garlic clove, very thinly sliced

FOR THE DRESSING
75ml/5 tbsp extra virgin olive oil
15ml/1 tbsp balsamic vinegar
5ml/1 tsp lemon juice
chopped fresh mixed herbs
salt and ground black pepper

1 Cut the peppers in half and remove the seeds and stalks. Cut into quarters and cook, skin side up, under a hot grill (broiler) until the skin chars. Transfer to a bowl and cover with a plate. Leave to cool. Peel the peppers and cut into strips.

2 Thinly slice the sun-dried tomatoes. Arrange the pepper strips and fresh tomatoes on a serving dish. Scatter the anchovies, sun-dried tomatoes, capers, pine nuts and garlic over the top.

3 To make the dressing, mix together the olive oil, vinegar, lemon juice, herbs and seasoning. Pour over the salad just before serving.

Mozzarella, Tomato & Basil Salad

This simple salad is considered rather patriotic in Italy, as its three ingredients are the colours of the national flag. The deliciously mild taste of mozzarella is complemented perfectly by the fresh, sweet taste of tomatoes and the aromatic flavour of basil.

SERVES 4

INGREDIENTS
4 large tomatoes
400g/14oz/2 cups mozzarella cheese, from cow or buffalo milk
8–10 fresh basil leaves
60ml/4 tbsp extra virgin olive oil
salt and ground black pepper

1 Using a sharp knife, slice the tomatoes and mozzarella into thick rounds. Arrange the tomatoes and cheese around a serving dish in overlapping slices. Scatter over fresh basil leaves.

2 Sprinkle the olive oil over the tomato and mozzarella slices and season with a little salt. Serve with the black pepper passed around separately.

COOK'S TIP
In Italy, the most sought after mozzarella is made from the milk of water buffalo, which has a subtler flavour and softer texture than mozzarella made from cow's milk. Mozzarella di bufala is made in the area around Naples and can be found mainly in the south and in Campania.

Marinated Vegetable Antipasto

This delicious appetizer traditionally consists of a selection of marinated vegetable dishes served with good Italian salami and thin slices of Parma ham. Serve in attractive bowls, with plenty of fresh crusty bread.

SERVES 4

INGREDIENTS

FOR THE PEPPERS
3 red (bell) peppers
3 yellow (bell) peppers
4 garlic cloves, sliced
handful fresh basil, plus extra to garnish
extra virgin olive oil
salt and ground black pepper

FOR THE MUSHROOMS
450g/1lb open cap mushrooms
60ml/4 tbsp extra virgin olive oil
1 large garlic clove, crushed
15ml/1 tbsp chopped fresh rosemary
250ml/8fl oz/1 cup dry white wine
fresh rosemary sprigs, to garnish

FOR THE OLIVES
1 dried red chilli, crushed
grated rind 1 lemon
120ml/4fl oz/½ cup extra virgin olive oil
225g/8oz/1⅓ cups Italian black olives
30ml/2 tbsp chopped fresh flat leaf parsley
lemon wedges, to serve

1 Place the peppers under a hot grill (broiler). Turn occasionally until they are blistered all over. Remove from the heat and place in a large plastic bag. When cool, remove the skin, halve the peppers and remove the seeds. Cut the flesh into strips lengthways and place them in a bowl with the garlic and basil leaves.

2 Add salt to taste, cover with oil and marinate for 3–4 hours before serving, tossing occasionally. Store in the refrigerator for up to 2 weeks covered in oil in a screw-top jar. When serving, garnish with more basil leaves.

3 Thickly slice the mushrooms and place in a large bowl. Heat the oil in a small pan and add the crushed garlic and rosemary. Pour in the white wine. Bring the mixture to the boil, then lower the heat and simmer for 3 minutes.

4 Add salt and pepper to taste and pour the mixture over the mushrooms. Mix well and leave until cool, stirring occasionally. Cover and marinate overnight. Serve at room temperature, garnished with rosemary sprigs.

5 Prepare the olives. Place the dried red chilli and grated lemon rind in a small pan with the olive oil. Cook over a very gently heat for about 3 minutes. Add the olives and cook gently for 1 minute more.

6 Tip the olives into a bowl and set aside to cool. Leave to marinate overnight. Sprinkle the parsley over just before serving with lemon wedges.

BRUSCHETTA WITH TOMATOES & OLIVE OIL

This wonderfully simple appetizer makes the most of Italy's favourite ingredients – ripe tomatoes, garlic, olive oil and fresh basil. Slices of crusty white bread are toasted, rubbed with garlic and sprinkled with olive oil and chopped fresh tomatoes.

SERVES 4

INGREDIENTS
3–4 tomatoes
a few fresh basil leaves, torn into pieces
8 slices crusty white bread
2–3 garlic cloves, peeled and cut in half
90ml/6 tbsp extra virgin olive oil
salt and ground black pepper

1 Using a sharp knife, chop the tomatoes and discard the tough stem. Place them in a small bowl with their juice. Season with salt and black pepper, and stir in the torn basil leaves. Leave to stand for 10 minutes.

2 Arrange the bread on a grill (broiler) rack and toast under a preheated grill until crisp and golden brown on both sides. Rub one side of each piece of toasted bread with the cut garlic.

3 Arrange the toasts on a serving platter. Sprinkle with the olive oil. Spoon on the chopped tomatoes and serve at once.

COOK'S TIP
In Tuscany, this dish is intended to make the most of the new season's olive oil. Always try to use a good quality oil as the distinctive fruity taste is an essential part of the dish and complements the flavours of fresh tomatoes, basil and garlic perfectly.

STUFFED ROAST PEPPERS WITH PESTO

These sweet and juicy peppers are filled with fresh scallops, pesto and slivers of garlic to give a wonderfully flavoursome result. Serve with plenty of Italian bread, such as ciabatta or focaccia, to mop up the hot garlicky juices.

SERVES 4

INGREDIENTS
4 squat red (bell) peppers
2 large garlic cloves, cut into thin slivers
60ml/4 tbsp olive oil
4 shelled scallops
45ml/3 tbsp pesto
salt and ground black pepper
freshly grated Parmesan cheese, to serve
salad leaves and fresh basil sprigs, to garnish

1 Preheat the oven to 180°C/350°F/Gas 4. Cut the peppers in half lengthways, through their stalks. Scrape out and discard the cores and seeds. Wash the pepper shells and pat dry.

2 Put the peppers, cut-side up, in an oiled roasting pan. Divide the slivers of garlic equally among them and sprinkle with salt and pepper to taste. Spoon the oil into the peppers, then roast for 40 minutes.

3 Meanwhile, cut each scallop in half to make two flat discs. Remove the peppers from the oven and place a scallop half in each roasted pepper half. Spoon a little pesto on top of each scallop.

4 Return the pan to the oven and roast for 10 minutes more. Transfer the peppers to individual serving plates, sprinkle with grated Parmesan and garnish each plate with a few salad leaves and fresh basil sprigs. Serve warm.

GRILLED AUBERGINE PARCELS

These mouthwatering parcels have a delicious filling of tomatoes, mozzarella cheese and fresh basil, and are sprinkled with toasted pine nuts.

SERVES 4

INGREDIENTS
2 large, long aubergines (eggplant)
225g/8oz mozzarella cheese
2 plum tomatoes
16 large basil leaves
30ml/2 tbsp olive oil
salt and ground black pepper
30ml/2 tbsp toasted pine nuts and torn basil leaves, to garnish

FOR THE DRESSING
60ml/4 tbsp extra virgin olive oil
5ml/1 tsp balsamic vinegar
15ml/1 tbsp sun-dried tomato paste or tomato purée (paste)
15ml/1 tbsp lemon juice

COOK'S TIP
If the aubergines are very large they may have a slightly bitter taste. To draw out the bitter juices, spread out the raw slices on a tray and sprinkle lightly with salt. Set aside for about 30 minutes, then rinse the aubergine slices thoroughly under cold running water before cooking.

1 Remove the stalks from the aubergines and cut lengthways into thin slices – the aim is to get 16 slices in total, disregarding the first and last slices (each about 5mm/¼in thick). If you have a mandolin, it will cut perfect, even slices for you, otherwise, use a long-bladed, sharp knife.

2 Bring a large pan of salted water to the boil, add the aubergine slices and cook for about 2 minutes, until just softened. Drain the sliced aubergines, then dry them on kitchen paper.

3 Using a sharp knife, cut the mozzarella cheese into eight equal slices. Cut each plum tomato widthways, into eight thin slices, discarding the first and last slices of each tomato.

4 Take two aubergine slices and place on a flameproof tray or dish, in a cross. Place a slice of tomato in the centre, season with salt and pepper, then add a basil leaf, followed by a slice of mozzarella, another basil leaf, a slice of tomato and a little more seasoning.

5 Fold the ends of the aubergine slices around the mozzarella and tomato filling to make a neat parcel. Repeat with the rest of the assembled ingredients to make eight parcels. Chill the parcels for 20 minutes.

6 To make the tomato dressing, whisk together the olive oil, vinegar, sun-dried tomato paste or tomato purée and lemon juice. Season with salt and ground black pepper to taste.

7 Preheat the grill (broiler). Brush the parcels with olive oil and cook them for about 5 minutes on each side, until golden. Serve hot, with the dressing, sprinkled with toasted pine nuts and torn basil leaves.

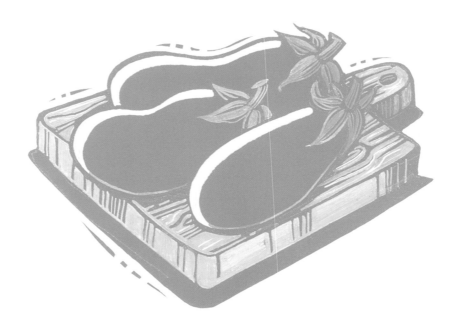

GRILLED VEGETABLE TERRINE

This attractive terrine is made up of layers of peppers, aubergines and courgettes: the vegetables traditionally associated with the south of Italy. Grilling the vegetables first gives the terrine a wonderfully rich, sweet-smoky taste.

SERVES 6

INGREDIENTS
2 large red (bell) peppers, quartered, cored and seeded
2 large yellow (bell) peppers, quartered, cored and seeded
1 large aubergine (eggplant), sliced lengthways
2 large courgettes (zucchini), sliced lengthways
90ml/6 tbsp olive oil
1 large red onion, thinly sliced
75g/3oz/½ cup raisins
15ml/1 tbsp tomato purée (paste)
15ml/1 tbsp red wine vinegar
400ml/14fl oz/1⅔ cups tomato juice
15g/½oz/2 tbsp powdered gelatine
fresh basil leaves, to garnish

FOR THE DRESSING
90ml/6 tbsp extra virgin olive oil
30ml/2 tbsp red wine vinegar
salt and ground black pepper

1 Place the prepared red and yellow peppers skin side up under a hot grill (broiler) and cook until the skins are blackened. Transfer the cooked peppers to a bowl and cover with a plate.

2 Preheat the grill. Arrange the aubergine and courgette slices on separate baking sheets. Brush them with a little oil and cook under the grill, in batches if necessary, turning occasionally, until tender and golden.

3 When the peppers are cool enough to handle, peel off the blackened skins and rinse under running water. Remove the seeds and stem and discard. Cut the flesh into thick strips and set aside.

4 Heat the remaining olive oil in a frying pan and add the sliced onion, raisins, tomato purée and red wine vinegar. Cook gently until soft and syrupy. Leave the mixture to cool in the frying pan.

5 Lightly oil a 1.75 litre/3 pint/7½ cup terrine, then line with clear film, leaving a little hanging over the sides. Pour half the tomato juice into a small pan and sprinkle the gelatine over the top. Heat gently over a very low heat, stirring occasionally until completely dissolved. Do not allow the gelatine mixture to boil or it may not set properly.

6 Place a thin layer of red peppers in the bottom of the lined terrine and pour in enough of the tomato and gelatine mixture to cover. Continue layering the aubergine, courgettes, yellow peppers and onion mixture, until all the ingredients are used up. Pour a little of the tomato and gelatine mixture over each layer of vegetables and finish with a layer of red peppers.

7 Add the remaining tomato juice to any left in the pan and pour into the terrine. Give the terrine a sharp tap, to disperse the juice, then cover and transfer to the refrigerator to set.

8 To make the dressing, whisk together the oil and vinegar, and season. Turn out the terrine and remove the clear film. Cut the terrine into thick slices and serve, drizzled with a little of the dressing. Garnish with basil leaves.

Fried Mozzarella

This tasty dish originates from the Neapolitan area, where much mozzarella is produced. Slices of cheese are first coated in breadcrumbs, then deep-fried to produce a crisp outer coating that encloses a mouthful of soft cheese with a wonderfully elastic texture. It makes a perfect informal lunch dish.

SERVES 2–3

INGREDIENTS
300g/11oz mozzarella cheese
oil, for deep-frying
2 eggs
flour seasoned with salt and ground black pepper,
   for coating
plain dry breadcrumbs, for coating

1 Using a sharp knife, cut the mozzarella into slices about 1cm/½in thick. Gently pat off any excess moisture with kitchen paper.

2 Heat the oil until a small piece of bread sizzles as soon as it is dropped in (about 180°C/350°F). While the oil is heating, beat the eggs in a shallow bowl. Spread some flour on one plate and some breadcrumbs on another.

3 Press the cheese slices into the seasoned flour, coating them evenly with a thin layer. Shake off any excess. Dip the floured slices into the beaten egg, then into the breadcrumbs. Dip them once more into the egg, and then again into the breadcrumbs, coating them evenly.

4 Fry immediately in the hot oil until golden brown. (You may have to do this in two batches but do not let the breaded cheese wait for too long or the breadcrumb coating will separate from the cheese while it is being fried.) Drain quickly on kitchen paper and serve hot.

FONTINA CHEESE DIP

This delicious dip is rather like a Swiss fondue and is known as Fonduta *in Italy. It needs only some warm ciabatta or focaccia bread, a herby salad and some robust red wine to make a thoroughly enjoyable meal.*

SERVES 4

INGREDIENTS
250g/9oz Fontina cheese, diced
250ml/8fl oz/1 cup milk
15g/½oz/1 tbsp butter
2 eggs, lightly beaten
ground black pepper
bread, to serve

1 Put the diced Fontina cheese in a bowl with the milk and leave to soak for about 3 hours. Transfer the soaked cheese to a double boiler or a heatproof bowl set over a pan of simmering water.

2 Add the butter and beaten eggs to the cheese and milk and cook gently, stirring continuously, until the cheese has melted to form a smooth sauce with the consistency of custard.

3 Remove the sauce from the heat and season with ground black pepper. Transfer to a serving dish and serve immediately with chunks of bread.

COOK'S TIPS
• *This sauce needs to be cooked over a very gentle heat – don't overheat it, or the eggs might curdle.*
• *Fontina cheese has a rich salty flavour, a little like Gruyère, which makes a good substitute.*

FRITTATA WITH SUN-DRIED TOMATOES

The addition of sun-dried tomatoes to this traditional Italian omelette gives it a slightly piquant flavour and a distinctly Mediterranean feel.

SERVES 3–4

INGREDIENTS
6 sun-dried tomatoes, dry or in oil and drained
60ml/4 tbsp olive oil
1 small onion, finely chopped
a pinch of fresh thyme leaves
6 eggs
50g/2oz/½ cup freshly grated Parmesan cheese
salt and ground black pepper

1 Place the tomatoes in a small bowl and pour on enough hot water to just cover them. Soak for about 15 minutes. Lift the tomatoes out of the water and slice them into thin strips. Reserve the soaking water.

2 Heat the oil in a large non-stick or heavy frying pan. Stir in the onion and cook for 5–6 minutes, or until soft and golden. Add the tomatoes and thyme and stir over a medium heat for 2–3 minutes. Season with salt and pepper.

3 Break the eggs into a bowl and beat lightly with a fork. Stir in 60ml/4 tbsp of the water from soaking the tomatoes and the grated Parmesan. Raise the heat under the pan. When the oil is sizzling, pour in the beaten eggs. Mix them quickly into the other ingredients, then stop stirring. Lower the heat to medium and cook for about 4–5 minutes on the first side, or until the frittata is puffed and golden.

4 Take a large heatproof plate, place it upside down over the pan, and holding it firmly with oven gloves, turn the pan and the frittata over on to it. Slide the frittata back into the pan and continue cooking for 3–4 minutes, until golden brown on the second side. Remove the pan from the heat. The frittata can be served hot, at room temperature or cold. Cut it into wedges to serve.

Frittata with Spinach & Prosciutto

The combination of lightly sautéed spinach, diced prosciutto and eggs is absolutely delicious. In Italy, fritatte *are often used as fillings for sandwiches.*

SERVES 6

INGREDIENTS

200g/7oz/1 cup cooked spinach
45ml/3 tbsp olive oil
4 spring onions (scallions), finely sliced
1 garlic clove, finely chopped
50g/2oz/⅓ cup prosciutto, cut into small dice
8 eggs
salt and ground black pepper

1 Squeeze any excess moisture out of the cooked spinach with your hands. Chop it roughly and set aside.

2 Heat the oil in a large non-stick or heavy frying pan. Stir in the spring onions and cook for 3–4 minutes. Add the garlic and prosciutto, then stir over a medium heat until just golden. Stir in the spinach and cook for 3–4 minutes, or until just heated through. Season with salt and pepper.

3 Break the eggs into a bowl and beat lightly with a fork. Raise the heat under the vegetables. After about 1 minute pour in the eggs. Mix them quickly into the other ingredients and stop stirring. Cook over a medium heat for 5–6 minutes on the first side, or until the frittata is puffed and golden brown. If the frittata seems to be sticking to the pan, shake the pan backwards and forwards to release it.

4 Take a large heatproof plate, place it upside down over the pan and, holding it firmly with oven gloves, turn the pan and the frittata over on to it. Slide the frittata back into the pan and continue cooking for 3–4 minutes, until golden brown on the second side. Remove from the heat. The frittata can be served hot, at room temperature or cold. Cut it into wedges to serve.

PROSCIUTTO WITH FIGS

Salty cured ham makes an excellent starter sliced paper-thin and served with sweet, fresh figs. The hams cured in the region of Parma in the north of Italy are held to be the finest in the country. Figs are grown all over Italy, but the hot climate of Sicily is said to produce the best fruits of all, with their luscious pink flesh.

SERVES 4

INGREDIENTS
8 ripe green or black figs
12 paper-thin slices prosciutto crudo
crusty bread and unsalted butter, to serve

1 Wipe the figs with a damp cloth. Cut them almost into quarters but do not cut all the way through the base. If the skins are tender, they may be eaten along with the inner fruit. If you prefer, peel each quarter carefully by pulling the peel gently away from the pulp.

2 Arrange the slices of prosciutto crudo on a large serving platter, then arrange the quartered figs on top. Serve with plenty of crusty bread and unsalted butter.

TUNA CARPACCIO

Carpaccio is usually made with finely sliced fillet of beef, marinated in oil and vinegar, but meaty fish like tuna and swordfish make an unusual and delicious alternative. The secret is to slice the fish wafer thin by freezing it first, a technique also used by the Japanese for making sashimi.

SERVES 4

INGREDIENTS
2 fresh tuna steaks, about 450g/1lb total weight
60ml/4 tbsp extra virgin olive oil
15ml/1 tbsp balsamic vinegar
5ml/1 tsp caster (superfine) sugar
30ml/2 tbsp drained bottled green peppercorns or capers
salt and ground black pepper
lemon wedges and green salad, to serve

1 Using a sharp knife, remove and discard the skin from each tuna steak. Place each steak between two sheets of clear film or non-stick baking paper and pound with a rolling pin until flattened slightly.

2 Peel off the clear film or non-stick baking paper and roll up each flattened tuna steak as tightly as possible. Wrap tightly in clear film and place in the freezer for 4 hours, or until firm.

3 Unwrap the frozen tuna and, using a very sharp knife, cut crossways into the thinnest possible slices. Arrange the fish on individual plates.

4 Place the olive oil, balsamic vinegar, sugar and peppercorns or capers in a jug (pitcher) and whisk together. Season with salt and pepper and pour over the tuna. Cover and allow to come to room temperature for 30 minutes before serving with lemon wedges and green salad.

STUFFED MUSSELS

This wonderful dish is a speciality of southern Italy. Mussels are lightly cooked, then filled with a garlicky mixture of parsley and breadcrumbs and baked. This dish can also be made with large clams rather than mussels and can be enjoyed hot or cold.

SERVES 4

INGREDIENTS
675g/1½lb large fresh mussels
75g/3oz/⅓ cup butter, at room temperature
25g/1oz/¼ cup dry breadcrumbs
2 garlic cloves, finely chopped
45ml/3 tbsp chopped fresh parsley
25g/1oz/¼ cup freshly grated Parmesan cheese
salt and ground black pepper

1 Scrub the mussels well under cold running water, cutting off the "beard" with a small knife. Discard any that do not close when tapped sharply with the back of a knife. Preheat the oven to 230°C/450°F/Gas 8.

2 Place the mussels in a large pan with 250ml/8fl oz/1 cup water and cook over a medium heat. As soon as they open, lift them out one by one with a slotted spoon. Discard any mussels that do not open. Remove and discard the empty half of each shell, leaving the mussel in the other half.

3 To make the stuffing, place the butter, breadcrumbs, garlic, parsley and grated Parmesan in a small bowl and stir well. Place the mixture in a pan and heat gently, stirring with a wooden spoon, until the stuffing mixture begins to soften. Season with ground black pepper.

4 Arrange the mussel halves on a flat baking tray. Spoon a small amount of the stuffing into each mussel. Bake for about 7 minutes, or until lightly browned. Serve hot or at room temperature.

Sautéed Mussels with Garlic

These garlicky mussels make a great appetizer. They are served without their shells in a delicious sauce flavoured with paprika and chilli. Serve with crusty Italian bread to soak up the richly flavoured juices.

SERVES 4

INGREDIENTS
900g/2lb fresh mussels
1 lemon slice
90ml/6 tbsp olive oil
2 shallots, finely chopped
1 garlic clove, finely chopped
15ml/1 tbsp chopped fresh parsley
2.5ml/½ tsp paprika
1.5ml/¼ tsp dried chilli flakes

1 Scrub the mussels well under cold running water, cutting off the "beard" with a small knife. Discard any that do not close when tapped sharply with the back of a knife.

2 Put the mussels in a large pan, with 250ml/8fl oz/1 cup water and the slice of lemon. Bring to the boil and cook for 3–4 minutes; remove the mussels as they open. Discard any that remain closed. Take the mussels out of the shells and drain on kitchen paper.

3 Heat the oil in a sauté pan, add the mussels and cook, stirring, for 1 minute. Remove the mussels from the pan using a slotted spoon. Add the shallots and garlic to the pan and cook, covered, over a low heat, for about 5 minutes, until soft.

4 Remove the pan from the heat and stir in the parsley, paprika and chilli flakes. Return to the heat and stir in the mussels with any juices. Cook briefly to heat through, then serve at once.

SOUPS

In Italy, soups range from clear broths with a scattering of tiny pasta, to fresh vegetable soups, chunky minestrone and substantial soups made with grains and pulses. Light broths, such as Tiny Pasta in Broth, are often served before the main meal or as a pick-me-up when you are unwell. Delicate, puréed soups, such as Fresh Tomato and Basil Soup and Cream of Courgette Soup, are also served before the main meal, while more substantial soups, such as Tuscan Bean Soup and Spinach and Rice Soup, can be served as a meal in themselves and are often eaten in the evening if the main meal of the day has been at lunchtime.

PASTA SQUARES & PEAS IN BROTH

This thick soup comes from the Lazio region, where it is traditionally made with fresh home-made pasta and peas. In this modern version, ready-made pasta is used with frozen peas, to save time.

SERVES 4–6

INGREDIENTS
25g/1oz/2 tbsp butter
50g/2oz pancetta or rindless smoked streaky (fatty) bacon, roughly chopped
1 small onion, finely chopped
1 celery stick, finely chopped
400g/14oz/3½ cups frozen peas
5ml/1 tsp tomato purée (paste)
5–10ml/1–2 tsp finely chopped fresh flat leaf parsley
1 litre/1¾ pints/4 cups chicken stock
300g/11oz fresh lasagne sheets
about 50g/2oz prosciutto crudo, cut into cubes
salt and ground black pepper
freshly grated Parmesan cheese, to serve

1 Melt the butter in a large pan and add the chopped pancetta or bacon, onion and celery. Cook over a low heat, stirring constantly, for 5 minutes.

2 Add the peas to the pan and cook, stirring, for 3–4 minutes. Stir in the tomato purée and parsley, then add the chicken stock. Season with salt and pepper. Bring the mixture to the boil. Cover, lower the heat and simmer for 10 minutes. Meanwhile, cut the lasagne sheets into 2cm/¾in squares.

3 Taste the stock for seasoning. Drop in the pasta, stir and bring to the boil. Simmer for 2–3 minutes or until the pasta is *al dente*, drain then stir in the prosciutto. Serve hot in warmed bowls, with grated Parmesan handed around separately.

TINY PASTA IN BROTH

In Italy, this soup is known as Pastina in Brodo *and is often served with bread for a light evening supper. Use any dried tiny soup pasta, such as conchigliette or farfalline, in place of the funghetti, if you prefer.*

SERVES 4

INGREDIENTS
1.2 litres/2 pints/5 cups beef stock
75g/3oz/¾ cup dried funghetti
2 pieces bottled roasted red (bell) pepper, about 50g/2oz
salt and ground black pepper
coarsely shaved Parmesan cheese, to serve

1 Pour the beef stock into a large, heavy pan and bring to the boil. Season with salt and ground black pepper to taste, then drop in the dried funghetti. Stir well and bring back to the boil.

2 Lower the heat and simmer for about 8 minutes, or according to the packet instructions, until the pasta is *al dente*. Stir frequently during cooking to prevent the pasta shapes from sticking together.

3 Drain the pieces of roasted pepper and dice them finely. Place them in the bottom of four warmed soup bowls. Taste the soup for seasoning and add more salt and pepper if necessary. Ladle the soup into the warmed soup bowls and serve immediately, with shavings of Parmesan handed separately.

Cappelletti in Broth

This light soup is usually served in northern Italy on Santo Stefano (St Stephen's Day – the day after Christmas) and on New Year's Day. The stock is traditionally made with the Christmas capon carcass.

SERVES 4

INGREDIENTS
1.2 litres/2 pints/5 cups chicken stock
90–115g/3½–4oz/1 cup fresh or dried cappelletti
30ml/2 tbsp dry white wine (optional)
about 15ml/1 tbsp finely chopped fresh flat leaf parsley (optional)
salt and ground black pepper
about 30ml/2 tbsp freshly grated Parmesan cheese, to serve
shredded flat leaf parsley, to garnish

1 Pour the chicken stock into a large pan and bring to the boil. Season with salt and black pepper to taste, then drop in the cappelletti. Stir well and bring back to the boil. Lower the heat to a simmer and cook according to the instructions on the packet, until the pasta is *al dente*. Stir frequently during cooking to ensure the pasta cooks evenly.

2 If using, pour the wine into the pan and add the parsley. Stir well. Taste for seasoning, adding more if necessary. Ladle the soup into four warmed bowls, then sprinkle with grated Parmesan and garnish with parsley. Serve immediately.

COOK'S TIPS
• *Cappelletti is just another name for tortellini, which come from Romagna. You can buy them dried or fresh, or you can make your own.*
• *Other small stuffed pasta, such as agnolotti or sacchettini can be used instead of cappelletti and will be just as delicious.*

PASTA SOUP WITH CHICKEN LIVERS

This light and tasty soup can be served as either a first or main course. Even if you do not normally like chicken livers, they are so delicious in this recipe that you will find yourself loving them.

SERVES 4–6

INGREDIENTS
115g/4oz/⅔ cup chicken livers, thawed if frozen
3 sprigs each of fresh parsley, marjoram and sage
leaves from 1 fresh thyme sprig
5–6 fresh basil leaves
15ml/1 tbsp olive oil
knob butter
4 garlic cloves, crushed
15–30ml/1–2 tbsp dry white wine
2 × 300g/11oz cans condensed chicken consommé
225g/8oz/2 cups frozen peas
50g/2oz/½ cup dried pasta shapes, e.g. farfalle
2–3 spring onions (scallions), diagonally sliced
salt and ground black pepper

1 Cut the chicken livers into small pieces with scissors. Chop the herbs. Heat the oil and butter in a frying pan, add the garlic and herbs, with salt and pepper to taste, and fry gently for a few minutes. Add the livers, increase the heat to high and stir-fry for a few minutes until they change colour and become dry. Pour the wine over the livers, cook until dry, then remove the pan from the heat.

2 Tip both cans of consommé into a large pan and add water as directed on the labels. Add an extra can of water, then stir in a little salt and black pepper to taste and bring to the boil.

3 Add the frozen peas to the pan and simmer for about 5 minutes, then add the pasta shapes and bring the soup back to the boil, stirring. Allow to simmer, stirring frequently, until the pasta is only just *al dente*: about 5 minutes or according to the instructions on the packet. Add the livers and spring onions and heat through for 2–3 minutes. Taste for seasoning. Serve hot, in warmed bowls.

Rich Minestrone

This special minestrone is made with chicken and flavoured with fresh basil and rosemary. It makes a hearty meal, served with crusty Italian bread, such as ciabatta or pane Toscano, and freshly grated Parmesan cheese.

Serves 4–6

Ingredients
15ml/1 tbsp olive oil
2 chicken thighs
3 rindless streaky (fatty) bacon rashers, chopped
1 onion, finely chopped
a few fresh basil leaves, shredded
a few fresh rosemary leaves, finely chopped
15ml/1 tbsp chopped fresh flat leaf parsley
2 potatoes, cut into 1cm/½ in cubes
1 large carrot, cut into 1cm/½in cubes
2 small courgettes (zucchini), cut into 1cm/½in cubes
1–2 celery sticks, cut into 1cm/½in cubes
1 litre/1¾ pints/4 cups chicken stock
200g/7oz/1¾ cups frozen peas
90g/3½oz/scant 1 cup stellette
salt and ground black pepper
coarsely shaved Parmesan cheese, to serve
fresh basil leaves, to garnish

Cook's Tip
For extra flavour, add any extra pieces of Parmesan rind to the simmering soup. If you cannot find stellette, any other dried tiny soup pasta, such as orecchiette or funghetti, can be used instead. Alfabetini, in the shape of letters, are often a popular choice with children.

1 Heat the olive oil in a large frying pan, add the chicken thighs and fry for about 5 minutes on each side. Remove the chicken thighs from the pan with a slotted spoon or tongs and set aside.

2 Lower the heat, add the chopped bacon, onion, basil, rosemary and parsley to the frying pan and stir to coat in oil. Cook gently over a low heat, stirring frequently, for about 5 minutes. Add the potatoes, carrot, courgettes and celery to the pan and cook for about 6 minutes more, stirring frequently.

3 Return the chicken thighs to the pan of vegetables, pour in the chicken stock and bring to the boil. Cover and cook over a low heat for 35–40 minutes, stirring the soup occasionally.

4 Remove the chicken thighs from the pan with a slotted spoon and place them on a board. Stir the peas and pasta into the soup and bring back to the boil. Simmer for 7–8 minutes, or according to the instructions on the packet, until the pasta is *al dente*, stirring frequently.

5 Meanwhile, remove and discard the skin from the chicken thighs, then remove the meat from the bones and cut it into 1cm/½in pieces. Return the meat to the soup and heat through. Taste for seasoning, then ladle into warmed soup bowls. Scatter over the Parmesan shavings and serve immediately, garnished with one or two fresh basil leaves.

GENOESE MINESTRONE

In Genoa, cooks often stir pesto into minestrone towards the end of cooking. This soup is packed full of vegetables and has a good strong flavour. It makes an excellent vegetarian supper dish, served with plenty of crusty Italian bread.

SERVES 4–6

INGREDIENTS
1 onion
2 celery sticks
1 large carrot
45ml/3 tbsp olive oil
150g/5oz green beans, cut into 5cm/2in pieces
1 courgette (zucchini), thinly sliced
1 potato, cut into 1cm/½in cubes
¼ Savoy cabbage, shredded
1 small aubergine (eggplant), cut into 1cm/½in cubes
200g/7oz can cannellini beans, drained and rinsed
2 Italian plum tomatoes, chopped
1.2 litres/2 pints/5 cups vegetable stock
90g/3½oz dried spaghetti or vermicelli
salt and ground black pepper

FOR THE PESTO
about 20 fresh basil leaves
1 garlic clove
10ml/2 tsp pine nuts
15ml/1 tbsp freshly grated Parmesan cheese
15ml/1 tbsp freshly grated Pecorino cheese
30ml/2 tbsp olive oil

COOK'S TIP
If you are in a hurry or don't want to go to the trouble of making your own pesto, the bottled variety makes a good substitute. Use traditional green basil pesto rather than the red sun-dried tomato pesto. You will need about 45ml/3 tbsp.

1 Chop the onion, celery and carrot finely, either in a food processor or by hand. Heat the olive oil in a large pan, add the finely chopped vegetables and cook over a low heat, stirring frequently, for about 6 minutes. Add the green beans, courgette, potato and cabbage and stir-fry over a medium heat for about 3 minutes.

2 Add the aubergine, cannellini beans and tomatoes to the pan of vegetables and stir-fry for 2–3 minutes. Pour in the vegetable stock and season with salt and ground black pepper. Bring the mixture to the boil. Stir well, cover and lower the heat. Simmer for about 40 minutes, stirring occasionally.

3 Meanwhile, make the pesto. Process all the ingredients in a food processor until the mixture forms a smooth sauce, adding 15–45ml/1–3 tbsp water through the feeder tube if the mixture seems too thick.

4 Break the spaghetti or vermicelli into small pieces and add it to the soup. Simmer, stirring frequently, for 5 minutes. Add the pesto sauce and stir well, then simmer for 2–3 minutes more, or until the pasta is *al dente*. Taste for seasoning. Serve hot, in warmed soup bowls.

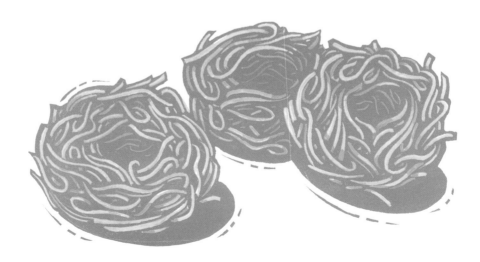

Fresh Tomato & Basil Soup

This is the perfect soup for late summer, when fresh tomatoes are at their most flavoursome. It is delicious served hot, but can also be served chilled: after straining, chill for at least 4 hours, then stir in the cream and serve immediately.

Serves 4–6

Ingredients
15ml/1 tbsp olive oil
25g/1oz/2 tbsp butter
1 onion, finely chopped
900g/2lb ripe Italian plum tomatoes, roughly chopped
1 garlic clove, roughly chopped
about 750ml/1¼ pints/3 cups chicken or vegetable stock
120ml/4fl oz/½ cup dry white wine
30ml/2 tbsp sun-dried tomato paste
30ml/2 tbsp shredded fresh basil, plus a few whole leaves, to garnish
150ml/¼ pint/⅔ cup double (heavy) cream
salt and ground black pepper

1 Heat the olive oil and butter in a large pan until foaming. Add the onion and cook gently for about 5–6 minutes, stirring frequently, until softened.

2 Add the chopped tomatoes and garlic to the onions, then stir in the stock, white wine and sun-dried tomato paste. Season with salt and pepper. Bring to the boil, then lower the heat, half cover the pan and simmer gently for 10–12 minutes, stirring occasionally to stop the tomatoes sticking to the base of the pan.

3 Process the soup with the shredded basil in a food processor or blender, then press through a strainer into a clean pan.

4 Pour the double cream into the soup and heat through, stirring. Do not allow the soup to boil. Check the consistency and add more stock if necessary, then taste for seasoning. Pour into heated bowls and garnish with basil. Serve at once.

LENTIL SOUP WITH TOMATOES

This is a classic rustic Italian soup flavoured with fresh rosemary. Look out for small green lentils in Italian groceries or delicatessens as they are particularly good in this recipe. Serve with freshly baked garlic bread.

SERVES 4

INGREDIENTS
225g/8oz/1 cup dried green or brown lentils
45ml/3 tbsp olive oil
3 rindless streaky (fatty) bacon rashers, cut into small dice
1 onion, finely chopped
2 celery sticks, finely chopped
2 carrots, finely diced
2 rosemary sprigs, finely chopped
2 bay leaves
400g/14oz can chopped plum tomatoes
1.75 litres/3 pints/7½ cups vegetable stock
salt and ground black pepper
bay leaves and rosemary sprigs, to garnish

1 Pick over the lentils carefully, discarding any stones or other particles, then place in a large bowl and cover with cold water. Leave to soak for at least 2 hours. Rinse and drain well.

2 Heat the olive oil in a large pan. Add the bacon and cook for about 3 minutes, then stir in the onion and cook for 5 minutes until softened. Stir in the celery, carrots, rosemary, bay leaves and soaked lentils. Toss over the heat for 1 minute until thoroughly coated in the oil.

3 Add the chopped tomatoes and stock to the pan and bring to the boil. Lower the heat, half cover the pan, and simmer for about 1 hour, or until the lentils are perfectly tender. Remove the bay leaves and season with salt and pepper to taste. Serve with a garnish of fresh bay leaves and rosemary sprigs.

TUSCAN BEAN SOUP

There are many versions of this bean soup from Tuscany. This one uses cannellini beans, leeks, cabbage and olive oil – and tastes even better reheated the next day.

SERVES 4

INGREDIENTS
45ml/3 tbsp extra virgin olive oil
1 onion, roughly chopped
2 leeks, roughly chopped
1 large potato, peeled and diced
2 garlic cloves, finely chopped
1.2 litres/2 pints/5 cups vegetable stock
400g/14oz can cannellini beans, drained, liquid reserved
175g/6oz Savoy cabbage, shredded
45ml/3 tbsp chopped fresh flat leaf parsley
30ml/2 tbsp chopped fresh oregano
75g/3oz/1 cup Parmesan cheese, shaved
salt and ground black pepper
extra virgin olive oil, to serve

FOR THE GARLIC TOASTS
45ml/2–3 tbsp extra virgin olive oil
thick slices country bread
garlic clove, peeled and bruised

1 Heat the oil in a large pan, add the onion, leeks, potato and garlic and cook over a gentle heat for 4–5 minutes. Pour the stock and liquid from the beans over the vegetables. Cover and simmer for 10 minutes. Add the cabbage, beans and half the herbs to the pan. Season and cook for 10 minutes.

2 Spoon one-third of the soup into a food processor or blender and process until smooth. Return to the soup in the pan, taste for seasoning and heat through.

3 Meanwhile, make the garlic toasts. Drizzle a little oil over the slices of bread, then rub both sides of each slice with the garlic. Toast until browned on both sides. Ladle the soup into bowls. Sprinkle with the remaining herbs and the Parmesan shavings. Add a drizzle of olive oil and serve with the toasts.

WHITE BEAN SOUP

This hearty, warming soup from Tuscany is made with puréed beans, which give it a wonderful texture and delicous flavour. It makes a great winter lunch or supper dish.

SERVES 6

INGREDIENTS
350g/12oz/1½ cups dried cannellini or other white beans
1 bay leaf
75ml/5 tbsp olive oil
1 onion, finely chopped
1 carrot, finely chopped
1 stick celery, finely chopped
3 tomatoes, peeled and finely chopped
2 garlic cloves, finely chopped
5ml/1 tsp fresh thyme leaves or 2.5ml/½ tsp dried thyme
750ml/1¼ pints/3 cups boiling water
salt and ground black pepper
extra virgin olive oil, to serve

1 Pick over the beans, discarding any stones or other particles, place in a bowl, pour over cold water and leave to soak overnight. Drain. Place the beans in a large pan of water, bring to the boil and cook for 20 minutes. Drain, then return to the pan, cover with cold water and bring back to the boil. Add the bay leaf and cook for 1–2 hours until the beans are tender. Drain and remove the bay leaf.

2 Place about three-quarters of the beans in a food processor and process to a purée, or pass through a food mill, adding a little water if necessary.

3 Heat the olive oil in a large heavy pan. Stir in the chopped onion and cook for about 5 minutes over a low heat until soft. Add the chopped carrot and celery and cook for about 5 minutes more.

4 Add the tomatoes, garlic and thyme to the pan and cook for 6–8 minutes, stirring frequently. Pour in the boiling water and stir in the beans and the bean purée. Season with salt and pepper and simmer for 10–15 minutes. Serve in individual soup bowls, sprinkled with a little olive oil.

PASTA & CHICKPEA SOUP

In this simple, country-style soup, the shape of the pasta and the beans complement
one another beautifully. If you like garlic, add one or two crushed cloves with the
vegetables for extra flavour.

SERVES 4–6

INGREDIENTS
1 onion
2 carrots
2 celery sticks
60ml/4 tbsp olive oil
400g/14oz can chickpeas, rinsed and drained
200g/7oz can cannellini beans, rinsed and drained
150ml/¼ pint/⅔ cup passata (bottled strained tomatoes)
120ml/4fl oz/½ cup water
1.5 litres/2½ pints/6¼ cups vegetable or chicken stock
1 fresh rosemary sprig, plus extra to garnish
200g/7oz/scant 2 cups dried conchiglie
salt and ground black pepper
freshly grated Parmesan cheese, to serve

1 Chop the onion, carrots and celery finely, either in a food processor or by hand.
Heat the oil in a large pan, add the finely chopped vegetables and cook over a
low heat, stirring frequently, for 5–7 minutes.

2 Add the chickpeas and cannellini beans to the pan and cook for 5–6 minutes.
Stir in the passata and water. Cook, stirring, for 2–3 minutes.

3 Pour 475ml/16fl oz/2 cups of the stock into the pan, add the rosemary sprig
and season with salt and black pepper. Bring the mixture to the boil, cover, then
simmer gently, stirring occasionally, for 1 hour.

4 Pour the remaining stock into the pan, add the conchiglie and bring to the boil,
stirring. Lower the heat and simmer, stirring frequently, for 7–8 minutes or
until *al dente*. Taste for seasoning. Remove the rosemary sprig and serve the soup
hot, in warmed bowls, topped with grated Parmesan and a few rosemary sprigs.

RICE & BROAD BEAN SOUP

This wonderful soup makes the most of fresh broad beans while they are in season.
It works well with frozen beans for the rest of the year.

SERVES 4

INGREDIENTS
1kg/2¼lb broad (fava) beans in their pods, or 400g/14oz shelled
  frozen broad beans, thawed
90ml/6 tbsp olive oil
1 onion, finely chopped
2 tomatoes, peeled and finely chopped
225g/8oz/1 cup risotto rice
25g/1oz/2 tbsp butter
1 litre/1¾ pints/4 cups boiling water
salt and ground black pepper
freshly grated Parmesan cheese, to serve (optional)

1 If using fresh beans, shell them and discard the pods. Bring a large pan of water to the boil and blanch the beans for 3–4 minutes. Drain and rinse under cold water and peel off the skins.

2 Heat the oil in a large pan. Add the onion and cook for 2–3 minutes over low to a medium heat until soft. Add the beans and cook for about 5 minutes, stirring. Season with salt and black pepper. Add the chopped tomatoes and cook for 5 minutes more, continuing to stir.

3 Add the rice to the pan and stir. Cook for 1–2 minutes, then add the butter and stir until it melts. Pour in the water, a little at a time, until it has all been added. Taste for seasoning and continue cooking until the rice is tender. Serve hot, with freshly grated Parmesan if liked.

COOK'S TIP
Fresh broad beans, picked in late spring and early
summer when they are still small, have tender skins
so do not need to be peeled.

SPINACH & RICE SOUP

Use very fresh, young spinach leaves to prepare this light and fresh-tasting soup. The addition of risotto rice adds body and creaminess, while fresh chilli adds a touch of spice and produces attractive red flecks in the finished soup.

SERVES 4

INGREDIENTS
675g/1½lb fresh spinach, washed
45ml/3 tbsp extra virgin olive oil
1 small onion, finely chopped
2 garlic cloves, finely chopped
1 small fresh red chilli, seeded and finely chopped
115g/4oz/generous 1 cup risotto rice
1.2 litres/2 pints/5 cups vegetable stock
60ml/4 tbsp grated Pecorino cheese
salt and ground black pepper

1 Place the spinach in a large pan with just the water that clings to its leaves after washing. Add a large pinch of salt. Heat gently until the spinach has wilted, then remove from the heat and drain, reserving any liquid.

2 Chop the spinach finely using a large knife or place in a food processor and process to a fairly coarse purée.

3 Heat the olive oil in a large pan and gently cook the onion, garlic and chilli for about 5 minutes, until softened. Add the rice and stir until well coated with the oil, then pour in the stock and reserved spinach liquid. Bring the mixture to the boil, lower the heat and simmer for 10 minutes.

4 Add the spinach to the rice mixture and season with salt and pepper to taste. Cook for about 5 minutes more, until the rice is tender. Check the seasoning again, adding more if necessary, and serve with the Pecorino cheese.

PUMPKIN SOUP

This smooth, beautifully coloured orange soup would be perfect for an autumn dinner. It uses spaghetti broken into pieces, but broken vermicelli or dried tiny soup pasta will give equally good results.

SERVES 4

INGREDIENTS
450g/1lb pumpkin peeled
50g/2oz/¼ cup butter
1 onion, finely chopped
750ml/1¼ pints/3 cups chicken broth or water
475ml/16fl oz/2 cups milk
a pinch of grated nutmeg
40g/1½oz/7 tbsp spaghetti, broken into small pieces
90ml/6 tbsp freshly grated Parmesan cheese
salt and ground black pepper

1 Chop the pumpkin into 2.5cm/1in cubes. Heat the butter in a large pan. Add the onion and cook over a medium heat for 6–8 minutes, until softened. Stir in the pumpkin and cook for 2–3 minutes more.

2 Pour the chicken broth or water into the pan and cook about 15 minutes until the pumpkin is soft. Remove the pan from the heat.

3 Tip the soup into a food processor or blender and process to a smooth purée. Return the puréed soup to the pan and stir in the milk and grated nutmeg. Season with salt and ground black pepper to taste, then bring the soup back to the boil over a gentle heat.

4 Add the broken spaghetti pieces to the soup and stir. Continue cooking over a gentle heat until the pasta is *al dente*. Stir in the grated Parmesan cheese, ladle into warmed soup bowls and serve at once.

WILD MUSHROOM SOUP

This delicious soup obtains its rich, mushroomy flavour from the addition of dried porcini, which have a very intense taste. Beef stock helps to strengthen the earthy flavour of the mushrooms and gives the soup a robust feel.

SERVES 4

INGREDIENTS
25g/1oz/2 cups dried porcini mushrooms
30ml/2 tbsp olive oil
15g/½oz/1 tbsp butter
2 leeks, thinly sliced
2 shallots, roughly chopped
1 garlic clove, roughly chopped
225g/8oz/3 cups fresh wild mushrooms
about 1.2 litres/2 pints/5 cups beef stock
2.5ml/½ tsp dried thyme
150ml/¼ pint/⅔ cup double (heavy) cream
salt and ground black pepper
fresh thyme sprigs, to garnish

1 Put the dried porcini in a bowl, pour over 250ml/8fl oz/1 cup warm water and leave to soak for 20–30 minutes. Lift the mushrooms out of the liquid and squeeze over the bowl to remove as much of the soaking liquid as possible. Strain the liquid and reserve. Finely chop the porcini.

2 Heat the olive oil and butter in a large pan until foaming. Add the prepared leeks, shallots and garlic, and cook gently for about 5 minutes, stirring frequently, until softened but not coloured.

3 Chop or slice the fresh mushrooms and add to the pan. Cook over a medium heat for a few minutes until they begin to soften. Pour in the stock and bring to the boil. Add the porcini, soaking liquid, thyme and seasoning. Lower the heat, half cover the pan and simmer for 30 minutes, stirring occasionally.

4 Pour three-quarters of the soup into a food processor and process until smooth. Return to the pan, stir in the cream and heat through. Add more stock if the soup is too thick and taste for seasoning. Serve hot, garnished with fresh thyme.

CREAM OF COURGETTE SOUP

The beauty of this soup is its delicate pale green colour, rich and creamy texture and subtle taste. If you prefer a more pronounced cheese flavour, use Gorgonzola instead of dolcelatte as it has a more pungent taste.

SERVES 4–6

INGREDIENTS
30ml/2 tbsp olive oil
15g/½oz/1 tbsp butter
1 onion, roughly chopped
900g/2lb courgettes (zucchini), trimmed and sliced
5ml/1 tsp dried oregano
about 600ml/1 pint/2½ cups vegetable or chicken stock
115g/4oz dolcelatte cheese, rind removed, diced
300ml/½ pint/1¼ cups single (light) cream
salt and ground black pepper
fresh oregano and extra dolcelatte, to garnish

1 Heat the oil and butter in a large pan until foaming. Add the onion and cook gently for about 5 minutes, stirring frequently, until softened. Add the courgettes and oregano and season with salt and black pepper. Cook over a medium heat for 10 minutes, stirring frequently.

2 Pour the chicken stock into the pan and bring the mixture to the boil, stirring. Lower the heat, half cover the pan and simmer gently for about 30 minutes, stirring occasionally. Add the diced dolcelatte and stir until melted.

3 Tip the soup into a food processor or blender and process until smooth, then press through a strainer into a clean pan. Pour in two-thirds of the cream and stir over a low heat until hot, but do not allow to boil.

4 Check the consistency of the soup and add more stock if it is too thick. Taste for seasoning, then pour into warmed soup bowls. Swirl in the remaining cream and serve immediately, garnished with oregano and extra cheese.

PASTA & GNOCCHI

Traditionally, pasta and gnocchi are served after the antipasti and before the main course of meat or fish. Freshly made pasta needs little more than a dressing of butter, Parmesan cheese, pesto, or garlic and oil but fresh, local ingredients, such as tomatoes, artichokes, anchovies, nuts and shellfish, make wonderful pasta sauces. Pasta can also be made into more substantial baked dishes. Gnocchi are light and fluffy little dumplings that are usually made with potato but can also be made with semolina, ricotta, spinach and pumpkin. Like pasta, they can be served with a simple dressing or a more elaborate sauce.

Spaghetti with Garlic & Oil

In Italy, this wonderfully simple dish is known as Spaghetti Aglio, Olio e Peperoncino. *However, in Rome, they often run the words together to pronounce the name of this dish as "spaghetti-ayo-e-oyo" or simply "ayo-e-oyo".*

SERVES 4

INGREDIENTS
400g/14oz fresh or dried spaghetti
90ml/6 tbsp extra virgin olive oil
2–4 garlic cloves, crushed
1 dried red chilli
1 small handful fresh flat leaf parsley, roughly chopped
salt

1 Cook the spaghetti in a large pan of salted boiling water, according to the instructions on the packet. Meanwhile, heat the oil very gently in a small frying pan or pan. Add the crushed garlic and whole dried chilli and stir over a low heat until the garlic is just beginning to brown. Remove the chilli and discard.

2 Drain the pasta and tip it into a large warmed serving bowl. Tip the warm oil and garlic mixture over the spaghetti, add the chopped parsley and toss vigorously until the pasta glistens. Serve immediately.

COOK'S TIPS
• *Don't use salt in the oil and garlic mixture, because it will not dissolve sufficiently.*
• *In Rome, grated Parmesan is never served with this dish, nor is it seasoned with pepper.*
• *In summer, Romans use fresh chillies, which they grow in pots on their terraces and window ledges.*

SPAGHETTI WITH FRESH TOMATO SAUCE

This Neapolitan sauce is made in summer when tomatoes are very ripe and sweet. It only uses a few ingredients so that nothing detracts from the flavour of the tomatoes themselves. Spaghetti is the traditional choice of pasta with this sauce.

SERVES 4

INGREDIENTS
675g/1½lb ripe Italian plum tomatoes
60ml/4 tbsp olive oil
1 onion, finely chopped
350g/12oz fresh or dried spaghetti
1 small handful fresh basil leaves
salt and ground black pepper
coarsely shaved Parmesan cheese, to serve

1 With a sharp knife, cut a cross in the bottom (flower) end of each tomato. Bring a medium pan of water to the boil and remove from the heat. Plunge a few of the tomatoes into the water, leave for 30 seconds, then lift out with a slotted spoon. Repeat with the remaining tomatoes. Peel off the skin and roughly chop the flesh.

2 Heat the olive oil in a large pan, add the onion and cook over a low heat, stirring frequently, for about 5 minutes until soft and lightly coloured. Add the tomatoes and season with salt and pepper. Bring the mixture to a simmer, then turn the heat down and cover the pan. Cook over a low heat, stirring occasionally, for 30–40 minutes until the sauce has thickened.

3 Meanwhile, cook the spaghetti in a large pan of salted boiling water, according to the instructions on the packet. Shred the basil leaves finely. Remove the sauce from the heat, stir in the basil and taste for seasoning. Drain the pasta, tip it into a warmed serving bowl, pour the sauce over and toss well. Serve immediately, with shaved Parmesan handed separately.

PENNE ALL'ARRABBIATA

This is one of Rome's best loved pasta dishes. Literally translated, arrabbiata means "enraged" or "furious", but in this context it should be translated as "fiery", which describes the spicy, chilli-flavoured tomato sauce. Make it as hot as you like by adding more chillies to taste.

SERVES 4

INGREDIENTS
25g/1oz dried porcini mushrooms
90g/3½oz/7 tbsp butter
150g/5oz pancetta or rindless smoked streaky
  (fatty) bacon, diced
1–2 dried red chillies, to taste
2 garlic cloves, crushed
8 ripe Italian plum tomatoes, peeled and chopped
a few fresh basil leaves, torn, plus extra to garnish
350g/12oz/3 cups fresh or dried penne
50g/2oz/⅔ cup freshly grated Parmesan cheese
25g/1oz/⅓ cup freshly grated Pecorino cheese
salt

> ## VARIATION
> For a vegetarian version of this classic spicy tomato sauce, use black olives in place of the pancetta or bacon. Leave out step 2 and add 25g/1oz/¼ cup roughly chopped black olives in step 5.

1 Place the dried porcini mushrooms in a small bowl and pour over warm water to cover. Leave to soak for about 20 minutes. Drain, then squeeze dry with your hands. Finely chop and set aside.

2 Melt 50g/2oz/4 tbsp of the butter in a medium pan or skillet. Add the diced pancetta or bacon and stir-fry over a medium heat until golden and slightly crispy. Lift the pancetta from the pan with a slotted spoon and set aside.

3 Add the chopped porcini to the pan or skillet and stir-fry over a medium heat for about 5 minutes. Lift out the mushrooms with a slotted spoon and set aside with the cooked pancetta or bacon.

4 Crumble one dried chilli into the pan, add the garlic and cook, stirring, for a few minutes until the garlic turns golden brown. Add the chopped tomatoes and basil leaves and season with salt. Cook gently, stirring occasionally, for about 12 minutes. Meanwhile, cook the penne in a large pan of salted boiling water, according to the instructions on the packet.

5 Add the pancetta or bacon and the mushrooms to the tomato sauce and stir well. Taste for seasoning, adding more chillies if you prefer a hotter flavour. If the sauce is too dry, stir in a little of the pasta water.

6 Drain the pasta and tip it into a warmed serving bowl. Dice the remaining butter, add it to the pasta with the cheeses, then toss until well coated. Pour the spicy tomato sauce over the pasta, toss well and serve immediately, with a few basil leaves sprinkled on top.

ELICHE WITH PESTO

This fragrant green sauce is traditionally made from fresh basil, pine nuts, grated Parmesan and Pecorino and olive oil. Bottled pesto is a useful stand-by, but if you have a food processor, it is very easy to make and the taste is much better.

SERVES 4

INGREDIENTS
50g/2oz/1⅓ cups fresh basil leaves, plus extra to garnish
2–4 garlic cloves
60ml/4 tbsp pine nuts
120ml/4fl oz/½ cup extra virgin olive oil
115g/4oz/1⅓ cups freshly grated Parmesan cheese, plus extra to serve
25g/1oz/⅓ cup freshly grated Pecorino cheese
400g/14oz/3½ cups dried eliche
salt and ground black pepper

1 Put the basil leaves, garlic and pine nuts in a blender or food processor. Add 60ml/4 tbsp of the olive oil. Process until the ingredients are finely chopped, then stop the machine, remove the lid and scrape down the sides of the bowl.

2 Turn the machine on again and slowly pour the remaining oil in a thin, steady stream through the feeder tube. You may need to stop the machine and scrape down the sides of the bowl once or twice. Tip the mixture into a large bowl and beat in the cheeses with a wooden spoon. Check for seasoning.

3 Cook the pasta in a large pan of salted boiling water, according to the instructions on the packet. Drain well, add to the bowl of pesto and toss well. Serve immediately, garnished with the fresh basil leaves. Hand Parmesan separately.

COOK'S TIP
Pesto can be made 2–3 days in advance. To store, transfer to a small bowl and pour over a film of olive oil. Cover tightly with clear film and refrigerate.

Linguine with Sun-dried Tomato Pesto

This delicious red pesto is made with sun-dried tomatoes instead of basil. It was once a rarity but is becoming increasingly popular and can be bought ready-made in jars. However, it is very simple to make and is even more delicious.

Serves 4

Ingredients
25g/1oz/⅓ cup pine nuts
25g/1oz/⅓ cup freshly grated Parmesan cheese
50g/2oz/½ cup sun-dried tomatoes in olive oil
1 garlic clove, roughly chopped
60ml/4 tbsp olive oil
350g/12oz fresh or dried linguine
salt and ground black pepper
coarsely shaved Parmesan cheese, to serve
basil leaves, to garnish

1 Put the pine nuts in a small non-stick frying pan and toss over a low to medium heat for 1–2 minutes until the nuts are lightly toasted and golden. Tip the pine nuts into a food processor and add the grated Parmesan, sun-dried tomatoes and garlic. Process until finely chopped, season with plenty of black pepper and process briefly to combine.

2 With the machine running, gradually pour the olive oil through the feeder tube and process until it has all been incorporated and the ingredients have formed a smooth paste, scraping down the sides of the bowl once or twice.

3 Cook the pasta in a large pan of salted boiling water, according to the instructions on the packet. Drain, reserving a little of the cooking water. Tip the pasta into a warmed bowl, add the pesto and a few spoonfuls of the hot water and toss. Serve immediately, garnished with basil. Hand Parmesan shavings separately.

PENNE WITH ARTICHOKES

Artichokes are a very popular vegetable in Italy, and are often used in sauces for pasta. This wonderful dish is garlicky and richly flavoured, the perfect dinner party first course during the globe artichoke season.

SERVES 6

INGREDIENTS
juice of ½–1 lemon
2 globe artichokes
30ml/2 tbsp olive oil
1 small fennel bulb, thinly sliced, with feathery tops reserved
1 onion, finely chopped
4 garlic cloves, finely chopped
1 handful fresh flat leaf parsley, roughly chopped
400g/14oz can chopped Italian plum tomatoes
150ml/¼ pint/⅔ cup dry white wine
350g/12oz/3 cups dried penne
10ml/2 tsp capers, chopped
salt and ground black pepper
freshly grated Parmesan cheese, to serve

1 Prepare a bowl of cold water and stir in the juice of half a lemon. Cut off the artichoke stalks, then pull off and discard the outer leaves until only the pale inner leaves that are almost white at the base of the artichoke remain.

2 With a pair of kitchen scissors or a sharp knife, cut off the tops of these leaves so that the base remains. Cut the base in half lengthways, then prise the hairy choke out of the centre with the tip of a knife and discard.

3 Cut the artichokes lengthways into 5mm/¼in slices and drop them into the prepared bowl of water and lemon juice. Bring a large pan of water to the boil. Add a good pinch of salt, then drain the artichokes and add them immediately to the water. Boil for about 5 minutes, drain and set aside.

4 Heat the olive oil in a large skillet or pan and add the fennel, onion, garlic and parsley. Cook over a low to medium heat, stirring frequently, for 10 minutes until the fennel has softened and is lightly coloured.

5 Add the tomatoes and white wine and season with salt and pepper to taste. Bring the mixture to the boil, stirring, then lower the heat, cover the pan and simmer for 10–15 minutes. Add the artichokes to the tomato mixture and stir to combine. Cover and simmer for 10 minutes more.

6 Meanwhile, cook the pasta in a large pan of salted boiling water, according to the instructions on the packet. Drain the pasta, reserving a little of the cooking water. Stir the capers into the sauce, then taste for seasoning, adding more if necessary, and add the remaining lemon juice if you like.

7 Tip the pasta into a warmed serving bowl, pour the sauce over and toss well to mix, adding a little of the reserved cooking water if you prefer a runnier sauce. Serve immediately, garnished with the reserved fennel fronds. Hand around a bowl of grated Parmesan separately.

FETTUCINE ALL'ALFREDO

This very simple dish of fettucine served with a cream and Parmesan sauce was invented by a Roman restaurateur called Alfredo.

SERVES 4

INGREDIENTS
50g/2oz/¼ cup butter
200ml/7fl oz/scant 1 cup panna da cucina or double (heavy) cream
50g/2oz/⅔ cup freshly grated Parmesan cheese, plus extra to serve
350g/12oz fresh fettucine
salt and ground black pepper

1 Melt the butter in a large pan or skillet. Add the cream and bring it to the boil. Simmer for 5 minutes, stirring, then add the Parmesan, with salt and pepper to taste, and turn off the heat under the pan.

2 Bring a large pan of salted water to the boil. Drop in the pasta all at once and quickly bring back to the boil, stirring occasionally. Cook for 2–3 minutes until *al dente*, or according to the instructions on the packet. Drain well.

3 Turn on the heat under the pan of cream to low, add the pasta at once and toss until it is coated in the sauce. Taste for seasoning. Serve immediately, with extra grated Parmesan handed around separately.

COOK'S TIPS
- *With so few ingredients, it is important to use only the best-quality ones for this dish to be a success. Use good unsalted butter and top-quality Parmesan cheese. The best is Parmigio Reggiano – available from Italian delicatessens – which has its name stamped on the rind. Grate it only just before using.*
- *Fresh fettucine is traditional for this dish, so either make it yourself or buy it from an Italian delicatessen. If you cannot get fettucine, you can use tagliatelle instead.*

Orecchiette with Anchovies & Broccoli

With its robust flavours, this dish is typical of southern Italian and Sicilian cooking. Anchovies, pine nuts, garlic and Pecorino cheese make a great combination and go well with lightly cooked broccoli. Serve with crusty bread for a light lunch or supper.

SERVES 4

INGREDIENTS
300g/11oz/2 cups broccoli florets
40g/1½oz/½ cup pine nuts
350g/12oz/3 cups dried orecchiette
60ml/4 tbsp olive oil
1 small red onion, thinly sliced
50g/2oz jar anchovies in olive oil
1 garlic clove, crushed
50g/2oz/⅔ cup freshly grated Pecorino cheese
salt and ground black pepper

1 Break the broccoli into small sprigs and cut off the stalks. If the stalks are large, chop or slice them. Cook in a pan of salted boiling water for 2 minutes, then drain and refresh under cold running water. Leave to drain on kitchen paper.

2 Put the pine nuts in a dry non-stick frying pan and toss over a low to medium heat for 1–2 minutes or until the nuts are lightly toasted and golden. Remove and set aside. Cook the pasta in a large pan of salted boiling water, according to the instructions on the packet.

3 Meanwhile, heat the oil in a skillet, add the red onion and fry gently, stirring frequently, for about 5 minutes until softened. Add the anchovies with their oil, then add the garlic and fry over a medium heat, stirring frequently, for 1–2 minutes until the anchovies break down to form a paste. Add the broccoli and plenty of pepper and toss over the heat for a minute or two. Taste for seasoning.

4 Drain the pasta and tip it into a warmed bowl. Add the broccoli mixture and grated Pecorino and toss well to combine. Sprinkle the pine nuts over the top and serve immediately.

Paglia e Fieno with Walnuts & Gorgonzola

Cheese and nuts are popular ingredients for pasta sauces. The combination is very rich, so reserve this dish for a dinner party starter. It needs no accompaniment other than wine – a dry white would be good.

SERVES 4

INGREDIENTS
275g/10oz dried paglia e fieno
25g/1oz/2 tbsp butter
5ml/1 tsp finely chopped fresh sage or 2.5ml/½ tsp dried sage, plus fresh
* sage leaves, to garnish (optional)*
115g/4oz torta di Gorgonzola cheese, diced
45ml/3 tbsp mascarpone cheese
75ml/5 tbsp milk
50g/2oz/½ cup walnut halves, ground
30ml/2 tbsp freshly grated Parmesan cheese
salt and ground black pepper

1 Cook the pasta in a large pan of salted boiling water, according to the instructions on the packet. Meanwhile, melt the butter in a large skillet or pan over a low heat, add the sage and stir it around. Sprinkle in the diced Gorgonzola, then add the mascarpone. Stir the ingredients with a wooden spoon until the cheeses start to melt. Pour in the milk and keep stirring.

2 Sprinkle the walnuts and grated Parmesan into the sauce and add plenty of black pepper. Continue to stir over a low heat until the mixture forms a creamy sauce. Cook for only a few minutes and do not allow the sauce to boil.

3 Drain the pasta, tip it into a warmed serving bowl, then pour over the sauce and toss well. Serve immediately, with more black pepper ground on top. Garnish with fresh sage leaves, if you wish.

Spaghetti alla Carbonara

This delicious cream and pancetta sauce contains eggs, which cook gently around the hot spaghetti when the sauce and pasta are tossed together. This version contains plenty of pancetta or smoked bacon and is not too creamy, but you can vary the amounts as you like.

SERVES 4

INGREDIENTS
30ml/2 tbsp olive oil
1 small onion, finely chopped
8 pancetta or rindless smoked streaky (fatty) bacon rashers (strips),
  cut into 1cm/½in strips
350g/12oz fresh or dried spaghetti
4 eggs
60ml/4 tbsp crème fraîche
60ml/4 tbsp freshly grated Parmesan cheese, plus extra to serve
salt and ground black pepper

1 Heat the olive oil in a large pan or skillet, add the finely chopped onion and cook over a low heat, stirring frequently, for about 5 minutes until softened.

2 Add the strips of pancetta or bacon to the onion in the pan and cook for about 10 minutes, stirring frequently. Meanwhile, cook the pasta in a large pan of salted boiling water, according to the instructions on the packet until *al dente*.

3 Put the eggs, crème fraîche and grated Parmesan cheese in a mixing bowl. Grind in plenty of black pepper, then beat everything together well.

4 Drain the pasta, tip it into the pan with the pancetta or bacon and toss well to combine. Turn the heat off under the pan. Immediately add the egg mixture and toss vigorously so that it cooks lightly and coats the pasta. Divide the pasta among four warmed bowls and sprinkle with black pepper. Serve immediately, with grated Parmesan handed separately.

SPAGHETTI WITH MEATBALLS

Small meatballs simmered in a sweet and spicy tomato sauce are truly delicious with spaghetti. Children love them and you can easily leave out the chillies.

SERVES 6–8

INGREDIENTS

350g/12oz minced (ground) beef
1 egg
60ml/4 tbsp roughly chopped fresh flat leaf parsley
2.5ml/½ tsp crushed dried red chillies
1 thick slice white bread, crusts removed and torn into small pieces
30ml/2 tbsp milk
about 30ml/2 tbsp olive oil
300ml/½ pint/1¼ cups passata (bottled strained tomatoes)
400ml/14fl oz/1⅔ cups vegetable stock
5ml/1 tsp granulated sugar
350–450g/12oz–1lb fresh or dried spaghetti
salt and ground black pepper
freshly grated Parmesan cheese, to serve

1 Put the minced beef in a large bowl. Add the egg, half the parsley and half the crushed chillies. Season with plenty of salt and black pepper. Soak the bread in the milk for a few minutes, then squeeze and crumble over the meat mixture.

2 Mix the meat and breadcrumbs together, then knead until smooth and sticky. Wash your hands, then roll small pieces of mixture between your palms to make 40–60 balls. Place on a tray and chill in the refrigerator for about 30 minutes.

3 Heat the oil in a large non-stick frying pan. Cook the meatballs in batches until browned on all sides. Pour the passata and stock into a separate large pan. Heat gently, then add the remaining chillies, sugar and seasoning. Add the meatballs to the sauce and bring to the boil. Lower the heat, cover and simmer for 20 minutes.

4 Cook the pasta in a large pan of salted boiling water, according to the instructions on the packet. Drain and tip it into a warmed serving bowl. Pour over the sauce and toss gently. Sprinkle with the remaining parsley and serve with grated Parmesan handed separately.

TAGLIATELLE BOLOGNESE

This versatile meat sauce is traditionally served with tagliatelle but it is just as good served with spaghetti or a short pasta shape such as penne or fusilli. Simply toss with 450g/1lb of freshly cooked pasta.

SERVES 4–6

INGREDIENTS
1 onion
1 small carrot
1 celery stick
2 garlic cloves
45ml/3 tbsp olive oil
400g/14oz minced (ground) beef
120ml/4fl oz/½ cup red wine
200ml/7fl oz/scant 1 cup passata (bottled strained tomatoes)
15ml/1 tbsp tomato purée (paste)
5ml/1 tsp dried oregano
15ml/1 tbsp chopped fresh flat leaf parsley
about 350ml/12fl oz/1½ cups beef stock
8 baby Italian tomatoes (optional)
salt and ground black pepper

1 Chop all the vegetables finely, either in a food processor or by hand. Heat the olive oil in a large pan, add the chopped vegetable mixture and cook over a low heat, stirring frequently, for 5–7 minutes.

2 Add the minced beef to the vegetable mixture and cook for about 5 minutes, stirring frequently and breaking up any lumps in the meat with a wooden spoon. Stir in the wine and mix well. Cook for 1–2 minutes, then add the passata, tomato purée, herbs and 60ml/4 tbsp of the beef stock. Season with salt and pepper to taste. Stir well and bring to the boil.

3 Cover the pan, and simmer for 30 minutes, stirring from time to time and adding more stock as necessary. Add the tomatoes, if using, and simmer for 5–10 minutes more. Taste for seasoning and toss with hot, freshly cooked pasta.

TRENETTE WITH SHELLFISH

This colourful and delicious dish is ideal for a dinner party. The spicy tomato sauce is quite runny, so serve it with plenty of crusty Italian bread, such as ciabatta, and spoons as well as forks.

SERVES 4

INGREDIENTS

45ml/3 tbsp olive oil
1 small onion, finely chopped
1 garlic clove, crushed
½ fresh red chilli, seeded and chopped
200g/7oz can chopped Italian plum tomatoes
30ml/2 tbsp chopped fresh flat leaf parsley
400g/14oz fresh mussels
400g/14oz fresh clams
60ml/4 tbsp dry white wine
400g/14oz/3½ cups dried trenette
a few fresh basil leaves, torn
90g/3½oz/⅔ cup peeled cooked prawns (shrimp), thawed
    and thoroughly dried if frozen
salt and ground black pepper
chopped fresh herbs, to garnish

1 Heat 30ml/2 tbsp of the oil in a skillet or medium pan. Add the onion, garlic and chilli and cook over a medium heat for 1–2 minutes, stirring constantly. Stir in the tomatoes, flat leaf parsley and pepper to taste. Bring to the boil, lower the heat, cover and simmer for 15 minutes.

2 Meanwhile, remove the beards from the mussels with a sharp knife, then scrub the mussels and clams under cold running water. Discard any that are open or that do not close when sharply tapped with the back of a knife.

3 In a large pan, heat the remaining oil. Add the clams and mussels with the rest of the parsley and cook over a high heat for a few seconds. Pour in the wine, then cover the pan. Cook for about 5 minutes, stirring frequently, until the clams and mussels have opened.

4 Remove the pan from the heat. Lift the clams and mussels from the cooking liquid with a slotted spoon and transfer to a large bowl. Discard any shellfish that have not opened. Strain the cooking liquid into a measuring jug (pitcher).

5 Reserve eight clams and four mussels in their shells for the garnish, then remove the remaining mussels and clams from their shells and set aside.

6 Cook the pasta in a large pan of salted boiling water, according to the instructions on the packet. Meanwhile, add 120ml/4fl oz/½ cup of the reserved seafood liquid to the tomato sauce. Bring to the boil over a high heat, stirring. Lower the heat, add the basil and cooked prawns with the shelled clams and mussels. Stir well, then taste for seasoning, adding more if necessary.

7 Drain the pasta and tip into a large warmed bowl. Pour over the sauce and toss well to combine. Serve in individual bowls, sprinkled with fresh herbs and garnished with two reserved clams and one mussel in their shells.

LINGUINE WITH CRAB

This recipe comes from Rome. It makes a very rich and tasty first course on its own, or can be served for a lunch or supper with crusty Italian bread. Some cooks like a finer sauce, and work the crabmeat through a sieve after pounding.

SERVES 4

INGREDIENTS
about 250g/9oz shelled crabmeat
45ml/3 tbsp olive oil
1 small handful fresh flat leaf parsley, roughly chopped, plus extra to garnish
1 garlic clove, crushed
350g/12oz ripe Italian plum tomatoes, skinned and chopped
60–90ml/4–6 tbsp dry white wine
350g/12oz fresh or dried linguine
salt and ground black pepper

1 Put the crabmeat in a mortar and pound to a rough pulp with a pestle, or use a sturdy bowl and the end of a rolling pin. Set aside.

2 Heat 30ml/2 tbsp of the oil in a large pan. Add the parsley and garlic, with salt and pepper to taste, and fry for a few minutes until the garlic begins to brown. Add the tomatoes, pounded crabmeat and wine, cover the pan and simmer gently for 15 minutes, stirring occasionally.

3 Meanwhile, cook the pasta in a large pan of salted boiling water, according to the instructions on the packet, draining it the moment it is *al dente*, and reserving a little of the cooking water.

4 Return the pasta to the clean pan, add the remaining oil and toss quickly over a medium heat until the oil coats the strands. Add the tomato and crab mixture to the pasta and toss again, adding a little of the reserved cooking water if necessary. Adjust the seasoning to taste. Serve hot, in warmed bowls, sprinkled with parsley.

Capelli d'Angelo with Lobster

Capelli d'Angelo all'Aragosta is a sophisticated, stylish dish for a special occasion. Some cooks make the sauce with champagne rather than sparkling white wine, especially when they are planning to serve champagne with the meal.

SERVES 4

INGREDIENTS
meat from the body, tail and claws 1 cooked lobster
juice ½ lemon
40g/1½oz/3 tbsp butter
4 fresh tarragon sprigs, leaves stripped and chopped
60ml/4 tbsp double (heavy) cream
90ml/6 tbsp sparkling dry white wine
60ml/4 tbsp fish stock
300g/11oz fresh capelli d'angelo
salt and ground black pepper
about 10ml/2 tsp lumpfish roe, to garnish (optional)

1 Cut the lobster meat into small pieces and put it in a bowl. Sprinkle with the lemon juice. Melt the butter in a skillet or large pan, add the lobster meat and tarragon and stir over the heat for a few seconds. Add the cream and stir for a few seconds more, then pour in the wine and fish stock, with salt and pepper to taste. Simmer for 2 minutes, then remove from the heat and cover.

2 Cook the capelli d'angelo in a large pan of salted boiling water, according to the instructions on the packet. Drain well, reserving a few spoonfuls of the cooking water.

3 Place the pan of lobster sauce over a medium to high heat, add the pasta and toss for just long enough to combine and heat through. Moisten with a little of the reserved water from the pasta. Serve immediately in warmed bowls, sprinkled with lumpfish roe if you like.

Pansotti with Herbs & Cheese

These stuffed pasta shapes from Liguria are traditionally served with a kind of pesto made from walnuts, making it very rich. The recipe given here is a simple version.

Serves 6–8

Ingredients
300g/11oz/2¾ cups Farina Bianca 00 or Tipo 00 flour
3 eggs
3 small handfuls fresh herbs, such as basil, flat leaf parsley, sage or thyme
5ml/1tsp salt
50g/2oz/¼ cup butter
freshly grated Parmesan cheese, to serve

For the filling
250g/9oz/generous 1 cup ricotta cheese
150g/5oz/1⅔ cups freshly grated Parmesan cheese
1 large handful fresh basil leaves, finely chopped
1 large handful fresh flat leaf parsley, finely chopped
a few fresh marjoram or oregano sprigs, leaves removed and finely chopped
1 garlic clove, crushed
1 small egg
salt and ground black pepper

For the sauce
90g/3½oz shelled walnuts
1 garlic clove
60ml/4 tbsp extra virgin olive oil
120ml/4fl oz/½ cup panna da cucina or double (heavy) cream

1 Mound the flour on a clean work surface and make a large, deep well in the centre. Crack the eggs into the well, then add the herbs and salt. With a table knife, mix together the eggs, herbs and salt, then gradually incorporate the flour.

2 As soon as the egg mixture is no longer liquid, use your fingers to work the ingredients together to form a rough sticky dough. If the dough is too dry, add a few drops of cold water. If the dough is too moist, sprinkle a little flour over it.

3 Press the dough into a rough ball and kneed for about 5 minutes until the dough is very smooth and elastic. Wrap tightly in clear film and leave to rest for 15–20 minutes at room temperature.

4 Meanwhile, make the filling and sauce. Put the ricotta, Parmesan, herbs, garlic and egg in a bowl with salt and pepper to taste and beat well to mix.

5 To make the sauce, put the walnuts, garlic and olive oil in a food processor and process to a paste, adding up to 120ml/4fl oz/½ cup warm water through the feeder tube to slacken the consistency. Spoon the mixture into a large bowl and add the cream. Beat well to mix, then add salt and pepper to taste.

6 Using a pasta machine, roll out a quarter of the pasta dough into a strip measuring 90cm–1 metre/36–39in. Cut the strip with a sharp knife into two 45–50cm/18–20in lengths.

7 Using a 5cm/2in square ravioli cutter, cut 8–10 squares from one of the pasta strips. Using a teaspoon, put a mound of filling in the centre of each square, but do not overfill, or the *pansotti* will burst open during cooking.

8 Brush a little water around the edge of each square, then fold the square diagonally in half over the filling to make a triangular shape. Press the edges gently to seal. Spread out on clean floured dishtowels, sprinkle lightly with flour and leave to dry, while repeating the process with the remaining dough to make 64–80 pansotti altogether.

9 Cook the pansotti in a large pan of salted boiling water for 4–5 minutes. Meanwhile, put the walnut sauce in a large warmed bowl and add a ladleful of the pasta cooking water. Drain the pasta and tip into the bowl of walnut sauce.

10 Melt the butter in a small pan and drizzle it over the pansotti. Toss well, then sprinkle with grated Parmesan. Alternatively, toss the pansotti in the melted butter, spoon into warmed individual bowls and drizzle over the sauce. Serve immediately, with more grated Parmesan handed separately.

Spinach & Ricotta Ravioli

Leafy green spinach and creamy ricotta cheese are a classic Italian combination. They make a wonderful filling for these little pasta parcels, which are traditionally served on Christmas Eve – a time when meat-filled pasta should not be eaten.

SERVES 8

INGREDIENTS
300g/11oz/2¾ cups Farina Bianca 00 or Tipo 00 flour
3 eggs
5ml/1tsp salt
grated Parmesan cheese, to serve

FOR THE FILLING
40g/1½oz/3 tbsp butter
175g/6oz fresh spinach leaves, trimmed, washed and shredded
200g/7oz/scant 1 cup ricotta cheese
25g/1oz/⅓ cup freshly grated Parmesan cheese
freshly grated nutmeg
1 small egg
salt and ground black pepper

FOR THE SAUCE
50g/2oz/¼ cup butter
250ml/8fl oz/1 cup panna da cucina or double (heavy) cream
50g/2oz/⅔ cup freshly grated Parmesan cheese

1 Mound the flour on a clean work surface and make a large, deep well in the centre. Crack the eggs into the well, then add the salt. With a table knife or fork, mix together the eggs and salt, then gradually incorporate the flour.

2 As soon as the egg mixture is no longer liquid, use your fingers to work the ingredients together to form a rough sticky dough. If the dough is too dry, add a few drops of cold water. If the dough is too moist, sprinkle a little flour over it.

3 Press the dough into a rough ball and kneed for about 5 minutes until the dough is very smooth and elastic. Wrap tightly in clear film and leave to rest for 15–20 minutes at room temperature.

4 Meanwhile, make the filling. Melt the butter in a medium pan, add the spinach and salt and pepper to taste and cook over a medium heat for 5–8 minutes, stirring frequently, until the spinach is wilted and tender. Increase the heat to high and stir until the water is driven off and the spinach is quite dry.

5 Tip the spinach into a large bowl and leave until cold, then add the ricotta, grated Parmesan and nutmeg to taste. Beat well to mix, taste for seasoning, then add the egg and beat well again.

6 Using a pasta machine, roll out a quarter of the pasta dough into a strip measuring 90cm–1 metre/36–39in. Cut the strip with a sharp knife into two 45–50cm/18–20in lengths.

7 Using a teaspoon, put 10–12 little mounds of the filling along one side of one of the pasta strips, spacing them evenly. Brush a little water around each mound, then fold the plain side of the pasta strip over the filling.

8 Starting from the folded edge, press down gently with your fingertips around each mound of filling, pushing the air out at the unfolded edge. Sprinkle lightly with flour. With a fluted pasta wheel, cut along each long side, then in between each mound to make small square shapes.

9 Put the ravioli on floured dishtowels, sprinkle lightly with flour and leave to dry. Repeat the process with the remaining pasta to make 80–96 ravioli altogether. Drop the ravioli into a large pan of salted boiling water, bring back to the boil and cook for 4–5 minutes.

10 Meanwhile, make the sauce. Gently heat the butter, cream and Parmesan in a medium pan until the butter and Parmesan have melted. Increase the heat and simmer for 1–2 minutes until the sauce is slightly reduced, then season.

11 Drain the ravioli and divide them among 8 warmed bowls. Drizzle the sauce over them and serve immediately, sprinkled with grated Parmesan.

LASAGNE FROM BOLOGNA

This classic lasagne has a rich, meaty filling layered between sheets of pasta and a creamy white sauce, and is baked in the oven until golden and bubbling.

SERVES 4–6

INGREDIENTS
1 onion
1 small carrot
1 celery stick
2 garlic cloves
45ml/3 tbsp olive oil
400g/14oz minced (ground) beef
120ml/4fl oz/½ cup red wine
200ml/7fl oz/scant 1 cup passata (bottled strained tomatoes)
15ml/1 tbsp tomato purée (paste)
5ml/1 tsp dried oregano
15ml/1 tbsp chopped fresh flat leaf parsley
about 550ml/18fl oz/2½ cups beef stock
8 baby Italian tomatoes (optional)
12 pre-cooked dried lasagne sheets
50g/2oz/⅔ cup freshly grated Parmesan cheese
salt and ground black pepper

FOR THE WHITE SAUCE
50g/2oz/¼ cup butter
50g/2oz/½ cup plain (all-purpose) flour
900ml/1½ pints/3¾ cups hot milk
salt and ground black pepper

1 Chop the vegetables and garlic finely, either in a food processor or by hand. Heat the olive oil in a large pan, add the finely chopped vegetable mixture and cook over a low heat, stirring frequently, for 5–7 minutes.

2 Add the minced beef to the pan and cook for 5 minutes, stirring frequently and breaking up any lumps in the meat with a wooden spoon. Stir in the red wine and mix well. Cook for 1–2 minutes more.

3 Add the passata, tomato purée, herbs and 60ml/4 tbsp of the stock to the meat mixture. Season, stir well and bring to the boil. Cover the pan, and simmer for 30 minutes, stirring occasionally and adding more stock as necessary. Add the tomatoes, if using, and simmer for 5–10 minutes more. Add enough stock to make the meat sauce quite runny and stir to combine, then taste for seasoning. Preheat the oven to 190°C/375°F/Gas 5.

4 Make the white sauce. Melt the butter in a medium pan, add the flour and cook, stirring, for 1–2 minutes. Add the milk a little at a time, whisking vigorously after each addition. Bring to the boil and cook, stirring, until the sauce is smooth and thick. Season to taste, whisk well to mix, then remove from the heat.

5 Spread about a third of the meat sauce over the bottom of a baking dish. Cover with about a quarter of the white sauce, followed by four sheets of lasagne. Repeat the layers twice more, then cover the top layer of lasagne with the remaining white sauce and sprinkle the grated Parmesan evenly over the top.

6 Bake for 40–45 minutes or until the pasta feels tender when pierced with a skewer. Allow to stand for about 10 minutes before serving.

COOK'S TIPS
- *The meat sauce for this dish can be made up to 3 days in advance and kept in a covered container in the refrigerator.*
- *This lasagne is best baked straight after layering or the pasta will begin to absorb the sauces.*
- *To reheat leftover lasagne, prick it all over with a skewer, then slowly pour a little milk over to moisten. Cover with foil and reheat in a 190°C/ 375°F/Gas 5 oven for about 20 minutes, or until heated through and bubbling.*

MIXED MEAT CANNELLONI

*This dish is very rich and is best served with a crisp green salad. Pasta tubes are filled
with three different meats cooked in butter and cream, covered in a creamy sauce
and baked in the oven.*

SERVES 4

INGREDIENTS
60ml/4 tbsp olive oil
1 onion, finely chopped
1 carrot, finely chopped
2 garlic cloves, crushed
2 ripe Italian plum tomatoes, peeled and finely chopped
130g/4½oz minced (ground) beef
130g/4½oz minced (ground) pork
250g/9oz minced (ground) chicken
30ml/2 tbsp brandy
25g/1oz/2 tbsp butter
90ml/6 tbsp panna da cucina or double (heavy) cream
5ml/1 tsp chopped fresh herbs
16 dried cannelloni tubes
75g/3oz/1 cup freshly grated Parmesan cheese
salt and ground black pepper
green salad, to serve

FOR THE WHITE SAUCE
50g/2oz/¼ cup butter
50g/2oz/½ cup plain (all-purpose) flour
900ml/1½ pints/3¾ cups milk
nutmeg

1 Heat the oil in a medium skillet or pan, add the onion, carrot, garlic and
tomatoes and cook over a low heat, stirring frequently, for about 10 minutes or
until very soft.

2 Add all the minced meats to the vegetables and cook gently for about
10 minutes, stirring frequently to break up any lumps. Add the brandy, increase
the heat and stir until it has reduced.

3 Add the butter, cream and chopped herbs to the meat mixture and cook gently over a low heat, stirring occasionally, for about 10 minutes. Remove the pan from the heat and allow to cool.

4 Preheat the oven to 190°C/375°F/Gas 5. Make the white sauce. Melt the butter in a pan, add the flour and cook, stirring constantly, for 1–2 minutes. Add the milk a little at a time, whisking after each addition. Bring to the boil and cook, stirring, until the sauce is smooth and thick.

5 Grate a little fresh nutmeg into the white sauce and stir, then season with salt and black pepper to taste and whisk well. Remove the pan from the heat.

6 Spoon a little of the white sauce into a baking dish and spread over the base. Fill the cannelloni tubes with the meat mixture and place in a single layer in the dish. Pour the remaining white sauce over the filled tubes, then sprinkle with the grated Parmesan cheese. Bake for 35–40 minutes or until the pasta feels tender when pierced with a skewer. Allow to stand for about 10 minutes before serving with green salad.

VARIATIONS
- Instead of filling dried pasta tubes, use fresh lasagne sheets instead. Spoon a line of the meat filling along one end of each lasagne sheet and roll the pasta around the filling. Arrange in a baking dish and cook as for dried pasta tubes.
- If you prefer, this recipe can be made with just one or two types of different minced meat. Ensure the total weight of minced meat is 510g/1lb 2oz.
- Good choices of fresh herbs include thyme, oregano and marjoram. Use one herb or a mixture of several for delicious results.

CANNELLONI SORRENTINA-STYLE

There's more than one way of making cannelloni. For this fresh-tasting dish, sheets of cooked lasagne are rolled around a tomato, ricotta and anchovy filling to make a delicious main course for a summer dinner party. The ingredients are similar to those on a Neapolitan pizza.

SERVES 4–6

INGREDIENTS
60ml/4 tbsp olive oil
1 small onion, finely chopped
900g/2lb ripe Italian plum tomatoes, peeled and finely chopped
2 garlic cloves, crushed
1 large handful fresh basil leaves, shredded, plus extra basil leaves, to garnish
250ml/8fl oz/1 cup vegetable stock
250ml/8fl oz/1 cup dry white wine
30ml/2 tbsp sun-dried tomato paste
2.5ml/½ tsp sugar
16–18 fresh or dried lasagne sheets
250g/9oz/generous 1 cup ricotta cheese
130g/4½oz packet mozzarella cheese, drained and diced small
8 bottled anchovy fillets in olive oil, drained and halved lengthways
50g/2oz/⅔ cup freshly grated Parmesan cheese
salt and ground black pepper

1 Heat the olive oil in a medium pan, add the onion and cook gently, stirring frequently, for about 5 minutes until softened. Stir in the tomatoes, garlic and half the basil. Season with salt and pepper to taste and toss over a medium to high heat for 5 minutes.

2 Pour half the tomato mixture into a bowl and set aside to cool. Stir the vegetable stock, white wine, tomato paste and sugar into the remaining tomato mixture and simmer for about 20 minutes, stirring occasionally.

3 Meanwhile, cook the lasagne sheets in batches in a large pan of salted boiling water, according to the instructions on the packet. Drain and separate the sheets of pasta and lay out them flat on a clean dishtowel to dry slightly. Preheat the oven to 190°C/375°F/Gas 5.

4 Add the ricotta and mozzarella to the cooled tomato mixture in the bowl. Stir in the remaining basil and season to taste with salt and black pepper. Spread a little of the mixture over each lasagne sheet.

5 Place an anchovy fillet across the width of each lasagne sheet, close to one of the short ends. Starting from the end with the anchovy fillet, roll each lasagne sheet up around the tomato filling.

6 Pour the tomato sauce into a food processor or blender and process to a smooth purée. Spread a little of the tomato sauce over the bottom of a large baking dish. Arrange the cannelloni seam-side down in a single layer and spoon the remaining sauce over them.

7 Sprinkle the grated Parmesan cheese over the cannelloni and bake for about 20 minutes or until the topping is golden brown and bubbling. Serve hot, garnished with a few fresh basil leaves.

VARIATION
For a vegetarian version, use 8 pitted black olives instead of the anchovies. Chop them roughly and sprinkle them in a line along the length of the tomato and ricotta filling, then roll up as before.

POTATO GNOCCHI

These delicious little Italian dumplings are made with mashed potato and flour and delicately flavoured with nugmeg. They are best served simply with butter and grated Parmesan cheese. To ensure a really light and fluffy result, don't overmix the dough.

SERVES 4–6

INGREDIENTS
1kg/2¼lb waxy potatoes, scrubbed
250–300g/9–11oz/2¼–2¾ cups plain (all-purpose) flour, plus extra for sprinkling
1 egg
a pinch of freshly grated nutmeg
25g/1oz/2 tbsp butter
salt
fresh basil leaves and shaved Parmesan cheese, to garnish

1 Cook the potatoes in their skins in a pan of salted boiling water until tender but not falling apart. Drain and peel while they are still hot. Spread a layer of flour on a clean work surface. Pass the hot potatoes through a food mill, directly on to the flour. Sprinkle with half of the remaining flour and mix together very lightly.

2 Break the egg into the potato, add the grated nutmeg and knead lightly, adding more flour if the mixture is too loose and sticky. When the dough is light to the touch and no longer moist, divide into 4 pieces.

3 On a lightly floured surface, form each piece of dough into a roll 2cm/¾in in diameter. Cut each roll crossways into pieces about 2cm/¾in long. Make ridges on one side with a fork and a depression on the other with your thumb.

4 Bring a large pan of salted water to a fast boil, then drop in half the prepared gnocchi. When they rise to the surface, after 3–4 minutes, they are done. Lift out with a slotted spoon, drain well, and place in a warmed serving bowl.

5 Dot the cooked gnocchi with butter. Cover to keep warm while cooking the remainder. As soon as they are all cooked, toss the gnocchi with the butter, garnish with Parmesan shavings and fresh basil leaves, and serve immediately.

SEMOLINA GNOCCHI

*This Roman dish is made with coarsely ground semolina, which is cooked in a
similar way to polenta. The rich paste is cut into flat discs and baked in the oven
with butter and cheese.*

SERVES 4

INGREDIENTS
1 litre/1¾ pints/4 cups milk
35g/1½oz/3 tbsp butter
250g/9oz/generous 3 cups coarsely ground semolina
3 egg yolks
115g/4oz/1¼ cups freshly grated Parmesan cheese
a pinch of grated nutmeg
salt

1 Heat the milk in a heavy pan with a pinch of salt and one-third of the butter.
Bring to the boil, then sprinkle in the semolina, whisking continuously to
prevent lumps forming. Bring the mixture back to the boil, then lower the heat and
simmer for 15–20 minutes, stirring occasionally.

2 Remove the pan from the heat and beat in the remaining butter, followed by
the egg yolks, one at a time. Stir in 45g/1¾oz/3 tbsp of the Parmesan. Season.
Sprinkle a little cold water onto a work surface, then spread out the semolina
mixture in an even layer about 1cm/½in thick. Leave to cool for at least 2 hours.

3 Preheat the oven to 220°C/425°F/Gas 7. Butter a shallow baking dish and use
a biscuit cutter to cut the semolina into 6cm/2½in rounds.

4 Place the trimmings in an even layer at the bottom of the prepared dish. Pour
over a little melted butter and sprinkle with some of the Parmesan. Cover with
a layer of the semolina rounds, overlapping them slightly. Sprinkle with nutmeg,
Parmesan and butter. Continue in this way until all the ingredients have been used up.

5 Bake for about 20 minutes, or until the top is browned. Remove from the oven
and allow to stand for 5 minutes before serving.

Spinach & Ricotta Gnocchi

Leafy spinach and mild, creamy ricotta work wonderfully in these tasty little herb dumplings. They are delicious served simply with a sage butter and grated Parmesan. For the best results, handle the dough as little as possible. It should be fairly soft and will be easier to handle if chilled for an hour before preparing the dumplings.

SERVES 4

INGREDIENTS
6 garlic cloves, unpeeled
25g/1oz mixed fresh herbs, such as parsley, basil, thyme, coriander
  (cilantro) and chives, finely chopped
225g/8oz fresh spinach leaves, washed
250g/9oz/generous 1 cup ricotta cheese
1 egg yolk
50g/2oz/²⁄₃ cup grated Parmesan cheese
75g/3oz/²⁄₃ cup plain (all-purpose) flour
50g/2oz/¼ cup butter
30ml/2 tbsp fresh sage, chopped
salt

COOK'S TIP
To achieve really light and fluffy results, squeeze out as much water as possible from the cooked spinach, then spread it out on a clean dishtowel, roll it up and wring out any excess moisture before chopping.

1 Drop the unpeeled garlic cloves into a pan of boiling water and cook for about 4 minutes. Drain well and press out of their skins. Place in a food processor with the chopped herbs and blend to a purée or mash the garlic with a fork and add the herbs to mix well.

2 Place the spinach in a large pan with just the water that clings to the leaves and cook gently over a low heat until wilted. Leave to cool, then squeeze out as much liquid as possible and chop finely.

3 Place the ricotta in a large mixing bowl and beat in the egg yolk, chopped spinach and herb and garlic purée. Stir in half the grated Parmesan cheese, sift in the flour and mix well to combine.

4 Using floured hands, break off pieces of the dough slightly smaller than a walnut and roll into small dumplings, being careful to handle the mixture as little as possible.

5 Bring a large pan of salted water to the boil and carefully add the gnocchi. When they rise to the top of the pan, after 3–4 minutes, they are cooked. The gnocchi should be light and fluffy all through.

6 Meanwhile, melt the butter in a frying pan and add the chopped sage. Fry gently for 1 minute. Add the drained gnocchi to the frying pan and toss in the butter over a gentle heat for 1 minute, then serve sprinkled with the remaining grated Parmesan.

PUMPKIN GNOCCHI WITH A CHANTERELLE PARSLEY CREAM

Italians love pumpkin and often incorporate it into their dumplings and other traditional pasta dishes as it adds a slight sweet richness. These gnocchi are superb on their own but they are also great served with meat or game.

SERVES 4

INGREDIENTS
450g/1lb floury potatoes, scrubbed
450g/1lb pumpkin, peeled, seeded and chopped
2 egg yolks
200g/7oz/1¾ cups plain (all-purpose) flour, plus more if necessary
a pinch of ground allspice
1.5ml/¼ tsp cinnamon
pinch freshly grated nutmeg
finely grated rind of ½ orange
salt and ground pepper

FOR THE SAUCE
30ml/2 tbsp olive oil
1 shallot, finely chopped
175g/6oz/2½ cups fresh chanterelles, sliced, or 15g/½oz/½ cup dried,
   soaked in warm water for 20 minutes, then drained
10ml/2 tsp almond butter
150ml/¼ pint/⅔ cup crème fraîche
a little milk or water
75ml/5 tbsp chopped fresh parsley
50g/2oz/½ cup freshly grated Parmesan cheese

1 Bring a large pan of salted water to the boil, add the potatoes and cook for about 20 minutes, or until cooked. Drain and set aside.

2 Place the prepared pumpkin in a large bowl, cover and microwave on full power for 8 minutes. Alternatively, wrap the pumpkin in foil and bake at 180°C/350°F/Gas 4 for 30 minutes. Drain well.

3 Pass the pumpkin and potatoes through a food mill into a bowl. Add the egg yolks, flour, spices, orange rind and seasoning and mix well to make a soft dough. If the mixture is too loose, add a little more flour to stiffen it up.

4 Bring a large pan of salted water to a fast boil. Meanwhile, spread a layer of flour on a clean work surface. Spoon the prepared gnocchi mixture into a piping bag fitted with a 1cm/½in plain nozzle.

5 Pipe directly on to the flour to make a 15cm/6in sausage. Roll in flour and cut crossways into 2.5cm/1in pieces. Repeat to make more sausage shapes and pieces. Mark each lightly with the tines of a fork and drop into the boiling water. When they rise to the surface, after 3–4 minutes, they are done.

6 Meanwhile, make the sauce. Heat the oil in a non-stick frying pan, add the shallot and fry until soft but not coloured. Add the chanterelles and cook briefly, then add the almond butter. Stir to melt and stir in the crème fraîche. Simmer briefly and adjust the consistency with milk or water. Add the parsley and season to taste.

7 Lift the gnocchi out of the water with a slotted spoon as soon as they rise to the surface, drain and turn into warmed bowls. Spoon over the sauce, sprinkle with grated Parmesan, and serve at once.

VARIATION
Turn these gnocchi into a main meal for vegetarians by serving them with a rich home-made tomato sauce. If you want to make the dish more special, serve the gnocchi with a side dish of ratatouille made from courgettes (zucchini), peppers and aubergines (eggplant), cooked gently with tomatoes, plenty of garlic and really good extra virgin olive oil.

RISOTTO & POLENTA

R ice is grown in the north of Italy, and risotto is often served after the antipasti in place of pasta. A good risotto depends on the quality of the rice and the technique of making it – you need to use a good risotto rice, such as arborio or carnaroli, and the stock must be added gradually to achieve a perfect creamy texture. Traditional risotto is simply flavoured with Parmesan cheese and onion but risottos may also include bacon, chicken, shellfish, vegetables or nuts. Polenta is a grainy cornmeal made from maize flour and forms the starchy base of a meal. It is cooked like a sort of porridge and is eaten soft, or allowed to set, then cut into shapes and baked or grilled.

RISOTTO WITH PARMESAN

This is one of the best-loved risottos in Italy. It is flavoured simply with onion, white wine and Parmesan and gives a delicious, creamy result.

SERVES 3–4

INGREDIENTS
1.2 litres/2 pints/5 cups beef, chicken or vegetable stock
65g/2½oz/5 tbsp butter
1 small onion, finely chopped
275g/10oz/1½ cups risotto rice
120ml/4fl oz/½ cup dry white wine
75g/3oz/1 cup freshly grated Parmesan cheese, plus extra to garnish
basil leaves, to garnish
salt and ground black pepper

1 Heat the stock in a large pan and leave to simmer until needed. Melt two-thirds of the butter in a separate large pan or deep frying pan. Stir in the onion and cook gently for about 5 minutes until soft and golden.

2 Add the rice to the onions and stir to coat the grains with butter. Cook gently for 1–2 minutes, then pour in the white wine. Raise the heat slightly and cook until the wine evaporates. Add one ladleful of the hot stock, and cook until it has been absorbed, stirring constantly.

3 Gradually add the remaining stock, a little at a time, allowing the rice to absorb the liquid before adding more, and stirring constantly. After 20–30 minutes the rice should be creamy and *al dente*. Season to taste.

4 Remove the pan from the heat. Stir in the remaining butter and the Parmesan cheese. Taste again for seasoning. Allow the risotto to rest for 3–4 minutes before serving, garnished with basil leaves and shavings of Parmesan, if you like.

Risotto alla Milanese

This golden risotto is flavoured with saffron and is always served with the hearty veal stew, Osso Buco, *but also makes a delicious first course or light supper dish.*

SERVES 3–4

INGREDIENTS
about 1.2 litres/2 pints/5 cups beef or chicken stock
a good pinch of saffron strands
75g/3oz/6 tbsp butter
1 onion, finely chopped
275g/10oz/1½ cups risotto rice
75g/3oz/1 cup freshly grated Parmesan cheese
salt and ground black pepper

1 Bring the stock to the boil, then reduce to a low simmer. Ladle a little stock into a small bowl. Add the saffron strands and leave to infuse.

2 Melt 50g/2oz/¼ cup of the butter in a large pan until foaming. Add the onion and cook gently for 3 minutes, stirring, until softened but not browned.

3 Add the rice to the onions. Stir until the grains start to swell and burst, then add a few ladlefuls of the stock, with the saffron liquid and salt and pepper to taste. Stir over a low heat until the stock has been absorbed. Add the remaining stock, a few ladlefuls at a time, allowing the rice to absorb all the liquid before adding more, and stirring constantly. After 20–25 minutes, the rice should be just tender and the risotto golden yellow, moist and creamy.

4 Gently stir in about two-thirds of the grated Parmesan and the remaining butter. Heat through until the butter has melted, then taste for seasoning. Transfer the risotto to a warmed serving bowl or platter and serve hot, with the remaining grated Parmesan served separately.

PORCINI & PARMESAN RISOTTO

This wonderful mushroom risotto is a variation on the classic Risotto alla Milanese.
*It includes saffron, porcini mushrooms and Parmesan cheese, which give a golden
risotto with a distinctive mushroom flavour.*

SERVES 4

INGREDIENTS
15g/½oz/2 tbsp dried porcini mushrooms
150ml/¼ pint/⅔ cup warm water
1 litre/1¾ pints/4 cups vegetable stock
a generous pinch of saffron strands
30ml/2 tbsp olive oil
1 onion, finely chopped
1 garlic clove, crushed
350g/12oz/1¾ cup dry white wine
25g/1oz/2 tbsp butter
50g/2oz/⅔ cup freshly grated Parmesan cheese
salt and ground black pepper
pink and yellow oyster mushrooms, to serve (optional)

COOK'S TIPS
*There are endless variations on this delicious
mushroom risotto. The proportion of stock to rice,
onions, garlic and butter must remain constant but
you can ring the changes with the flavourings. Try
adding a few fresh tarragon sprigs towards the end
of cooking time in place of the saffron.*

1 Put the dried porcini in a bowl and pour over the warm water. Leave the
mushrooms to soak for about 20 minutes, then lift out with a slotted spoon,
reserving the soaking liquid.

2 Filter the soaking water from the mushrooms through a layer of kitchen paper
in a strainer, then place it in a large pan with the vegetable stock. Bring the
liquid to a gentle simmer.

3 Spoon 45ml/3 tbsp of the hot vegetable stock into a cup and stir in the saffron strands. Set aside to infuse. Finely chop the soaked porcini mushrooms.

4 Heat the olive oil in a separate pan and lightly sauté the onion, garlic and mushrooms for about 5 minutes. Gradually add the rice, stirring to coat the grains in oil. Cook for 2 minutes, stirring constantly. Season with salt and pepper.

5 Pour the white wine into the pan and cook, stirring constantly, until it has been absorbed. Ladle in a quarter of the stock and continue to cook, stirring, until the stock has been absorbed.

6 Gradually add the remaining stock, a little at a time, allowing the rice to absorb the liquid before adding more, stirring constantly.

7 After about 20 minutes, when all the stock has been absorbed and the rice is *al dente*, stir in the butter, saffron water (with the strands) and half the Parmesan. Sprinkle with the remaining Parmesan and serve with pink and yellow oyster mushrooms, if you like.

RISOTTO WITH ASPARAGUS

Fresh asparagus only has a very short season and this elegant risotto really makes the most of it. The combination of its subtle flavour and attractive appearance, makes asparagus the perfect addition to a creamy risotto.

SERVES 4

INGREDIENTS
225g/8oz fresh asparagus
750ml/1¼ pints/3 cups vegetable or chicken stock
65g/2½ oz/5 tbsp butter
1 small onion, finely chopped
275g/10 oz/1½ cups risotto rice
75g/3oz/1 cup freshly grated Parmesan cheese
salt and ground black pepper

1 Cut off any woody ends of the asparagus stalks, peel the lower portions, then cook in a pan of boiling water for 5 minutes. Drain, reserving the cooking water, and refresh the asparagus under cold water. Cut diagonally into 4cm/1½in pieces. Separate the tip and next-highest sections from the stalks.

2 Place the stock in a pan and add 450ml/¾ pint/scant 2 cups of the asparagus cooking water. Heat to simmering point, and keep it hot.

3 Melt two-thirds of the butter in large heavy pan. Add the onion and fry until soft and golden. Stir in all the asparagus stalks. Cook for 2–3 minutes. Add the rice and cook for 1–2 minutes, mixing well to coat it with butter.

4 Stir a ladleful of the hot stock into the rice. Stir until the stock has been absorbed. Gradually add the remaining stock to the rice, a little at a time, allowing the rice to absorb the liquid before adding more, and stirring all the time.

5 After 10 minutes, add the remaining asparagus sections to the risotto. Continue to cook as before, for about 15 minutes, until the rice is *al dente*. Remove the pan from the heat and stir in the remaining butter and the Parmesan. Grind in a little black pepper, and taste again for salt. Serve at once.

PEA & HAM RISOTTO

This is a classic risotto from the Veneto. In Italy, it is traditionally served as a starter but it also makes an excellent supper dish with hot, crusty bread. Sweet peas and the smoky, salty flavour of ham make an unbeatable combination.

SERVES 4

INGREDIENTS
75g/3oz/6 tbsp butter
1 small onion, finely chopped
about 1 litre/1¾ pints/4 cups simmering chicken stock
275g/10oz/1½ cups risotto rice
150ml/¼ pint/⅔ cup dry white wine
225g/8oz/2 cups frozen petits pois (baby peas), thawed
115g/4oz cooked ham, diced
salt and ground black pepper
50g/2oz/⅔ cup freshly grated Parmesan cheese, to serve

1 Melt 50g/2oz/4 tbsp of the butter in a pan until foaming. Add the onion and cook gently for about 3 minutes, stirring frequently, until softened. Have the hot stock ready in an adjacent pan.

2 Add the rice to the onion mixture. Stir until the grains start to swell, then pour in the wine. Stir until it stops sizzling and most of it has been absorbed, then pour in a little hot stock, with salt and pepper to taste. Stir continuously, over a low heat, until all the stock has been absorbed.

3 Gradually add the remaining stock to the rice, a little at a time, allowing the rice to absorb all the liquid before adding more, and stirring constantly. Add the peas after 20 minutes. Cook for 5–10 minutes more, until the rice is *al dente* and the risotto rich and creamy.

4 Gently stir the diced cooked ham and the remaining butter into the risotto. Heat through until the butter has melted, then taste for seasoning. Transfer to a warmed serving bowl. Sprinkle a little Parmesan over the top of the risotto and serve the rest separately.

PUMPKIN & PISTACHIO RISOTTO

Vegetarians tired of the standard dinner party fare will love this elegant combination of creamy, golden rice, sweet and juicy pumpkin, and nutty green pistachios. Serve with crusty Italian bread and crisp green salad.

SERVES 4

INGREDIENTS

1.2 litres/2 pints/5 cups vegetable stock or water
a generous pinch of saffron strands
30ml/2 tbsp olive oil
1 onion, chopped
2 garlic cloves, crushed
900g/2lb/about 7 cups pumpkin, peeled, seeded and cut into 2cm/³⁄₄in cubes
400g/14oz/2 cups risotto rice
200ml/7fl oz/scant 1 cup dry white wine
30ml/2 tbsp freshly grated Parmesan cheese
50g/2oz/¹⁄₂ cup pistachios, coarsely chopped
45ml/3 tbsp chopped fresh marjoram or oregano, plus extra leaves to garnish
freshly grated nutmeg
salt and ground black pepper

1 In a large pan, bring the stock or water to a low simmer. Ladle a little into a small bowl. Add the saffron strands and leave to infuse. Heat the oil in another large pan. Add the onion and garlic and cook gently for 5 minutes until softened. Add the pumpkin and rice and stir to coat in oil. Cook for 2–3 minutes more.

2 Pour the wine over the rice and allow it to boil. When it has been absorbed, add quarter of the hot stock or water and the saffron liquid. Stir until all the liquid has been absorbed. Add the remaining stock or water, a little at a time, allowing the rice to absorb the liquid before adding more, stirring constantly. After 20–30 minutes the rice should be golden yellow, creamy and *al dente*.

3 Stir the Parmesan into the risotto, cover and leave to stand for 5 minutes. Stir in the pistachios and herbs. Season with a little nutmeg, salt and pepper, scatter over a few marjoram or oregano leaves and serve.

BROAD BEAN RISOTTO

*This delicious risotto is flavoured with smoked pancetta and baby broad beans.
It makes a healthy and filling lunch or supper, served with cooked fresh seasonal
vegetables or a mixed green salad.*

SERVES 4

INGREDIENTS
15ml/1 tbsp olive oil
1 onion, chopped
2 garlic cloves, finely chopped
175g/6oz smoked pancetta, diced
350g/12oz/1¾ cups risotto rice
1.5 litres/2½ pints/6¼ cups simmering chicken stock
225g/8oz/2 cups frozen baby broad (fava) beans
30ml/2 tbsp chopped fresh mixed herbs, such as parsley, thyme and oregano
salt and freshly ground black pepper
shavings Parmesan cheese, to serve

1 Heat the olive oil in a large heavy pan. Add the onion, garlic and pancetta and cook gently for about 5 minutes, stirring occasionally. Do not allow the onion and garlic to brown.

2 Add the rice to the pan and cook for 1 minute, stirring. Add a ladleful of stock and cook, stirring all the time, until the liquid has been absorbed. Continue adding the stock, a ladleful at a time, until the rice is tender, and almost all the liquid has been absorbed. This will take 30–35 minutes.

3 Meanwhile, cook the broad beans in a pan of lightly salted, boiling water for about 3 minutes until tender. Drain well and set aside. When the risotto is nearly cooked, stir in the broad beans and mixed herbs. Season with salt and pepper to taste. Spoon into warmed bowls and serve, sprinkled with shavings of fresh Parmesan cheese.

RISOTTO WITH SMOKED BACON & TOMATO

This classic risotto is richly flavoured with onions, smoked bacon and sun-dried tomatoes. It is so tasty, you'll want to keep going back for more.

SERVES 4–6

INGREDIENTS
8 sun-dried tomatoes in olive oil
275g/10oz good-quality rindless smoked back (lean) bacon
75g/3oz/6 tbsp butter
450g/1lb onions, roughly chopped
2 garlic cloves, crushed
350g/12oz/1¾ cups risotto rice
300ml/½ pint/1¼ cups dry white wine
1 litre/1¾ pints/4 cups simmering vegetable stock
50g/2oz/⅔ cup freshly grated Parmesan cheese
45ml/3 tbsp mixed chopped fresh chives and flat leaf parsley
salt and ground black pepper

1 Drain the sun-dried tomatoes and reserve 15ml/1 tbsp of the oil. Roughly chop the tomatoes and set aside. Cut the bacon into 2.5cm/1in pieces. Heat the oil from the sun-dried tomatoes in a large pan. Fry the bacon until well cooked and golden. Remove with a slotted spoon and drain on kitchen paper.

2 Heat 25g/1oz/2 tbsp of the butter in a pan and fry the onions and garlic over a medium heat for 10 minutes, until soft and golden brown. Stir in the rice. Cook for 1 minute, until the grains turn translucent.

3 Stir the wine into the stock. Add a ladleful to the rice and cook gently until the liquid has been absorbed. Stir in another ladleful and allow it to be absorbed. Repeat this process until all the liquid has been used up. This should take about 25 minutes. The risotto will become thick and creamy, and the rice tender.

4 Stir in the bacon, tomatoes, Parmesan, half the herbs and the remaining butter. Adjust the seasoning and serve sprinkled with the remaining herbs.

SAFFRON RISOTTO WITH CHICKEN & PARMA HAM

This wonderful combination of chicken and rice, cooked with Parma ham, white wine and Parmesan cheese, is very simple but absolutely delicious.

SERVES 6

INGREDIENTS
30ml/2 tbsp olive oil
225g/8oz skinless, boneless chicken breast portions,
  cut into 2.5cm/1in cubes
1 onion, finely chopped
1 garlic clove, finely chopped
450g/1lb/2⅓ cups risotto rice
120ml/4fl oz/½ cup dry white wine
1.5ml/¼ tsp saffron threads
1.75 litres/3 pints/7½ cups simmering chicken stock
50g/2oz Parma ham, cut into thin strips
25g/1oz/2 tbsp butter, cubed
25g/1oz/⅓ cup freshly grated Parmesan cheese, plus extra to serve
salt and ground black pepper
flat leaf parsley, to garnish

1 Heat the oil in a frying pan over a medium to high heat. Add the chicken cubes and cook, stirring, until they start to turn white. Reduce the heat to low and add the onion and garlic. Cook, stirring, until the onion is soft. Stir in the rice. Sauté for 1–2 minutes, stirring constantly, until the rice is coated in oil.

2 Add the wine to the pan and cook, stirring, until the wine has been absorbed. Stir the saffron into the simmering stock, then add ladlefuls of stock to the rice, allowing each ladleful to be absorbed before adding the next.

3 When the rice is three-quarters cooked, add the Parma ham and continue cooking until the rice is just tender and the risotto creamy. Add the butter and the Parmesan and stir well to combine. Season with salt and pepper to taste. Serve the risotto hot, sprinkled with a little more Parmesan, and garnish with parsley.

SEAFOOD RISOTTO

Fish and shellfish risottos are popular throughout the coastal regions of Italy. This recipe makes a good main course or can serve eight people as a starter. Vary the combination of shellfish or seafood, depending on availability.

SERVES 4–6

INGREDIENTS
450g/1lb fresh mussels
about 250ml/8fl oz/1 cup dry white wine
225g/8oz sea bass fillet, skinned and cut into pieces
seasoned flour
60ml/4 tbsp olive oil
8 scallops with corals separated, white parts halved or sliced, if large
225g/8oz squid, cleaned and cut into rings
12 large raw prawns (shrimp) or langoustines, heads removed
2 shallots, finely chopped
1 garlic clove, crushed
400g/14oz/2 cups risotto rice, preferably carnaroli
3 tomatoes, peeled, seeded and chopped
1.5 litres/2½ pints/6¼ cups simmering fish stock
30ml/2 tbsp chopped fresh parsley
30ml/2 tbsp double (heavy) cream
salt and ground black pepper

1 Remove the beards from the mussels and scrub, discarding any that do not close when sharply tapped with the back of a knife. Place them in a large pan and add 90ml/6 tbsp of the wine. Bring to the boil, cover the pan and cook for about 3 minutes until all the mussels have opened, shaking the pan occasionally. Drain, reserving the liquid and discarding any mussels that have not opened. Set aside a few mussels in their shells for garnishing; remove the others from their shells. Strain the cooking liquid.

2 Dust the pieces of sea bass in seasoned flour. Heat 30ml/2 tbsp of the olive oil in a frying pan and fry the fish for 3–4 minutes until cooked. Transfer to a plate. Add a little more oil to the pan and fry the white parts of the scallops for 1–2 minutes on both sides until tender. Transfer to a plate.

3 Fry the squid for 3–4 minutes in the same pan, adding a little more oil if necessary, then set aside. Lastly, add the prawns or langoustines and fry for about 3 minutes until pink, turning frequently. Towards the end of cooking, add a splash of wine – about 30ml/2 tbsp – and continue cooking so that the prawns become tender, but do not burn. Remove the prawns from the pan. As soon as they are cool enough to handle, remove the shells and legs, leaving the tails intact.

4 In a large pan, heat the remaining olive oil and fry the shallots and garlic for 3–4 minutes over a gentle heat until the shallots are soft but not brown. Add the rice and cook for a few minutes, stirring, until the rice is coated with oil and the grains are slightly translucent. Stir in the tomatoes, with the reserved cooking liquid from the mussels.

5 When all the free liquid has been absorbed, add the remaining wine, stirring constantly. When the wine has also been absorbed, gradually add the hot stock, one ladleful at a time, continuing to stir the rice constantly and waiting until each quantity of stock has been absorbed before adding the next.

6 When the risotto is three-quarters cooked, carefully stir in all the seafood, except the mussels reserved for the garnish. Continue to cook until all the stock has been absorbed and the rice is *al dente*.

7 Stir in the parsley and cream and adjust the seasoning. Cover the pan and leave the risotto to stand for 2–3 minutes. Serve in individual bowls, garnished with the reserved mussels in their shells.

GRILLED POLENTA WITH GORGONZOLA

Grilled polenta is delicious, and is a good way of using up cold polenta and is a good accompaniment to stews and soups. This recipe uses tart Gorgonzola but any soft, flavoursome cheese will be just as good.

SERVES 6–8 AS A SNACK

INGREDIENTS
1.5 litres/2½ pints/6¼ cups water
15ml/1 tbsp salt
350g/12oz/2½ cups polenta flour
225g/8oz/1¼ cups Gorgonzola at room temperature

1 Bring the water to the boil in a large heavy pan. Add the salt. Reduce the heat to a simmer and begin to add the polenta flour in a fine rain. Stir constantly with a whisk until the polenta has all been incorporated.

2 Switch to a long-handled wooden spoon and continue to stir the polenta over low to medium heat until it is a thick mass and pulls away from the sides of the pan. This may take from 25–50 minutes, depending on the type of flour used. For best results, never stop stirring the polenta until you remove it from the heat.

3 When the polenta is cooked, sprinkle a work surface or large board with a little water. Spread the polenta out on the surface in a layer 1.5cm/¾in thick. Allow to cool completely. Preheat the grill (broiler).

4 Cut the cooled polenta into triangles or squares and arrange on a grill rack. Grill until hot and speckled with brown on both sides. Spread with the Gorgonzola and serve immediately.

POLENTA ELISA

This baked polenta dish, flavoured with Gruyère and dolcelatte, comes from the valley around Lake Como. Serve it on its own as a starter, or with a mixed salad and some sliced salami or prosciutto for a midweek supper.

SERVES 4

INGREDIENTS
250ml/8fl oz/1 cup milk
225g/8oz/2 cups pre-cooked polenta
115g/4oz/1 cup grated Gruyère cheese
115g/4oz/1 cup dolcelatte cheese, crumbled
50g/2oz/¼ cup butter
2 garlic cloves, roughly chopped
a few fresh sage leaves, chopped
salt and ground black pepper
prosciutto, to serve

1 Preheat the oven to 200°C/400°F/Gas 6. Lightly butter a 20–25cm/8–10in baking dish. Bring the milk and 750ml/1¼ pints/3 cups water to the boil in a large pan, add 5ml/1 tsp salt, then tip in the polenta. Cook for about 8 minutes or according to the instructions on the packet.

2 Spoon half the polenta into the baking dish and level. Cover with half the grated Gruyère and crumbled dolcelatte. Spoon the remaining polenta evenly over the top and sprinkle with the remaining cheeses.

3 Melt the butter in a small pan until foaming, add the garlic and sage and fry, stirring, until the butter turns golden brown. Drizzle the butter mixture over the polenta and cheese and grind black pepper liberally over the top. Bake for about 5 minutes. Serve hot, with slices of prosciutto.

Baked Polenta with Tomato Sauce

This delicious baked polenta dish layers squares of set polenta with sweet tomato sauce and Gruyère cheese. It makes a good vegetarian main course.

SERVES 4

INGREDIENTS
5ml/1 tsp salt
250g/9oz/2¼ cups quick-cook polenta
5ml/1 tsp paprika
2.5ml/½ tsp ground nutmeg
30ml/2 tbsp olive oil
1 large onion, finely chopped
2 garlic cloves, crushed
2 × 400g/14oz cans chopped tomatoes
15ml/1 tbsp tomato purée (paste)
5ml/1 tsp sugar
75g/3oz Gruyère cheese, grated
salt and ground black pepper

1 Preheat the oven to 200°C/400°F/Gas 6. Line a baking tin (28 × 18cm/11 × 7in) with clear film. Bring 1 litre/1¾ pints/4 cups water to the boil with the salt. Pour in the polenta in a steady stream and cook, stirring continuously, for 5 minutes. Beat in the paprika and nutmeg, then pour into the prepared tin and smooth the surface. Leave to cool.

2 Heat the olive oil in a pan and cook the onion and garlic until soft. Add the tomatoes, tomato purée and sugar and stir well to combine. Season with salt and pepper and simmer for 20 minutes.

3 Turn out the polenta on to a chopping board, and cut into about 12 squares. Place half the squares in a greased ovenproof dish. Spoon over half the tomato sauce and sprinkle with half the cheese. Repeat the layers. Bake in the oven for about 25 minutes, until golden. Serve from the baking dish.

BAKED POLENTA WITH CHEESE

Cold polenta can be cut into slices and baked in layers with cheese. It makes a good dish on a cold winter evening. The traditional way of cutting set polenta is with a wooden knife or a piece of thick thread.

SERVES 4–6

INGREDIENTS
75g/3oz/6 tbsp butter
warm cooked polenta, made with 250g/9oz/2 cups polenta flour
45ml/3 tbsp olive oil
2 onions, thinly sliced
a pinch of grated nutmeg
150g/5oz/¾ cup mozzarella or sharp Cheddar cheese,
  cut into thin slices
45ml/3 tbsp finely chopped fresh parsley
35g/1½oz/⅓ cup freshly grated Parmesan cheese
salt and ground black pepper

1 Stir a third of the butter into the cooked polenta. Sprinkle a work surface with a little water. Spread the polenta out on to the surface in a layer 1cm/½in thick. Allow to cool. Using a pastry cutter, cut the polenta into 6cm/2½in rounds.

2 Heat the oil in a medium pan with 15g/½oz/1 tbsp of the remaining butter. Add the onions, and stir over low heat until soft. Season the onions with grated nutmeg, salt and black pepper.

3 Preheat the oven to 190°C/375°F/Gas 5. Butter an ovenproof dish. Spread a few of the onion slices in the bottom of the dish. Cover with a layer of the polenta rounds. Dot with butter.

4 Add a layer of the sliced mozzarella or Cheddar, and a sprinkling of parsley and grated Parmesan. Season with salt and pepper. Make another layer of the onions and continue the layers in order, ending with a sprinkling of Parmesan. Dot the top with butter. Bake for 20–25 minutes, or until the cheese has melted. Serve from the baking dish.

PIZZAS

This quintessentially Italian food can be eaten at any time of day as a snack or a main meal. Pizza dough is made with flour leavened with yeast, and can be baked directly on a flat baking sheet or in pizza pans. For the topping, almost any ingredient can be used – cheese, ham, sausage, seafood, tomatoes, mushrooms, artichoke, squash, spinach, onions, and olives are all popular. Classic combinations include the simple tomato and mozzarella topping of Pizza Margherita and the four cheeses of Pizza con Quattro Formaggi. The pizza base can also be folded over to enclose the filling to create Neapolitan calzone.

Basic Pizza Dough

Pizza dough is leavened with yeast. It usually rises once before being rolled out and filled. The dough can be baked in pizza pans or baked on a flat baking sheet. It can be used at once, or frozen for use at a later time.

Serves 4 as a main course or 8 as an appetizer

Ingredients
25g/1oz/2½ tbsp fresh yeast or 15g/½oz/1½ tbsp active dried yeast
250ml/8fl oz/1 cup lukewarm water
a pinch of sugar
5ml/1 tsp salt
350–400g/12–14oz/3–3½ cups plain (all-purpose) flour, preferably strong (bread)
oil

1 Pour a little hot water into a medium mixing bowl and swirl it around to warm the bowl. Drain. Place the yeast in the bowl, and pour on the warm water. Stir in the sugar, mix with a fork, and allow to stand for 5–10 minutes until the yeast has dissolved and starts to foam.

2 Use a wooden spoon to mix the salt and one-third of the flour into the yeast mixture. Mix in another third of the flour, stirring with the spoon until the dough forms a mass and begins to pull away from the sides of the bowl.

3 Sprinkle some of the remaining flour onto a smooth work surface. Remove the dough from the bowl and begin to knead it, working in the remaining flour a little at a time. Knead for 8–10 minutes until the dough is elastic and smooth. Form the dough into a ball.

4 Lightly oil a mixing bowl and put the dough in it. Stretch a moistened and wrung-out dishtowel across the top of the bowl, and leave it to stand in a warm place for 40–50 minutes or more, depending on the type of yeast used, until the dough has doubled in volume.

5 To test whether the dough has risen enough, poke two fingers into the dough. If the indentations remain, the dough is ready. Punch the dough down with your fist to release the air. Knead for 1–2 minutes.

6 If you want to make 2 medium pizzas, divide the dough into 2 balls. If you want to make 4 individual pizzas, divide the dough into 4 balls.

7 Pat the ball of dough out into a flat round on a lightly floured surface. With a rolling pin, roll it out to a thickness of about 5–7mm/⅜–¼in. If you are using a pizza pan, roll the dough out about 7mm/¼in larger than the size of the pan for the rim of the crust.

8 Place the dough in the lightly oiled pan, folding the extra dough under to make a thicker rim around the edge. If you are baking the pizza without a round pan, press some of the dough from the centre of the round towards the edge, to make a thicker rim. Place it on a lightly oiled flat baking sheet. The pizza dough is now ready for topping.

COOK'S TIPS
• This basic dough can not only be used as the base for pizzas but can also be used for other recipes, such as garlic bread, focaccia and bread sticks.
• If you do not have a warm enough place, turn the oven on to medium heat for 10 minutes before you knead the dough. Turn the oven off and place the bowl of dough in it. Close the door and let the dough rise.

PIZZA WITH ONIONS & BLACK OLIVES

Long, slow cooking gives the onions in this pizza a deliciously sweet flavour and juicy texture. They contrast wonderfully with the salty bitterness of the black olives and the mild, stringy mozzarella. If you prefer, use a few anchovy fillets in place of the olives – the result will be just as good.

SERVES 4

INGREDIENTS
90ml/6 tbsp extra virgin olive oil
4 onions, finely sliced
1 quantity Basic Pizza Dough, rolled out
350g/12oz/1¾ cups mozzarella cheese, cut into small dice
32 black olives, stoned (pitted) and halved
45ml/3 tbsp chopped fresh parsley
salt and ground black pepper

1 Preheat the oven to 240°C/475°F/Gas 9 for at least 20 minutes before baking the pizza. Heat half the olive oil in a large frying pan. Add the sliced onions and cook over low heat, stirring occasionally, for about 15 minutes until soft, translucent and beginning to brown. Season with salt and ground black pepper to taste. Remove the pan from the heat.

2 Place the prepared pizza dough on a baking sheet and spread the onions over the dough in an even layer, leaving the rim uncovered. Sprinkle evenly with the diced mozzarella.

3 Dot the pizza with the olives and sprinkle over the chopped parsley and remaining olive oil. Immediately place the pizza in the oven. Bake for about 15–20 minutes, or until the crust is golden brown and the cheese is bubbling.

Pizza alla Marinara

This very simple tomato and garlic pizza is absolutely delicious. The combination of slivered garlic, good quality olive oil and fresh oregano give an unmistakably Italian flavour. Enjoy it as a meal in itself or serve slices as an alternative to garlic bread.

Serves 2–3

Ingredients
675g/1½lb plum tomatoes
60ml/4 tbsp extra virgin olive oil
1 quantity Basic Pizza Dough, rolled out to about 25–30cm/10–12in diameter
4 garlic cloves, cut into slivers
15ml/1 tbsp chopped fresh oregano
salt and ground black pepper

1 Preheat the oven to 220°C/425°F/Gas 7. Place the tomatoes in a large bowl and pour over boiling water to cover. Leave to stand for 30 seconds, then drain. Peel the tomatoes and remove the seeds and tough stem and discard, then chop the flesh.

2 Heat 30ml/2 tbsp of the olive oil in a pan. Add the chopped tomatoes and cook, stirring frequently, for about 5 minutes until soft. Place in a strainer and leave to drain for about 5 minutes. Transfer to a food processor or blender and purée until smooth.

3 Brush the prepared pizza dough with half the remaining oil. Spoon over the tomatoes and sprinkle with garlic and oregano. Drizzle over the remaining oil and season. Bake for 15–20 minutes until crisp and golden. Serve immediately.

PIZZA ALLA MARGHERITA

This simple cheese and tomato pizza is named after the nineteenth-century Queen of Italy, and is one of the most popular of all pizzas. The delicious, combination of tomatoes, mozzarella and fresh basil is hard to beat.

SERVES 4

INGREDIENTS
450g/1lb peeled plum tomatoes, fresh or canned, weighed whole,
  without extra juice
1 quantity Basic Pizza Dough, rolled out
350g/12oz/1¾ cups mozzarella cheese, cut into small dice
10–12 fresh basil leaves, torn into pieces
60ml/4 tbsp freshly grated Parmesan cheese (optional)
45ml/3 tbsp olive oil
salt and ground black pepper

1 Preheat the oven to 240°C/475°F/Gas 9 for at least 20 minutes before baking. Pass the tomatoes through the medium holes of a food mill into a large bowl, scraping in all the pulp.

2 Spread the puréed tomatoes onto the prepared pizza dough, leaving the rim uncovered. Sprinkle evenly with the mozzarella. Dot with basil. Sprinkle with Parmesan, if using, salt, pepper and olive oil.

3 Immediately place the pizzas in the oven. Bake for 15–20 minutes, or until the crust is golden brown and the cheeses are melted and bubbling.

COOK'S TIP
If you want to invent your own pizza, use this classic recipe as the base for your own creations. Add a selection of toppings, such as artichoke hearts and olives, tuna, spinach and capers, or asparagus, Gorgonzola and fresh rocket.

SICILIAN PIZZA

This pizza has a rich, robust flavour and is topped with aubergine, mozzarella and Pecorino cheeses and garnished with olives and capers.

SERVES 2

INGREDIENTS

60ml/4 tbsp extra virgin olive oil
½ onion, very finely chopped
½ clove garlic, finely chopped
225g/8oz tomatoes, fresh or canned, chopped, with their juice
a few fresh basil leaves or parsley sprigs
1 small aubergine (eggplant), cut into thin rounds
½ quantity Basic Pizza Dough
175g/6oz mozzarella cheese, sliced
50g/2oz/½ cup pitted black olives
15ml/1 tbsp drained capers
60ml/4 tbsp grated Pecorino cheese
salt and ground black pepper

1 Heat 30ml/2tbsp of the oil in a medium pan. Add the onion and cook over a medium heat for about 5 minutes until soft and translucent. Stir in the garlic and tomatoes and herbs and season with salt and pepper. Cook for 20–30 minutes, then pass through a food mill and set aside.

2 Preheat the oven to 200°C/400°F/Gas 6. Brush two baking sheets with oil. Brush the aubergine rounds with olive oil and arrange them on the baking sheets. Bake for 10–15 minutes, turning once, until browned and tender. Remove the aubergine slices from the baking sheets and drain on kitchen paper.

3 Raise the oven temperature to 220°C/425°F/Gas 7. Roll the pizza dough into two 25cm/10in rounds. Transfer to baking sheets and spread with tomato sauce. Pile the aubergine on top and cover with mozzarella. Dot with black olives and capers. Sprinkle Pecorino cheese liberally over the top, and season with plenty of salt and pepper. Bake for 15–20 minutes until the crusts are golden brown.

BUTTERNUT SQUASH PIZZA

The combination of sweet butternut squash, sage and sharp goat's cheese works wonderfully on this sophisticated pizza.

SERVES 4

INGREDIENTS
15g/½oz/1 tbsp butter
90ml/6 tbsp olive oil
2 shallots, finely chopped
1 butternut squash, peeled, seeded and cubed, about 450g/1lb prepared weight
16 sage leaves
1 onion, finely chopped
1 garlic clove, finely chopped
450g/1 lb tomatoes, fresh or canned, chopped, with their juice
1 quantity Basic Pizza Dough
115g/4oz/1 cup mozzarella cheese, sliced
115g/4oz/½ cup firm goat's cheese
salt and ground black pepper

1 Preheat the oven to 200°C/400°F/Gas 6. Oil four baking sheets. Put the butter and 30ml/2 tbsp of the oil in a roasting pan and heat in the oven for a few minutes. Add the shallots, squash and half the sage leaves. Toss to coat. Roast for 15–20 minutes until tender.

2 Meanwhile, make the tomato sauce. Heat the remaining oil in a pan. Add the onion and cook gently for 5 minutes until soft. Stir in the garlic and tomatoes and season. Cook for 20–30 minutes, then pass through a food mill and set aside.

3 Raise the oven temperature to 220°C/425°F/Gas 7. Divide the pizza dough into four pieces and roll out each piece on a lightly floured surface to a 25cm/10in round. Transfer each round to a baking sheet and spread with the tomato sauce, leaving a 1cm/½in border. Spoon the squash and shallot mixture over the top.

4 Arrange the mozzarella over the squash and shallot mixture and crumble goat's cheese over. Scatter the remaining sage leaves over and season with plenty of salt and pepper. Bake for 15–20 minutes until the cheese has melted and the crust on each pizza is golden. Serve immediately.

PIZZA FIORENTINA

The key ingredients in this classic pizza are spinach and egg. A fresh egg is broken into the centre of the pizza and cooks while the pizza is baked.

SERVES 2–3

INGREDIENTS
105ml/7 tbsp olive oil
1 onion, finely chopped
1 garlic clove, finely chopped
450g/1lb tomatoes, fresh or canned, chopped, with their juice
a few fresh basil leaves or parsley sprigs
175g/6oz fresh spinach
1 small red onion, thinly sliced
1 pizza base, about 25–30cm/10–12in diameter
freshly grated nutmeg
150g/5oz mozzarella, thinly sliced
1 egg
25g/1oz Gruyère, grated
salt and ground black pepper

1 Heat 60ml/4 tbsp of the oil in a pan. Add the chopped onion and cook gently for 5 minutes until soft. Stir in the garlic, tomatoes and herbs and season. Cook for 20–30 minutes, then pass through a food mill and set aside.

2 Preheat the oven to 220°C/425°F/Gas 7. Remove the stalks from the spinach and wash the leaves in cold water. Drain well and pat dry with kitchen paper. Heat 15ml/1 tbsp of the oil and fry the red onion until soft. Add the spinach and continue to fry until just wilted. Drain off any excess liquid.

3 Brush the pizza base with half the remaining oil. Spread over the tomato sauce, then top with the spinach. Grate over some nutmeg. Arrange the mozzarella over the spinach and drizzle over the remaining oil. Bake for 10 minutes, then remove from the oven.

4 Make a well in the centre of the pizza topping and drop the egg into the hole. Sprinkle with Gruyère and return to the oven for 5–10 minutes until crisp and golden. Serve immediately.

Pizza con Quattro Formaggi

Any combination of cheeses can be used for this four-cheese pizza. Choose cheeses which are different in character, such as mild and creamy ricotta, pungent Dolcelatte, tangy Camembert and sweet, stringy Emmental.

Serves 4

Ingredients
1 quantity Basic Pizza Dough, rolled out
75g/3oz/½ cup Gorgonzola or other blue cheese, thinly sliced
75g/3oz/½ cup mozzarella cheese, finely diced
75g/3oz/½ cup goat's cheese, thinly sliced
75g/3oz/½ cup sharp Cheddar cheese, coarsely grated
4 fresh sage leaves, torn into pieces, or 45ml/3 tbsp chopped fresh parsley
45ml/3 tbsp olive oil
salt and ground black pepper

1 Preheat the oven to 240°C/475°F/Gas 9 for at least 20 minutes before baking the pizza. Arrange the Gorgonzola on one quarter of the prepared pizza dough and the mozzarella on another, leaving a border around the edge.

2 Arrange the goat's cheese and Cheddar cheeses on the remaining two quarters. Sprinkle with the herbs, salt and pepper, and olive oil. Immediately place the pizza in the oven. Bake for about 15–20 minutes, or until the crust is golden brown and the cheeses are bubbling. Serve immediately.

Pizza Quattro Stagioni

In Italian, this pizza is called "four seasons". The topping is divided into quarters – one for each season. You may substitute the mushrooms, ham, olives and artichokes with other seasonal ingredients, if you prefer.

SERVES 4

INGREDIENTS

450g/1lb peeled plum tomatoes, fresh or canned, weighed whole,
  without extra juice
75ml/5 tbsp olive oil
115g/4oz/1 cup mushrooms, thinly sliced
1 garlic clove, finely chopped
1 quantity Basic Pizza Dough, rolled out
350g/12oz/1¾ cups mozzarella cheese, cut into small dice
4 thin slices ham, cut into 5cm/2in squares
32 black olives, stoned (pitted) and halved
8 artichoke hearts preserved in oil, drained and cut in half
5ml/1 tsp oregano leaves, fresh or dried
salt and ground black pepper

1 Preheat the oven to 240°C/475°F/Gas 9 for at least 20 minutes before baking the pizza. Strain the tomatoes through the medium holes of a food mill into a large bowl, scraping in all the pulp.

2 Heat 30ml/2 tbsp of the oil and lightly sauté the mushrooms for 3–4 minutes. Stir in the garlic and set aside.

3 Spread the puréed tomato mixture over the prepared pizza dough, leaving the rim uncovered. Sprinkle evenly with diced mozzarella.

4 Spread mushrooms over one quarter of each pizza, arrange the ham on another quarter and the olives and artichoke hearts on the two remaining quarters. Sprinkle with oregano, salt and pepper, and the remaining olive oil.

5 Immediately place the pizza in the oven. Bake for 15–20 minutes, or until the crust is golden brown and the topping is bubbling. Serve immediately.

PROSCIUTTO, MUSHROOM & ARTICHOKE PIZZA

This wonderful pizza is full of rich and varied flavours and textures. Mild and juicy artichoke hearts complement salty-sweet prosciutto perfectly. For a really sophisticated pizza, use mixed cultivated mushrooms.

SERVES 2–3

INGREDIENTS
1 bunch spring onions (scallions)
60ml/4 tbsp olive oil
225g/8oz mushrooms, sliced
2 garlic cloves, chopped
1 quantity Basic Pizza Dough, rolled out to about 25–30cm/10–12in diameter
8 slices prosciutto
4 bottled artichoke hearts in oil, drained and sliced
60ml/4 tsp freshly grated Parmesan
salt and ground black pepper
thyme sprigs, to garnish

1 Preheat the oven to 220°C/425°F/Gas 7. Trim the spring onions, then chop all the white and some of the green stems.

2 Heat 30ml/2 tbsp of the oil in a frying pan. Add the spring onions, mushrooms and garlic and fry over a medium heat for 5–10 minutes until all the juices have evaporated. Season with salt and pepper and set aside to cool.

3 Brush the prepared pizza dough with half the remaining olive oil. Arrange the prosciutto, mushrooms and artichoke hearts on top.

4 Sprinkle grated Parmesan over the pizza, then drizzle over the remaining oil and season with salt and pepper. Bake for 15–20 minutes. Garnish with thyme sprigs and serve immediately.

PIZZA WITH SAUSAGE

Choose good quality seasoned sausages with a high meat content, such as luganega *or* cotechino, *if you like your topping hot or use slices of spicy cured sausage.*

SERVES 4

INGREDIENTS
450g/1lb peeled plum tomatoes, fresh or canned, weighed whole,
  without extra juice
1 quantity Basic Pizza Dough, rolled out
350g/12oz/1¾ cups mozzarella cheese, cut into small dice
225g/8oz/1½ cups sausage meat, removed from the casings and crumbled
5ml/1 tsp oregano leaves, fresh or dried
45ml/3 tbsp olive oil
salt and ground black pepper

1 Preheat the oven to 240°C/475°F/Gas 9 for at least 20 minutes before baking the pizza. Strain the tomatoes through the medium holes of a food mill into a large bowl, scraping in all the pulp.

2 Spread some of the puréed tomatoes on the prepared pizza base, leaving the rim uncovered. Sprinkle evenly with the diced mozzarella. Add the sausage meat in a layer. Sprinkle with oregano, salt and pepper, and olive oil.

3 Immediately place the pizza in the preheated oven. Bake for 15–20 minutes, or until the crust is golden brown and the cheese is bubbling. Serve immediately.

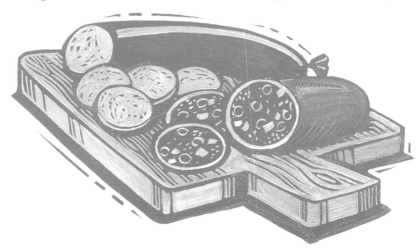

ANCHOVY, PEPPER & TOMATO PIZZA

This pretty, summery pizza is incredibly simple, yet quite delicious. It's well worth grilling the peppers as they take on a lovely smoky flavour that goes well with the sweet tomatoes and salty anchovies.

SERVES 2–3

INGREDIENTS
6 plum tomatoes
45ml/3 tbsp olive oil
5ml/1 tsp salt
1 large red (bell) pepper
1 large yellow (bell) pepper
1 quantity Basic Pizza Dough, rolled out to about 25–30cm/10–12in diameter
2 garlic cloves, chopped
50g/2oz can anchovy fillets, drained
ground black pepper
basil leaves, to garnish

1 Halve the tomatoes lengthways and scoop out the seeds. Roughly chop the flesh and place in a bowl with 15ml/1 tbsp of the oil and the salt. Mix well, then leave to marinate for 30 minutes.

2 Meanwhile, preheat the oven to 220°C/425°F/Gas 7. Slice the peppers in half lengthways and remove the seeds. Place the pepper halves, skin-side up, on a baking sheet and grill (broil) until the skins are evenly charred.

3 Place the grilled peppers in a covered bowl for 10 minutes, then peel off the charred skins and cut the flesh into thin strips. Brush the prepared pizza dough with half the remaining olive oil. Drain the tomatoes, then scatter over the base with the pepper strips and chopped garlic.

4 Arrange the anchovy fillets on top of the pizza and season with plenty of black pepper. Drizzle over the remaining oil and bake for 15–20 minutes until crisp and golden. Garnish with basil leaves and serve immediately.

Pizza with Seafood

This seafood pizza uses squid, mussels and prawns but any combination of shellfish or other seafood can be used as a pizza topping.

Serves 4

Ingredients

450g/1lb peeled plum tomatoes, fresh or canned, weighed whole, without extra juice
175g/6oz small squid
225g/8oz fresh mussels
1 quantity Basic Pizza Dough, rolled out
175g/6oz prawns (shrimp), raw or cooked, peeled and deveined
2 garlic cloves, finely chopped
45ml/3 tbsp chopped fresh parsley
45ml/3 tbsp olive oil
salt and ground black pepper

1   Preheat the oven to 240°C/475°F/Gas 9 for at least 20 minutes before baking the pizza. Strain the tomatoes through the medium holes of a food mill into a large bowl, scraping in all the pulp.

2   Clean the squid. Peel off the thin skin from the body section. Rinse well. Pull the head and tentacles away from the sac section. Remove and discard the translucent quill and any insides from the sac. Sever the tentacles from the head. Discard the head and insides. Remove the hard beak from the base of the tentacles. Rinse the sac and tentacles well. Drain and slice the sacs into rings 5mm/¼in thick.

3   Scrape the beards off the mussels and scrub well. Discard any that do not close when tapped sharply with the back of a knife. Place the mussels in a pan and heat until they open. Lift them out with a slotted spoon, and remove to a side dish. Discard any that do not open. Break off the empty half shells, and discard.

4   Spread the puréed tomatoes on the pizza dough, leaving the rim uncovered. Dot with the prawns and squid rings and tentacles. Sprinkle with the garlic, parsley, salt and pepper, and olive oil. Immediately place the pizza in the oven. Bake for about 8 minutes. Remove from the oven, and add the mussels in the half shells. Return to the oven and bake for 7–10 minutes more, or until the crust is golden.

SICILIAN CLOSED PIZZA

This pizza is rather like a pie. It is stuffed with hard-boiled eggs, anchovies, olives, tomatoes and grated cheese, but any flat pizza topping can be used.

SERVES 4–6

INGREDIENTS
1 quantity Basic Pizza Dough, risen once
olive oil, for brushing
30ml/2 tbsp coarse corn meal
3 hard-boiled (hard-cooked) eggs, shelled and sliced
50g/2oz/¼ cup anchovy fillets, drained and chopped
12 olives, stoned (pitted)
8 fresh basil leaves, torn into pieces
6 tomatoes, peeled, seeded and diced
2 garlic cloves, finely chopped
175g/6oz/1½ cups grated caciocavallo or Pecorino cheese
ground black pepper

1 Preheat the oven to 230°C/450°F/Gas 8. Punch the dough and knead lightly for 3–4 minutes. Divide the dough into two pieces, one slightly larger than the other. Lightly oil a round pizza pan 38cm/15in in diameter. Sprinkle with the corn meal. Roll the larger piece of dough into a round slightly bigger than the pan.

2 Transfer the rolled dough to the pizza pan, bringing it up the sides to the rim. Fill the pie by placing the sliced eggs in the bottom in a layer, leaving the edges of the dough uncovered. Dot with the anchovies, olives and basil. Spread the diced tomatoes over the other ingredients. Sprinkle with garlic and ground black pepper. Top with the grated cheese.

3 Roll or press the second piece of dough into a round the same size as the pan. Place it over the filling. Roll the edge of the bottom dough over it, and crimp together to make a border.

4 Brush the top and edges of the dough with olive oil. Bake for 30–40 minutes, or until the top is golden brown. Allow to stand for 5–8 minutes before serving.

CALZONE

This Neapolitan speciality is named after the baggy trousers worn by Neapolitan men in the 18th and 19th centuries. The pizza is folded over to enclose the topping.

SERVES 4

INGREDIENTS
1 quantity Basic Pizza Dough, risen once
350g/12oz/1½ cups ricotta cheese
175g/6oz/¾ cup ham, cut into small dice
6 tomatoes, peeled, seeded and diced
8 fresh basil leaves, torn into pieces
175g/6oz/1 cup mozzarella cheese, cut into small dice
60ml/4 tbsp freshly grated Parmesan cheese
olive oil, for brushing
salt and ground black pepper

1 Preheat the oven to 240°C/475°F/Gas 9 for at least 20 minutes before baking the calzoni. Punch the dough down and knead it lightly. Divide the dough into 4 balls. Roll each ball out into a flat round about 5mm/¼in thick.

2 Combine the ricotta, ham, tomatoes, basil, mozzarella and Parmesan in a bowl. Mix well and season. Divide the filling between the 4 rounds of dough, placing it on half of each round and allowing a border of 2cm/¾in all around. Fold the other half of the dough over. Crimp the edges together with your fingers to seal.

3 Place the calzoni on lightly oiled baking sheets. Brush the tops lightly with olive oil. Bake in the preheated oven for about 15–20 minutes, or until the tops are golden brown and the dough is puffed.

COOK'S TIP
Calzoni can be large or small and eaten hot or cold. They can be filled with any of the traditional flat pizza toppings. Traditionally, calzoni were made from rectangular pieces of dough

FISH & SHELLFISH

Italy has a long coastline and many lakes and rivers, so it is no wonder that fish and shellfish, such as sardines, red mullet, sea bass, monkfish, squid, mussels, clams and prawns, are so popular. Italians favour simply cooked fish and shellfish, such as Grilled Sardines, Trout Baked in Paper with Olives, and Pan-fried Prawns in their Shells. These dishes rely on the quality and flavour of the fresh ingredients and accompanying sauces are usually light and fresh. Seafood stews, such as Stewed Mussels and Clams, are also popular along the Italian coastline.

GRILLED FRESH SARDINES

Fresh sardines are popular throughout Italy and are at their best in spring. They are flavourful and firm-fleshed, and quite different in taste and consistency from those canned in oil. They are excellent simply grilled and served with lemon.

SERVES 4–6

INGREDIENTS
1kg/2¼lb very fresh sardines, gutted and with heads removed
olive oil, for brushing
salt and ground black pepper
45ml/3 tbsp chopped fresh parsley, to serve
lemon wedges, to garnish

1 Preheat the grill (broiler). Rinse the sardines in water and pat dry with kitchen paper. Brush the sardines lightly with olive oil and sprinkle generously with salt and pepper. Place the fish in one layer on the grill pan and grill for 3–4 minutes.

2 Turn the sardines, and cook the second side for 3–4 minutes, or until the skin begins to brown. Serve immediately, sprinkled with chopped fresh parsley and garnished with lemon wedges.

GRILLED SALMON STEAKS WITH FENNEL

Fennel grows wild all over the south of Italy and has a delicate but distinctive aniseed flavour that goes well with fish. In this traditional recipe, the salmon is marinated in lemon juice and fennel, which imparts a wonderful flavour.

SERVES 4

INGREDIENTS
juice of 1 lemon
45ml/3 tbsp chopped fresh fennel herb, or the green fronds from
the top of a fennel bulb
5ml/1 tsp fennel seeds
45ml/3 tbsp olive oil
4 salmon steaks of the same thickness, about 675g/1½lb total
salt and ground black pepper
lemon wedges, to garnish

1 Combine the lemon juice, chopped fennel herb and fennel seeds with the olive oil in a shallow dish. Place the salmon steaks in the dish, turning them to coat in the marinade. Sprinkle with salt and ground black pepper. Cover with clear film and place in the refrigerator. Allow to stand for 2 hours.

2 Preheat the grill (broiler). Arrange the salmon steaks in a single layer on a grill pan or shallow baking tray. Place the grill pan or baking tray about 10cm/4in from the heat source and cook the fish for about 4 minutes.

3 Turn the salmon steaks and spoon on the remaining fennel marinade. Grill for about 3 minutes, or until the edges begin to brown. Serve immediately garnished with lemon wedges.

Chargrilled Squid
with Chillies

If you like your squid hot and spicy, chop some – or all – of the chilli seeds with the flesh. If not, cut the chillies in half lengthways, scrape out the seeds and discard them before chopping the flesh.

SERVES 2

INGREDIENTS
2 whole prepared squid, with tentacles
75ml/5 tbsp olive oil
30ml/2 tbsp balsamic vinegar
2 fresh red chillies, finely chopped
60ml/4 tbsp dry white wine
salt and ground black pepper
hot cooked risotto rice, to serve
sprigs of fresh parsley, to garnish

1 Make a lengthways cut down the body of each squid, then open out flat. Score the flesh on both sides in a criss-cross pattern with a sharp knife. Chop the tentacles. Place the squid in a dish. Whisk together the oil and vinegar in a bowl. Season, then pour over the squid. Cover and leave to marinate for about 1 hour.

2 Heat a ridged cast-iron pan until hot. Cook one of the squid bodies over a medium heat for 2–3 minutes, pressing the squid with a fish slice to keep it flat. Repeat on the other side. Cook the remaining squid body in the same way.

3 Cut the cooked squid into diagonal strips. Pile the hot risotto rice in the centre of warmed soup plates and top with the strips of squid, arranging them criss-cross fashion. Keep hot.

4 Place the chopped tentacles and chillies in the cast-iron pan and toss over a medium heat for 2 minutes. Stir in the wine, then spoon over the squid and risotto. Garnish with the parsley and serve at once.

PAN-FRIED PRAWNS IN THEIR SHELLS

Garlic and vermouth are a wonderful combination and complement the delicate flavour of prawns perfectly. Serve this quick and simple dish for an informal supper with friends, with plenty of hot crusty Italian bread to scoop up the juices.

SERVES 4

INGREDIENTS
60ml/4 tbsp extra virgin olive oil
32 large fresh prawns (shrimp), in their shells
4 garlic cloves, finely chopped
120ml/4fl oz/½ cup Italian dry white vermouth
45ml/3 tbsp passata (bottled strained tomatoes)
salt and ground black pepper
crusty bread, to serve
chopped fresh flat leaf parsley, to garnish

1 Heat the olive oil in a large heavy frying pan until just sizzling. Add the prawns and toss over a medium to high heat until their shells just begin to turn pink.

2 Sprinkle the garlic over the prawns in the pan and toss again, then pour over the vermouth and let it bubble, tossing the prawns constantly so that they cook evenly and absorb the flavours of the garlic and vermouth.

3 Add the passata and season with salt and pepper to taste. Stir until the prawns are thoroughly coated in the sauce. Serve at once, sprinkled with the parsley and accompanied by plenty of hot crusty bread.

COOK'S TIP
Prawns in their shells are sweet and juicy but they can be quite messy, so provide guests with finger bowls and napkins.

PAN-FRIED SOLE WITH LEMON

The delicate flavour and texture of sole is brought out in this simple, classic dish.
Lemon sole is used here because it is less expensive than Dover sole.

SERVES 2

INGREDIENTS
30–45ml/2–3 tbsp seasoned flour
4 lemon sole fillets
45ml/3 tbsp olive oil
50g/2oz/¼ cup butter
60ml/4 tbsp lemon juice
30ml/2 tbsp bottled capers, rinsed
salt and ground black pepper
fresh flat leaf parsley and lemon wedges, to garnish

1 Tip the seasoned flour into a shallow dish and dredge the sole fillets to coat evenly on both sides. Heat the oil with half the butter in a shallow pan until foaming. Add sole fillets and fry over a medium heat for 2–3 minutes on each side.

2 Lift the sole fillets out of the pan with a fish slice (spatula) and place on a warmed serving platter. Keep warm while you fry the remaining sole fillets. Remove the pan from the heat.

3 Add the lemon juice and remaining butter to the pan. Return to a high heat and stir vigorously until the juices are sizzling and beginning to turn golden. Remove from the heat and stir in the capers. Pour over the sole and season with salt and pepper. Serve at once, garnish with parsley and lemon wedges.

COOK'S TIP
After removing the fish from the pan, it is important
to cook the juices for long enough. If they are not
cooked until they are golden, they may taste bitter.

RED MULLET WITH TOMATOES

Red mullet is a very popular fish in Italy. This simple dish accentuates its distinctive, almost prawn-like, flavour and its pretty reddish colour. Small sea bass may be substituted for red mullet, if you prefer.

SERVES 4

INGREDIENTS

4 red mullet, about 175–200g/6–7oz each
450g/1lb tomatoes, peeled, or 1 × 400g/14oz can plum tomatoes
60ml/4 tbsp olive oil
60ml/4 tbsp finely chopped fresh parsley
2 garlic cloves, finely chopped
120ml/4fl oz/½ cup white wine
4 thin lemon slices, cut in half
salt and ground black pepper

1 Hold the fish by the tail and use a blunt knife to remove the scales. Clean the fish without removing the liver, then wash thoroughly under cold running water and pat dry with kitchen paper.

2 Chop the tomatoes into small pieces. Heat the oil in a pan or casserole large enough to hold the fish in one layer. Add the parsley and garlic, and sauté for 1 minute. Stir in the tomatoes and cook over moderate heat for 15–20 minutes. Season with salt and pepper.

3 Add the fish to the tomato sauce and cook over moderate to high heat for about 5 minutes. Add the white wine and the lemon slices. Bring the sauce back to the boil and cook for about 5 minutes more. Turn the fish over and cook for a further 4–5 minutes.

4 Remove the fish from the casserole and place on a warmed serving platter. Keep warm until needed. Boil the sauce rapidly for 3–4 minutes to reduce it slightly. Spoon it over the fish, and serve straight away.

SOLE WITH SWEET & SOUR SAUCE

This traditional dish from Venice is flavoured with wine, vinegar and spices. It should be prepared 1–2 days in advance, to allow the sole to absorb all the flavours.

SERVES 4

INGREDIENTS
60ml/4 tbsp flour
a pinch of ground cloves
3–4 fillets of sole, about 500g/1¼lb total, divided in half
90–120ml/6–8 tbsp olive oil
40g/1½oz/generous ¼ cup pine nuts
3 bay leaves
a pinch of ground cinnamon
a pinch of grated nutmeg
4 cloves
1 small onion, very finely sliced
50ml/2fl oz/¼ cup dry white wine
50ml/2fl oz/¼ cup white wine vinegar
50g/2oz/⅓ cup sultanas (golden raisins)
salt and ground black pepper

1 Season the flour with the ground cloves and salt and pepper, then dredge the sole fillets to coat evenly. Heat 45ml/3 tbsp of the oil in a heavy frying pan or skillet. Cook the sole fillets a few at a time for about 3 minutes on each side, until golden. Add more olive oil if necessary.

2 Remove the fish from the pan with a fish slice (spatula) and place in a large shallow serving dish. Sprinkle with the pine nuts, bay leaves, cinnamon, nutmeg and whole cloves.

3 Heat the remaining oil in a pan. Add the onion and cook over low heat until golden. Add the wine, vinegar and sultanas and boil for 4–5 minutes. Pour the mixture over the fish. Cover the dish with foil and leave in a cool place for 24–48 hours. Remove 2 hours before serving and serve at room temperature.

Monkfish Medallions with Tomatoes & Thyme

Monkfish has a sweet flesh that combines well with the Mediterranean flavours.
Baking it with thyme, black olives and tomatoes gives a juicy, succulent texture.

SERVES 4

INGREDIENTS
600g/1lb 6oz monkfish fillet, preferably in one piece
45ml/3 tbsp extra virgin olive oil
75g/3oz/½ cup small black olives, preferably from the Riviera, stoned (pitted)
1 large or 2 small tomatoes, seeded and diced
1 fresh thyme sprig , or 5ml/1 tsp dried thyme leaves
salt and ground black pepper
15ml/1 tbsp very finely chopped fresh parsley, to serve

1 Preheat the oven to 200°C/400°F/Gas 6. Remove the grey membrane from the monkfish, if necessary. Cut the fish into slices 1cm/½in thick. Heat a non-stick frying pan until quite hot, without oil. Sear the fish quickly on both sides, then remove to a side dish.

2 Spread 15ml/1 tbsp of the olive oil in the bottom of a shallow baking dish. Arrange the fish in one layer in the dish. Scatter the olives and diced tomato on top of the fish. Sprinkle the fish with the thyme, salt and pepper, and the remaining olive oil. Bake for 10–12 minutes.

3 To serve, divide the monkfish among 4 warmed plates. Spoon on the tomatoes and olives and any cooking juices and sprinkle with chopped fresh parsley.

Trout Baked in Paper with Olives

Baking whole trout with pancetta and olives in paper packets keeps in all the rich flavours and moisture, giving a juicy, succulent result. They look very attractive served at the table still wrapped in their paper.

Serves 4

Ingredients

4 trout, about 275g/10oz each, gutted
75ml/5 tbsp olive oil
4 bay leaves
4 slices pancetta
60ml/4 tbsp chopped shallots
60ml/4 tbsp chopped fresh parsley
120ml/4fl oz/½ cup dry white wine
24 green olives, stoned (pitted)
salt and ground black pepper

1 Preheat the oven to 200°C/400°F/Gas 6. Wash the trout well under cold running water. Drain and pat dry with kitchen paper. Lightly brush oil onto 4 pieces of baking parchment each large enough to enclose one fish. Lay one fish on each piece of oiled paper. Place a bay leaf in each cavity and sprinkle with plenty of salt and ground black pepper.

2 Carefully wrap a slice of pancetta around each fish. Sprinkle with 15ml/1 tbsp each of shallots and parsley. Drizzle each fish with 15ml/1 tbsp of olive oil and 30ml/2 tbsp of white wine. Add 6 olives to each packet.

3 Close the paper loosely around the fish, rolling the edges together to seal them completely. Bake for 20–25 minutes. To serve, place each packet on an individual plate and open at the table.

BAKED COD WITH GARLIC MAYONNAISE

Cod is not native to the Mediterranean so, in Italy, a similar species is used for this dish. Creamy garlic mayonnaise makes a wonderful addition to this white fish.

SERVES 4

INGREDIENTS
4 anchovy fillets
45ml/3 tbsp chopped fresh parsley
90ml/6 tbsp olive oil
4 cod fillets, about 750g/1½lb total, skinned
40g/1½oz/⅓ cup plain breadcrumbs
salt and ground black pepper

FOR THE MAYONNAISE
2 garlic cloves, finely chopped
1 egg yolk
5ml/1 tsp Dijon mustard
175ml/6fl oz/¾ cup vegetable oil

1 Make the mayonnaise. Put the garlic in a mortar or small bowl and mash to a paste. Beat in the egg yolk and mustard. Add the oil in a thin streak while beating vigorously with a small wire whisk. When the mixture is thick and smooth, season with salt and pepper. Cover and keep cool.

2 Preheat the oven to 200°C/400°F/Gas 6. With a sharp knife, chop the anchovy fillets with the parsley very finely. Place in a small bowl, add pepper and 45ml/ 3 tbsp of the oil, then mix to a paste.

3 Place the cod in one layer in an oiled baking dish. Spread the anchovy paste over the fish and sprinkle with the breadcrumbs and remaining oil. Bake for 20–25 minutes until the breadcrumbs are golden. Serve hot with garlic mayonnaise.

ROAST SEA BASS

Sea bass has a firm flesh with a fine flavour. It is an expensive fish, best cooked as simply as possible. Avoid elaborate sauces, which would mask its delicate flavour.

SERVES 4

INGREDIENTS
1 fennel bulb with fronds, about 275g/10oz
2 lemons
120ml/4fl oz/½ cup olive oil
1 small red onion, diced
2 sea bass, about 500g/1¼lb each, cleaned with heads left on
120ml/4fl oz/½ cup dry white wine
salt and ground black pepper
lemon slices, to garnish

1 Preheat the oven to 190°C/375°F/ Gas 5. Cut the fronds off the top of the fennel and reserve for the garnish. Cut the fennel bulb lengthways into thin wedges, then into dice. Cut one half lemon into four slices and set aside. Squeeze the juice from the remaining lemon half and the other lemon.

2 Heat 30ml/2 tbsp of the oil in a frying pan, add the diced fennel and onion and cook gently, stirring frequently, for about 5 minutes until softened. Remove the pan from the heat.

3 Make three diagonal slashes on both sides of each sea bass with a sharp knife. Brush a roasting tin generously with oil, add the fish and tuck two lemon slices in each cavity. Scatter the fennel and onion over the fish.

4 Whisk together the remaining oil and lemon juice and season with salt and pepper. Pour over the fish. Cover with foil and roast for 30 minutes or until the flesh flakes, removing the foil for the last 10 minutes. Discard the lemon slices, transfer the fish to a heated serving platter and keep hot.

5 Put the roasting tin on top of the stove. Add the wine and stir over a medium heat to incorporate all the pan juices. Bring to the boil, then spoon the juices over the fish. Garnish with the reserved fennel fronds and lemon slices and serve.

MONKFISH WITH TOMATO SAUCE

This dish comes from the coast of Calabria in southern Italy and is richly flavoured with tomatoes and black olives. Garlic mashed potato is an ideal accompaniment.

SERVES 4

INGREDIENTS
450g/1lb fresh mussels
2 garlic cloves, roughly chopped
300ml/½ pint/1¼ cups dry white wine
a few fresh basil sprigs, plus extra leaves to garnish
30ml/2 tbsp olive oil
15g/½oz/1 tbsp butter
900g/2lb monkfish fillets, skinned and cut into large chunks
1 onion, finely chopped
500g/1¼lb jar sugocasa or passata (bottled strained tomatoes)
15ml/1 tbsp sun-dried tomato paste
115g/4oz/1 cup stoned (pitted) black olives
salt and ground black pepper

1 Scrape the beards off the mussels and scrub well. Discard any that do not close when tapped sharply with the back of a knife. Put the mussels, garlic, wine and some basil in a flameproof casserole. Cover and bring to the boil. Lower the heat and simmer for 5 minutes, shaking frequently. Remove the mussels, discarding any that fail to open. Strain the cooking liquid and reserve.

2 Heat the oil and butter in the casserole until foaming, add the monkfish and sauté over a medium heat until they just change colour. Remove. Add the onion and cook gently for 5 minutes, stirring frequently. Add the sugocasa or passata, the reserved cooking liquid from the mussels and the sun-dried tomato paste. Season with salt and pepper. Bring to the boil, stirring, then lower the heat, cover and simmer for 20 minutes, stirring occasionally.

3 Pull off and discard the top shells from the mussels. Add the monkfish to the sauce and cook gently for 5 minutes. Stir in the olives and remaining basil, then taste for seasoning. Place the mussels in their half shells on top of the sauce, cover the pan and heat the mussels through for 1–2 minutes. Serve garnished with basil.

SEAFOOD STEW

Fish and shellfish stews are specialities of the Mediterranean, where there is a plentiful supply of good quality ingredients. This recipe includes prawns, mussels and clams, as well as chunks of filleted fish. It is wonderful served with plenty of toasted bread.

SERVES 4

INGREDIENTS
45ml/3 tbsp olive oil
1 onion, sliced
1 carrot, sliced
½ stick celery, sliced
2 garlic cloves, chopped
1 × 400g/14oz can plum tomatoes, chopped, with their juice
225g/8oz fresh prawns (shrimp), peeled and deveined (reserve the shells)
450g/1lb white fish bones and heads, gills removed
1 bay leaf
1 fresh thyme sprig, or 1.5ml/¼ tsp dried thyme leaves
a few peppercorns
675g/1½lb fresh mussels, in their shells
500g/1¼lb fresh small clams, in their shells
250ml/8fl oz/1 cup white wine
1kg/2¼lb mixed fish fillets, such as cod, monkfish, red mullet
  or hake, bones removed and cut into chunks
45ml/3 tbsp finely chopped fresh parsley
salt and ground black pepper
rounds of French bread, toasted, to serve

COOK'S TIP
When buying the fish and shellfish for this recipe, shop with an open mind and buy whatever fish looks freshest and best on the day.

1 Heat the oil in a medium pan. Add the onion and cook slowly until soft. Stir in the carrot and celery, and cook for 5 minutes more. Add the garlic, the tomatoes and their juice, and 250ml/8fl oz/1 cup water. Cook over moderate heat for about 15 minutes, until the vegetables are soft. Purée in a food processor and set aside.

2 Place the prawn shells in a large pan with the fish bones and heads. Add the herbs and peppercorns and pour in 750ml/1¼ pints/3 cups of water. Bring to the boil, reduce the heat and simmer for 25 minutes, skimming off any scum that rises to the surface. Strain and pour into a pan with the tomato sauce. Season.

3 Scrape the beards off the mussels. Scrub the mussels and clams well and discard any that do not close when tapped sharply with the back of a knife. Place the prepared mussels and clams in a large pan with the wine. Cover and steam until all the shells have opened.

4 Lift the clams and mussels out of the pan with a slotted spoon, discard any that have not opened and set the remaining shellfish aside. Filter the cooking liquid through a layer of kitchen paper held in a strainer and add it to the stock and tomato sauce. Check the seasoning and add more if necessary.

5 Bring the sauce to the boil, add the fish and boil for 5 minutes. Add the prawns and boil for a further 3–4 minutes. Stir in the mussels and clams and cook for 2–3 minutes more. Transfer the stew to a warmed casserole. Sprinkle with parsley and serve with the toasted rounds of French bread.

STEWED MUSSELS & CLAMS

Casseroles of mixed shellfish are very popular on the Ligurian coast. In this stew, mussels and clams are cooked in white wine and flavoured with garlic to produce a wonderfully flavoursome dish.

SERVES 4

INGREDIENTS
750g/1½lb fresh mussels, in their shells
675g/1½lb fresh clams, in their shells
75ml/5 tbsp olive oil
3 garlic cloves, peeled and crushed
300ml/½ pint/1¼ cups dry white wine
75ml/5 tbsp chopped fresh parsley
ground black pepper
rounds of crusty bread, toasted, to serve

1 Scrape the beards off the mussels. Scrub the mussels and clams well, rinse under cold water and discard any with broken shells or that do not close when tapped sharply with the back of a knife.

2 Heat the olive oil in a large pan with the garlic until it is golden. Add the mussels, clams and the wine. Cover the pan, and cook for about 5–8 minutes until the shells have opened.

3 Lift the clams and mussels out of the pan with a slotted spoon, discarding any that do not open. Pour any liquid in the shells back into the pan. Place the shellfish in a warmed serving bowl. Discard the garlic.

4 Strain the cooking liquid through a layer of kitchen paper held in a strainer, pouring it over the clams and mussels in the bowl. Sprinkle with the chopped parsley and black pepper.

5 To serve, place rounds of toasted bread in the bottom of individual soup bowls and ladle in the mussels and clams with some of the hot liquid.

STUFFED SQUID

Squid are popular in all the coastal regions of Italy. These stuffed squid are filled with a tasty mixture of anchovy, garlic, tomatoes and parsley and baked in the oven.

SERVES 4

INGREDIENTS
900g/2lb fresh squid (about 16)
juice of ½ lemon
2 anchovy fillets, chopped
2 garlic cloves, finely chopped
3 tomatoes, peeled, seeded and finely chopped
30ml/2 tbsp chopped fresh parsley
50g/2oz/½ cup plain breadcrumbs
1 egg
30ml/2 tbsp olive oil
120ml/4fl oz/½ cup dry white wine
salt and ground black pepper
a few fresh parsley sprigs, to garnish

1 Clean the squid. Peel off the thin skin from the body section. Rinse well. Pull the head and tentacles away from the body sac. Remove and discard the translucent quill and any remaining insides from the sac. Sever the tentacles from the head. Discard the head and intestines. Remove and discard the hard beak from the base of the tentacles. Place the tentacles in a bowl of water with the lemon juice. Rinse the sacs well under cold running water. Pat the insides dry with kitchen paper.

2 Preheat the oven to 180°C/350°F/Gas 4. Drain the tentacles. Chop them coarsely and place in a mixing bowl. Add the anchovy fillets, garlic, tomatoes, parsley, breadcrumbs, egg and salt and pepper and mix. Loosely stuff the squid sacs with this mixture. Close the opening to the sacs with wooden toothpicks.

3 Oil a large baking dish and arrange the squid in a single layer. Pour over the olive oil and white wine and bake uncovered for 35–45 minutes, or until tender. Remove the toothpicks and serve garnished with parsley.

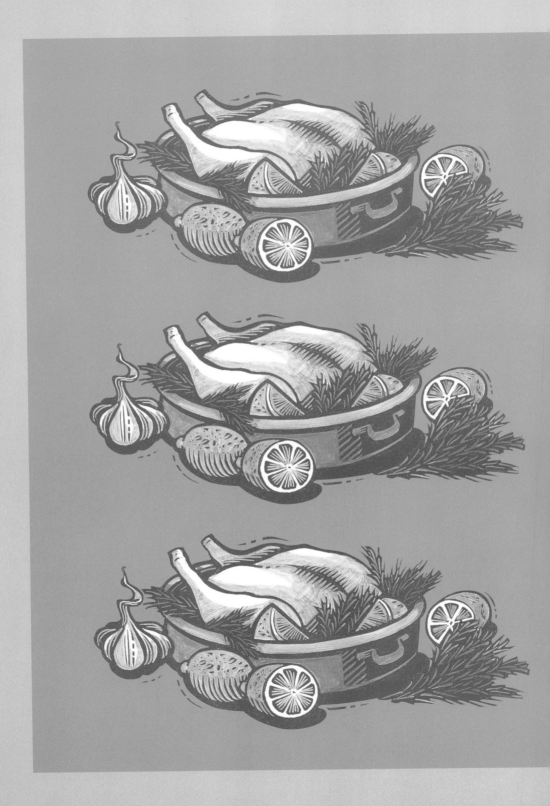

POULTRY & GAME

In Italy, poultry and game are usually served on their own as a second course. Chicken, turkey, and small game birds, such as poussin, quail and pheasant, are very popular, and are often pan-fried, stewed or roasted. The flavourings that accompany a dish tend to reflect the part of Italy from which it comes: Devilled Chicken uses spicy red chillies in the marinade, which are popular in southern Italian cooking; Chicken with Chianti makes use of the local wine; while Chicken with Parma Ham and Cheese uses the Fontina cheese that is made in the region.

ROAST CHICKEN WITH FENNEL

In Italy, this mildly aniseed-flavoured dish is prepared with wild fennel but when this is not available, cultivated fennel bulb works just as well.

SERVES 4–5

INGREDIENTS
1.8kg/4lb chicken
1 onion, quartered
120ml/4fl oz/½ cup olive oil
2 fennel bulbs
1 garlic clove, peeled
a pinch of grated nutmeg
3–4 thin slices pancetta or bacon
120ml/4fl oz/½ cup dry white wine
salt and ground black pepper

1 Preheat the oven to 180°C/350°F/Gas 4. Rinse the chicken in cold water. Pat it dry inside and out with kitchen paper. Sprinkle the cavity with salt and pepper. Place the onion quarters in the cavity. Rub the chicken with about 45ml/3 tbsp of the olive oil and place in a roasting pan.

2 Cut the green fronds from the tops of the fennel bulbs. Chop the fronds with the garlic. Place in a small bowl, add the nutmeg and season with salt and black pepper. Sprinkle the fennel mixture over the chicken, pressing it onto the oiled skin. Cover the breast with the slices of pancetta or bacon. Sprinkle with 30ml/2 tbsp of oil. Place in the oven and roast for 30 minutes, then remove and baste the chicken with any oils in the pan.

3 Meanwhile, boil or steam the fennel bulbs for 2–3 minutes until barely tender. Remove from the heat and cut into quarters or sixths lengthwise. Arrange the fennel around the chicken and sprinkle with the remaining oil. Pour about half the wine over the chicken, and return the pan to the oven and cook for 30 minutes.

4 Remove the pan from the oven and pour the remaining wine over the chicken. Cook for 15–20 minutes. Prick the thigh with a fork – if the juices run clear, the chicken is cooked. Transfer to a serving platter and arrange the fennel around it.

CHICKEN BREASTS COOKED IN BUTTER

This is a simple and delicious way of cooking chicken that brings out all of its delicacy. It should be accompanied by lightly flavoured vegetables so that the subtle tastes of chicken and butter are not overpowered.

SERVES 4

INGREDIENTS
4 small chicken breast portions, skinned and boned
seasoned flour, for dredging
75g/3oz/6 tbsp butter
fresh parsley sprigs, to garnish

1 Separate the two fillets of each chicken breast portion. They come apart very easily; one is large, the other small. Pound the large fillets lightly to flatten them. Dredge the chicken in the seasoned flour, shaking off any excess.

2 Heat the butter in a large heavy frying pan until it bubbles. Place all the chicken fillets in the pan, in one layer if possible. Cook over a medium to high heat for 3–4 minutes until they are golden brown.

3 Turn the chicken over. Reduce the heat, and continue cooking until the fillets are cooked through but still springy to the touch, about 9–12 minutes in all. If the chicken begins to brown too much, cover the pan for the final minutes of cooking. Serve at once garnished with fresh parsley.

CHICKEN WITH CHIANTI

The robust, full flavours of chianti and red pesto give this sauce an almost spicy flavour and a wonderfully rich colour, while the grapes add a delicious sweetness. Serve this dish with grilled polenta or warm crusty bread.

SERVES 4

INGREDIENTS
45ml/3 tbsp olive oil
4 part-boned chicken breast portions, skinned
1 red onion
30ml/2 tbsp red pesto
300ml/½ pint/1¼ cups Chianti
300ml/½ pint/1¼ cups water
115g/4oz red grapes, halved lengthways and seeded if necessary
salt and ground black pepper
fresh basil leaves, to garnish
rocket salad, to serve

1 Heat 30ml/2 tbsp of the olive oil in a large frying pan, add the skinned chicken breast portions and sauté over a medium heat for about 5 minutes until they have changed colour on all sides. Remove the chicken with a slotted spoon and drain on kitchen paper.

2 Cut the onions in half, through the root. Trim off the root, peel off the skin, then slice the onion halves lengthways to create thin wedges. Heat the remaining oil in the pan, add the onion wedges and red pesto and cook gently, stirring constantly, for 3 minutes until the onion is softened, but not browned.

3 Add the Chianti and water to the pan and bring to the boil, stirring, then return the chicken to the pan and season with salt and ground black pepper. Reduce the heat, then cover the pan and simmer gently for about 20 minutes or until the chicken is tender, stirring occasionally.

4 Add the grapes to the pan and cook over a low to medium heat until heated through, then taste the sauce for seasoning. Serve the chicken hot, garnished with basil and accompanied by the rocket salad.

HUNTER'S CHICKEN

This robust dish of chicken cooked in red wine with mushrooms is delicious served with creamed potatoes or warm polenta. For extra colour, use strips of green pepper in the sauce in place of the fresh mushrooms.

SERVES 4

INGREDIENTS
15g/½ oz/1 cup dried porcini mushrooms
30ml/2 tbsp olive oil
15g/½oz/1 tbsp butter
4 chicken pieces, on the bone, skinned
1 large onion, thinly sliced
400g/14oz can chopped tomatoes
150ml/¼ pint/⅔ cup red wine
1 garlic clove, crushed
1 fresh rosemary sprig, finely chopped, plus extra sprigs to garnish
115g/4oz/1¾ cups fresh field mushrooms, thinly sliced
salt and ground black pepper

1 Put the porcini in a bowl, pour over 250ml/8fl oz/1 cup warm water and soak for 20–30 minutes. Remove from the liquid and squeeze the porcini over the bowl. Strain the liquid and reserve. Finely chop the porcini.

2 Heat the oil and butter in a large flameproof casserole until foaming. Add the chicken. Sauté over a medium heat for 5 minutes, or until golden. Remove the chicken and drain on kitchen paper.

3 Add the onion and porcini to the pan. Cook gently, stirring, for 3 minutes until the onion has softened but not browned. Stir in the chopped tomatoes, wine and reserved mushroom soaking liquid, then add the crushed garlic and rosemary, with salt and pepper to taste. Bring to the boil, stirring all the time.

4 Return the chicken to the pan and coat with the sauce. Cover and simmer for 30 minutes. Add the fresh mushrooms and stir well. Continue simmering gently for 10 minutes or until the chicken is tender. Taste for seasoning. Serve hot garnished with fresh rosemary.

CHICKEN WITH PARMA HAM & CHEESE

In Italy, this dish is called Pollo alla Valdostana. *It derives its name from Val d'Aosta, home of the Fontina cheese that is used in this recipe. If you prefer, Swiss or French mountain cheeses, such as Gruyère or Emmental, can be used instead of Fontina.*

SERVES 4

INGREDIENTS
about 30ml/2 tbsp olive oil
2 thin slices prosciutto
2 thin slices Fontina cheese
4 part-boned chicken breast portions
4 basil sprigs
15g/½oz/1 tbsp butter
120ml/4fl oz/½ cup dry white wine
salt and ground black pepper
tender young salad leaves, to serve

1 Preheat the oven to 200°C/400°F/Gas 6. Lightly oil a baking dish. Cut the prosciutto and Fontina slices in half crossways. Skin the chicken breast portions, open out the slit in the centre of each one, and fill each cavity with half a ham slice and a basil sprig.

2 Heat the oil and butter in a large heavy frying pan until foaming. Cook the chicken over a medium heat for 1–2 minutes on each side until they change colour. Transfer to the baking dish. Add the wine to the pan juices, stir until sizzling, then pour over the chicken and season with salt and pepper.

3 Top each chicken breast portion with a slice of Fontina. Bake for 20 minutes or until the chicken is tender. Serve hot, with young salad leaves.

DEVILLED CHICKEN

This spicy, barbecued chicken dish is typical of southern Italy with its chilli-flavoured marinade. Versions without the chillies are just as good, if you prefer milder dishes.

SERVES 4

INGREDIENTS

120ml/4fl oz/½ cup olive oil
finely grated rind and juice 1 large lemon
2 garlic cloves, finely chopped
10ml/2 tsp finely chopped or crumbled dried red chillies
12 boneless chicken thighs, skinned, each cut into 3 or 4 pieces
salt and ground black pepper
flat leaf parsley leaves, to garnish
lemon wedges, to serve

1 To make the marinade, mix the oil, lemon rind and juice, garlic and chillies in a large, shallow glass or china dish. Season with salt and pepper. Whisk well, then add the chicken pieces, turning to coat with the marinade. Cover and leave to marinate in the fridge for at least 4 hours, or preferably overnight.

2 When ready to cook, prepare the barbecue or preheat the grill (broiler) and thread the chicken pieces on to eight oiled metal skewers. Cook on the barbecue or under a hot grill for 6–8 minutes, turning frequently, until tender and cooked through. Garnish with fresh parsley leaves and serve hot, with lemon wedges for squeezing.

COOK'S TIP
To prevent the chicken pieces falling off the skewers during cooking, thread the strips in a spiral fashion as this helps to keep the flesh together.

TURKEY WITH MARSALA CREAM SAUCE

Marsala and cream make a very rich and tasty sauce. The addition of lemon juice gives it a sharp edge, which helps to offset the richness of this dish.

SERVES 6

INGREDIENTS
6 turkey breast steaks
45ml/3 tbsp seasoned flour
30ml/2 tbsp olive oil
25g/1oz/2 tbsp butter
175ml/6fl oz/¾ cup dry Marsala
60ml/4 tbsp lemon juice
175ml/6fl oz/¾ cup double (heavy) cream
salt and ground black pepper
lemon wedges and chopped fresh parsley, to garnish
mangetouts and green beans, to serve

1 Put each turkey steak between two sheets of clear film and pound with a rolling pin to flatten and stretch. Cut each steak in half or into quarters, cutting away and discarding any sinew.

2 Spread out the flour in a shallow bowl and dredge the meat, coating evenly. Heat the olive oil and butter in a wide, heavy pan or frying pan until sizzling. Add as many pieces of turkey as the pan will hold and sauté over a medium heat for about 3 minutes on each side, until crispy and tender. Transfer to a warmed serving dish with tongs and keep hot. Repeat with the remaining turkey pieces, then lower the heat.

3 Mix the Marsala and lemon juice in a jug (pitcher), add to the pan and raise the heat. Bring to the boil, stirring in the sediment, then add the cream. Simmer, stirring constantly, until the sauce is reduced and glossy. Taste for seasoning. Spoon over the turkey, garnish with the lemon wedges and parsley and serve at once with the mangetouts and green beans.

TURKEY CUTLETS WITH OLIVES

This quick and tasty dish makes a good light main course. Tomatoes, garlic and black olives add a rich flavour to the turkey, while the chilli adds an extra bite.

SERVES 4

INGREDIENTS
60ml/4 tbsp olive oil
1 garlic clove, peeled and lightly crushed
1 dried chilli, lightly crushed
500g/1¼lb boneless turkey breast portion, cut into 5mm/¼in slices
120ml/4fl oz/½ cup dry white wine
4 tomatoes, peeled and seeded, cut into thin strips
about 24 black olives
6–8 fresh basil leaves, torn into pieces
salt and ground black pepper

1 Heat the olive oil in a large frying pan. Add the garlic and dried chilli, and cook over low heat until the garlic is golden. Raise the heat slightly. Place the turkey slices in the pan and season with salt and pepper. Cook for about 2 minutes over a medium heat, turning to brown on both sides. Remove the turkey to a heated dish.

2 Remove the garlic and chilli from the pan and discard. Add the wine, tomato strips and olives and cook over medium heat for 3–4 minutes, scraping up any meat residue from the bottom of the pan. Return the turkey to the pan and sprinkle with torn basil. Heat for about 30 seconds and serve immediately.

PAN-FRIED MARINATED POUSSIN

Marinating these small birds before cooking gives them a wonderfully rich, full flavour. They are delicious served sprinkled with fresh mint.

SERVES 3–4

INGREDIENTS
2 poussins, about 450g/1lb each
5–6 fresh mint leaves, torn into pieces, plus extra leaves to garnish
1 leek, sliced into thin rings
1 garlic clove, finely chopped
60ml/4 tbsp olive oil
30ml/2 tbsp fresh lemon juice
50ml/2fl oz/¼ cup dry white wine
salt and ground black pepper

1 Cut the poussins in half down the backbone, dividing the breast. Flatten the 4 halves with a mallet. Place them in a bowl with the mint, leek, garlic and ground black pepper. Sprinkle with oil and half the lemon juice, cover, and allow to stand in a cool place for 6 hours.

2 Heat a large heavy frying pan or skillet. Place the poussins and their marinade in the pan, cover and cook over a medium heat for about 45 minutes, turning occasionally. Season with salt during the cooking. Remove to a serving platter.

3 Tilt the pan and spoon off any fat on the surface. Pour in the wine and remaining lemon juice and cook until the sauce reduces. Strain the sauce, pressing the vegetables to extract all the juices, Place the poussins on individual dishes and spoon over the sauce. Sprinkle with mint, and serve.

QUAIL WITH GRAPES

Small birds such as quail are popular in Italian cooking. Pancetta, white wine and flavourful green grapes complement the subtle gamey flavour of quail perfectly.

SERVES 4

INGREDIENTS
6–8 fresh quail, gutted
60ml/4 tbsp olive oil
50g/2oz/¼ cup pancetta or bacon, cut into small dice
250ml/8fl oz/1 cup dry white wine
250ml/8fl oz/1 cup chicken broth, warmed
350g/12oz green grapes
salt and ground black pepper

1 Wash the quail carefully inside and out with cold water. Pat dry with kitchen paper. Sprinkle salt and pepper into the cavities.

2 Heat the oil in a heavy sauté pan or casserole large enough to accommodate all the quail in one layer. Add the diced pancetta or bacon, and cook over low heat for about 5 minutes.

3 Raise the heat under the pan. Place the quail in the pan and brown them evenly on all sides. Pour in the wine and cook over a medium heat until it reduces by about half. Turn the quail over. Cover the pan and cook for about 10–15 minutes. Add the broth, turn the quail again, cover, and cook for 15–20 minutes more, or until the birds are tender. Remove to a warmed serving platter and keep warm.

4 Meanwhile, drop the bunch of grapes into a pan of boiling water and blanch for about 3 minutes. Drain and set aside.

5 Strain the pan juices into a small glass jug. If bacon has been used, allow the fat to separate and rise to the top. Spoon off the fat and discard. Pour the strained gravy into a small pan. Add the grapes and warm them gently for 2–3 minutes. Spoon around the quail and serve.

GRILLED DUCK BREASTS WITH CHESTNUT SAUCE

This autumnal dish makes use of the sweet chestnuts that are gathered in Italian woods. The duck can be cooked under a grill or on a barbecue, which imparts a smoky flavour that complements the taste of chestnuts perfectly.

SERVES 4–5

INGREDIENTS
1 fresh rosemary sprig
1 garlic clove, thinly sliced
30ml/2 tbsp olive oil
4 duck breast portions, boned and fat removed
salt and ground black pepper

FOR THE SAUCE
450g/1lb chestnuts
5ml/1 tsp oil
350ml/12fl oz/1½ cups milk
1 small onion, finely chopped
1 carrot, finely chopped
1 small bay leaf
30ml/2 tbsp cream, warmed

COOK'S TIP
The chestnut sauce may be prepared in advance and kept in the refrigerator for 1–2 days. Alternatively, it can be made when chestnuts are in season and frozen. To use, remove from the freezer and allow to thaw at room temperature before reheating.

1 To make the marinade, strip the leaves from the rosemary sprig and place in a shallow bowl with the sliced garlic and olive oil. Stir to combine. Pat the duck breast portions dry with kitchen paper and brush with the marinade. Allow to stand for at least 2 hours in a cool place.

2 Preheat the oven to 180°C/350°F/Gas 4. Cut a cross in the flat side of each chestnut with a sharp knife. Place in a baking pan with the oil, and shake the pan until the nuts are thoroughly coated with the oil. Bake for about 20 minutes, allow to cool slightly, then peel.

3 Place the peeled chestnuts in a large heavy pan with the milk, onion, carrot and bay leaf. Cook over gentle heat for about 15 minutes, until the chestnuts are very tender. Season with salt and ground black pepper.

4 Remove the bay leaf from the pan and discard, then press the chestnut mixture through a strainer into a bowl. Return the puréed chestnut sauce to the pan and gently heat through over a low heat.

5 Meanwhile, cook the duck breasts. Preheat the grill (broiler), or prepare a barbecue. Arrange the marinated duck breasts on the grill rack and cook for 6–8 minutes until medium rare. The meat should be pink when sliced.

6 Slice the duck breast portions into rounds and arrange on warmed plates. Stir the warmed cream into the hot chestnut sauce, adding a little more cream if the sauce is too thick. Pour the sauce into a small jug (pitcher). Serve the duck immediately with the sauce handed separately.

Roast Pheasant with Sage & Juniper Berries

In Italy, aromatic sage and juniper berries are commonly used to flavour game. Their distinctive, slightly pungent taste complements the strong flavour of game perfectly. Wrapping the bird in pancetta before roasting helps to keep the meat moist.

SERVES 3–4

INGREDIENTS
1.2–1.4kg/2½–3lb pheasant with liver, finely chopped (optional)
45ml/3 tbsp olive oil
2 fresh sage sprigs
3 shallots, chopped
1 bay leaf
5ml/1 tsp lemon juice, plus 2 lemon quarters
30ml/2 tbsp juniper berries, lightly crushed
4 thin slices pancetta or bacon
90ml/6 tbsp dry white wine
250ml/8fl oz/1 cup chicken broth or stock, heated
25g/1oz/2 tbsp butter, at room temperature
30ml/2 tbsp flour
30ml/2 tbsp brandy
salt and ground black pepper

1 Wash the pheasant under cool water. Drain well and pat dry with kitchen paper, then rub with 15ml/1 tbsp of the olive oil. Place the remaining oil, sage leaves, shallots and bay leaf in a shallow bowl. Add the lemon juice and crushed juniper berries and stir to combine.

2 Place the pheasant and lemon quarters in the bowl and spoon the marinade over the bird. Allow to stand for several hours in a cool place, turning the pheasant occasionally to coat in the marinade. Remove the lemon quarters.

3 Preheat the oven to 180°C/350°F/Gas 4. Place the pheasant in a roasting pan, reserving the marinade. Sprinkle salt and ground black pepper in cavity and place the bay leaf inside.

4 Arrange some of the sage leaves from the marinade on the breast of the pheasant. Lay the slices of pancetta or bacon over the top of the leaves and secure with string.

5 Spoon the remaining marinade on top of the pheasant and roast until tender, about 30 minutes per 450g/1lb. Baste frequently with the pan juices and with the white wine. Transfer the pheasant to a warmed serving platter. Remove the string and pancetta and discard.

6 Carefully tilt the roasting pan and skim off any surface fat and discard. Pour in the chicken broth or stock. Stir over a medium heat, scraping up any meat residues from the bottom of the pan. Add the finely chopped pheasant liver, if using. Bring the mixture to the boil over a high heat and cook for about 3 minutes. Strain the juices into a small pan.

7 Blend the butter to a paste with the flour, then stir into the pan of meat juices a little at a time. Bring the mixture to the boil and cook for 2–3 minutes, stirring continuously to smooth out any lumps. Remove from the heat, stir in the brandy, and serve with the pheasant.

COOK'S TIP
In Italy, pheasants are usually eaten as soon as they are shot, so have a milder, less gamey flavour. If you can, buy a hen pheasant for this dish as they tend to have a more delicate flavour than cocks.

MEAT

Like poultry and game, meat is eaten as a second course, usually following pasta. The Italians are particularly fond of veal, and there are many traditional veal dishes, such as Osso Buco. Lamb is also popular: in the south, a leg of lamb is roasted with garlic and wild herbs, while the rustic Puglia stew is made with tomatoes. There are many recipes for beef stew and these reflect the ingredients available in the area from which they come. From the Veneto region comes Pan-fried Calf's Liver with Balsamic Vinegar, and two porks dishes, Pork in Sweet and Sour Sauce and Pork Braised in Milk with Carrots.

ROAST LAMB WITH HERBS

This classic dish of roast lamb cooked with garlic and wild herbs originates from southern Italy. It is the perfect dish for a special occasion.

SERVES 4–6

INGREDIENTS
1.5kg/3lb leg of lamb
45–60ml/3–4 tbsp olive oil
4 garlic cloves, peeled and cut in half
2 fresh sage sprigs, or pinch of dried sage leaves
2 fresh rosemary sprigs, or 5ml/1 tsp dried rosemary leaves
2 bay leaves
2 fresh thyme sprigs, or ½ tsp dried thyme leaves
175ml/6fl oz/¾ cup dry white wine
salt and ground black pepper

1 Cut any excess fat from the lamb. Rub with olive oil. Using a sharp knife, make small cuts just under the skin all around the meat. Insert the garlic pieces in some of the cuts and a few of the fresh herbs in the others. If using dried herbs, sprinkle them over the surface of the meat.

2 Place the remaining fresh herbs on the lamb, and leave in a cool place for at least 2 hours before cooking. Preheat the oven to 190°C/375°F/Gas 5.

3 Place the lamb in a roasting pan, surrounded by the herbs. Pour in 30ml/ 2 tbsp of the oil and season with plenty of salt and black pepper. Place in the oven and roast for 35 minutes, basting occasionally.

4 Pour the wine over the lamb. Roast for 15 minutes more, or until the meat is cooked. Remove the lamb to a heated serving dish. Tilt the pan, spooning off any fat on the surface. Strain the pan juices into a gravy boat. Slice the meat and serve with the sauce passed separately.

Lamb Stewed with Tomatoes & Garlic

This rustic stew comes from the plateau of Puglia, where sheep graze by vineyards. Richly flavoured garlic and rosemary complement the strong-tasting lamb perfectly.

Serves 5–6

Ingredients
2 large garlic cloves
90ml/6 tbsp olive oil
1 fresh rosemary sprig, or 45ml/3 tbsp chopped fresh parsley if fresh rosemary is not available
1.3kg/2½lb stewing lamb, trimmed of fat and gristle and cut into chunks
seasoned flour
175ml/6fl oz/¾ cup dry white wine
10ml/2 tsp salt
450g/1lb fresh tomatoes, chopped, or 1 × 400g/14oz can tomatoes, chopped
120ml/4fl oz/½ cup meat broth, heated

1 Preheat the oven to 180°C/350°F/Gas 4. Chop the garlic. Heat 60ml/4 tbsp of the oil in a wide casserole. Add the garlic and rosemary or parsley and cook over a medium heat, until the garlic is golden.

2 Dredge the lamb in the seasoned flour. Add the lamb chunks to the casserole in one layer, turning to brown them evenly. When brown, remove them to a side plate. Add a little more oil and brown the remaining lamb.

3 When all the lamb has been browned, return it to the casserole and pour over the white wine. Raise the heat and bring to the boil, scraping up any residue from the bottom of the pan. Sprinkle the lamb with the salt and add the tomatoes and broth. Stir well. Cover the casserole and place in the centre of the oven. Bake for 1¾–2 hours, or until the meat is tender.

Meatballs with Peperonata

These delicious, flavoursome meatballs are served with a tasty pepper and tomato sauce. They are a wonderful way to enjoy minced beef and taste very good with creamed potatoes. This is a perfect dish for children and adults alike.

Serves 4

Ingredients
400g/14oz minced (ground) beef
115g/4oz/2 cups fresh white breadcrumbs
50g/2oz/²⁄₃ cup grated Parmesan cheese
2 eggs, beaten
a pinch of paprika
a pinch of grated nutmeg
5ml/1 tsp dried mixed herbs
2 thin slices of mortadella or prosciutto (total weight about 50g/2oz), chopped
vegetable oil, for shallow frying
salt and ground black pepper
snipped fresh basil leaves, to garnish

For the peperonata
30ml/2 tbsp olive oil
1 small onion, thinly sliced
2 yellow (bell) peppers, cored, seeded and cut lengthways into thin strips
2 red (bell) peppers, cored, seeded and cut lengthways into thin strips
275g/10oz/1¼ cups finely chopped tomatoes or passata (bottled strained tomatoes)
15ml/1 tbsp chopped fresh parsley

> ### Variation
> *To make more delicately flavoured meatballs, use a mixture of half minced pork and half minced veal in place of the minced beef.*

1 Put the minced beef and half the breadcrumbs in a large bowl. Add the grated Parmesan, beaten eggs, paprika, nutmeg, mixed herbs and mortadella or prosciutto and season with salt and ground black pepper. Mix together with clean wet hands until thoroughly combined.

2 Divide the meat mixture into 12 equal portions and roll each into a ball. Flatten each meatball slightly so they are about 1cm/½in thick and make a neat, round patty.

3 Put the remaining breadcrumbs on a plate and roll the meatballs in them, a few at a time, until they are evenly coated. Place on a plate, cover with clear film and chill for about 30 minutes to firm up.

4 Meanwhile, make the peperonata. Heat the olive oil in a medium pan, add the sliced onion and cook gently over a low heat for about 3 minutes, stirring frequently, until soft and transparent.

5 Add the pepper strips and cook for 3 minutes, stirring constantly. Stir in the chopped tomatoes or passata and parsley and season with salt and pepper. Bring the mixture to the boil. Cover and cook for 15 minutes, then remove the lid and cook, stirring frequently, for 10 minutes more, or until reduced and thick. Taste for seasoning, adding more if necessary. Keep hot.

6 Pour oil into a frying pan to a depth of about 2.5cm/1in. When hot but not smoking, shallow fry the meatballs for 10–12 minutes, turning them 3–4 times and pressing them flat with a fish slice (spatula). Remove and drain on kitchen paper. Garnish with basil and serve immediately with the peperonata.

Beef Stew with Tomatoes, Wine & Peas

It seems there are as many recipes for this classic Italian stew as there are Italian cooks. This version is richly flavoured and perfect for a winter lunch or dinner.

Serves 4

Ingredients

30ml/2 tbsp plain (all-purpose) flour
10ml/2 tsp chopped fresh thyme or 5ml/1 tsp dried thyme
1kg/2¼ lb braising or stewing steak, cut into large cubes
45ml/3 tbsp olive oil
1 onion, roughly chopped
450g/1lb jar sugocasa or passata (strained bottled tomatoes)
250ml/8fl oz/1 cup beef stock
250ml/8fl oz/1 cup red wine
2 garlic cloves, crushed
30ml/2 tbsp tomato purée (paste)
275g/10oz/2 cups shelled fresh peas
5ml/1 tsp sugar
salt and ground black pepper
fresh thyme, to garnish

1 Preheat the oven to 160°C/325°F/Gas 3. Put the flour in a shallow dish and season with the thyme and salt and pepper. Add the beef cubes and coat evenly.

2 Heat the oil in a large flameproof casserole, add the beef and brown on all sides over a medium to high heat. Remove and drain on kitchen paper. Add the onion to the casserole, scraping the base to mix in any sediment. Cook gently for about 3 minutes, stirring frequently, until softened, then stir in the sugocasa or passata, stock, wine, garlic and tomato purée. Bring to the boil, stirring.

3 Return the beef to the casserole and stir well. Cover and cook in the oven for 1½ hours, then stir in the peas and sugar. Cook for 30 minutes more, or until the beef is tender. Garnish with thyme before serving.

Pan-fried Veal Escalopes with Marsala

Cooking veal escalopes in this way is quick and easy and gives wonderful results. The sweetness of Marsala helps to enliven the mild taste of veal.

SERVES 4

INGREDIENTS
*450g/1lb veal escalopes (veal scallops), preferably cut
  across the grain, about 5mm/¼in thick
50g/2oz/½ cup seasoned flour
50g/2oz/¼ cup butter
75ml/5 tbsp dry Marsala wine
75ml/5 tbsp stock or water*

1 Place the escalopes between two pieces of clear film or greaseproof (waxed) paper and pound flat with a rolling pin, to a thickness of about 5mm/¼in, then peel off the film or paper.

2 Spread the seasoned flour out on a plate. Lightly dredge the veal slices in the flour, shaking off any excess. Heat the butter in a large frying pan. As soon as the foam from the butter subsides, put the veal into the pan in one layer and brown the slices quickly on both sides, in two batches if necessary. Remove to a warmed serving plate and keep warm.

3 Pour the Marsala and stock or water into the pan. Cook over a medium to high heat for 3–4 minutes, scraping up any meat residues from the bottom of the pan. Pour the sauce over the meat and serve at once.

COOK'S TIP
If veal escalopes have not been cut across the grain or from one muscle, cut small notches around the edges to prevent them from curling during cooking as this will prevent them cooking evenly.

MILANESE VEAL CHOPS

These simple pan-fried veal chops come from Milan. They are coated lightly in breadcrumbs, then gently cooked in butter until crisp and golden.

SERVES 2

INGREDIENTS
2 veal chops or cutlets, on the bone
1 egg
90–120ml/6–8 tbsp breadcrumbs
50g/2oz/¼ cup butter
15ml/1 tbsp vegetable oil
salt and ground black pepper
lemon wedges, to serve

1 Trim any gristle or fat from the chops. Cut along the rib bone, if necessary, to free the meat on one side. Place the meat between two pieces of clear film and pound lightly with a rolling pin to flatten, then peel off the clear film.

2 Beat the egg in a shallow bowl and season with salt and pepper. Spread the breadcrumbs over a plate. Dip the chops into the egg and then into the breadcrumbs. Pat the breadcrumbs to help them to stick.

3 Heat the butter with the oil in a heavy frying pan large enough to hold both chops side by side. Do not let the butter brown. Add the chops and cook them slowly over a low to medium heat until the breadcrumbs are golden and the meat is cooked through. Serve hot with lemon wedges.

COOK'S TIPS
• The cooking time for this dish will depend on the thickness of the chops – the important thing is to avoid overcooking the breadcrumb coating while undercooking the meat.
• In Milan, cooks sometimes soak the veal chops in milk for about an hour before cooking to soften the meat and ensure a mild flavour.

Veal Rolls with Sage & Ham

*These delicious rolls of veal and prosciutto are so good that, as their Italian name –
Saltimbocca – implies, they literally "jump into your mouth". Sage has a slightly
bitter, aromatic flavour and is a very popular flavouring for veal in northern Italy.*

SERVES 3–4

INGREDIENTS
8 small veal escalopes (veal scallops)
8 small slices prosciutto
8 fresh sage leaves
40g/1½oz/3 tbsp butter
120ml/4fl oz/½ cup meat broth or stock, warmed
salt and ground black pepper

1 Lay the veal slices between sheets of clear film or greaseproof (waxed) paper
and gently pound with a wooden mallet until thin. Peel off the clear film or
greaseproof paper and discard.

2 Lay a piece of prosciutto over each flattened veal slice. Top with a fresh sage
leaf and season with salt and ground black pepper. Roll the escalopes around
the prosciutto and sage and secure each roll with a wooden toothpick.

3 Heat half the butter in a frying pan just large enough to hold the rolls in a single
layer. When the butter is bubbling add the veal rolls. Cook for 7–10 minutes,
or until the veal is cooked, turning the rolls to brown them on all sides. Remove to
a serving dish and keep warm.

4 Add the remaining butter to the frying pan and pour in the hot broth or stock.
Bring the mixture to the boil, scraping up any residue on the bottom of the pan
with a wooden spoon. Pour the sauce over the veal rolls and serve straight away.

Osso Buco

This is one of the best known dishes from Milan. Veal shanks are cooked with tomatoes and white wine to produce a rich and hearty stew. It is traditionally served with Risotto alla Milanese, but plain boiled rice goes equally well. The lemony gremolata garnish helps to cut the richness of the dish, as does a crisp green salad.

SERVES 4

INGREDIENTS
30ml/2 tbsp seasoned flour
4 veal shanks
2 small onions
30ml/2 tbsp olive oil
1 large celery stick, finely chopped
1 carrot, finely chopped
2 garlic cloves, finely chopped
400g/14oz can chopped tomatoes
300ml/½ pint/1¼ cups dry white wine
300ml/½ pint/1¼ cups chicken or veal stock
1 strip of thinly pared lemon rind
2 bay leaves, plus extra to garnish (optional)
salt and ground black pepper

FOR THE GREMOLATA
30ml/2 tbsp finely chopped fresh flat leaf parsley
finely grated rind of 1 lemon
1 garlic clove, finely chopped

1 Preheat the oven to 160°C/325°F/Gas 3. Spread out the seasoned flour in a shallow dish. Add the pieces of veal and turn them in the flour until evenly coated. Shake off any excess flour.

2 Slice one of the onions and separate it into rings. Heat the oil in a large flameproof casserole, then add the veal, with the onion rings. Cook the veal shanks over a medium heat, turning once, until brown on both sides. Remove the veal with tongs and set aside on kitchen paper to drain.

3 Chop the remaining onion and add it to the casserole with the celery, carrot and garlic. Stir the bottom of the pan with a wooden spoon to scrape up any sediment and mix with the pan juices. Cook gently, stirring frequently, for about 5 minutes until the vegetables soften.

4 Add the chopped tomatoes, wine, chicken or veal stock, lemon rind and bay leaves, then season with salt and ground black pepper. Bring the mixture to the boil, stirring frequently.

5 Return the veal to the casserole and stir to coat with the sauce. Cover with a lid and cook in the oven for about 2 hours, or until the veal feels tender when pierced with a fork.

6 Meanwhile, make the gremolata. In a small bowl, mix together the chopped parsley, lemon rind and chopped garlic.

7 Remove the casserole from the oven and lift out and discard the strip of lemon rind and the bay leaves. Taste the sauce for seasoning, adding more if necessary. Serve the stew hot, sprinkled with the gremolata and garnished with extra bay leaves, if you like.

COOK'S TIP
Veal shanks can be found in large supermarkets and good butchers. For the best result, choose pieces that are about 2cm/³⁄₄in thick.

PAN-FRIED CALF'S LIVER WITH BALSAMIC VINEGAR

This sweet and sour liver dish is a speciality of Venice. It is delicious served simply, with green beans sprinkled with browned breadcrumbs.

SERVES 2

INGREDIENTS
15ml/1 tbsp plain (all-purpose) flour
2.5ml/½ tsp finely chopped fresh sage, plus extra sprigs to garnish
4 thin slices of calf's liver, cut into serving pieces
45ml/3 tbsp olive oil
25g/1oz/2 tbsp butter
2 small red onions, sliced and separated into rings
150ml/¼ pint/⅔ cup dry white wine
45ml/3 tbsp balsamic vinegar
a pinch of granulated sugar
salt and ground black pepper
green beans sprinkled with browned breadcrumbs, to serve

1 Spread out the flour in a shallow bowl. Season it with the chopped sage and plenty of salt and pepper. Turn the liver in the flour until well coated.

2 Heat 30ml/2 tbsp of the oil with half of the butter in a wide, heavy pan or frying pan until foaming. Add the onion rings and cook gently, stirring frequently, for about 5 minutes until softened but not coloured. Remove with a fish slice (spatula) and set aside.

3 Heat the remaining olive oil and butter in the pan until foaming, add the floured liver and cook over medium heat for 2–3 minutes on each side. Transfer to warmed plates and keep hot.

4 Add the wine and vinegar to the pan, then stir to combine with the pan juices and any sediment. Add the onions and sugar and heat through, stirring. Spoon the sauce over the liver, garnish with fresh sage sprigs and serve at once with the green beans sprinkled with breadcrumbs.

PORK IN SWEET & SOUR SAUCE

The combination of sweet and sour flavours is particularly popular in Venetian cooking, especially with meat and liver. This delicious pork dish gains extra bite from the addition of crushed mixed peppercorns.

SERVES 2

INGREDIENTS
1 whole pork fillet, about 350g/12oz
25ml/1½ tbsp seasoned flour
30–45ml/2–3 tbsp olive oil
250ml/8fl oz/1 cup dry white wine
30ml/2 tbsp white wine vinegar
10ml/2 tsp granulated sugar
15ml/1 tbsp mixed peppercorns, coarsely ground
broad beans tossed with grilled bacon, to serve

1 Cut the pork diagonally into thin slices. Place between two sheets of clear film and pound lightly with a rolling pin to flatten them evenly. Spread out the seasoned flour in a shallow dish and dredge the meat to coat evenly.

2 Heat 15ml/1 tbsp of the oil in a wide, heavy pan or frying pan and add as many slices of pork as the pan will hold. Fry over a medium to high heat for about 3 minutes on each side, until crispy and tender. Remove with a fish slice (spatula) and set aside. Repeat with the remaining pork, adding more oil as necessary.

3 Put the wine, vinegar and sugar in a jug (pitcher) and mix well. Pour into the pan and stir vigorously over a high heat until reduced, scraping the pan to mix in any the sediment. Stir in the peppercorns and return the pork to the pan. Spoon the sauce over the pork until it is evenly coated and heated through. Serve with broad beans tossed with grilled bacon.

COOK'S TIP
Broad beans are at their best in late spring and early summer. If you serve this dish late in the season, skin the beans as their skin may be tough.

PORK BRAISED IN MILK WITH CARROTS

This method of slowly cooking a joint of pork in milk is a speciality of the Veneto region and produces a deliciously creamy gravy.

SERVES 4–5

INGREDIENTS

675g/1½lb lean pork loin
45ml/3 tbsp olive oil
25g/1oz/2 tbsp butter
1 small onion, finely chopped
1 celery stick, finely chopped
8 carrots, cut into 5cm/2in strips
2 bay leaves
15ml/1 tbsp peppercorns
475ml/16fl oz/2 cups milk, scalded
salt

1 Trim any excess fat from the pork, and tie it into a roll with string. Preheat the oven to 180°C/350°F/Gas 4. Heat the oil and butter in a large casserole. Add the vegetables and cook over low heat for 8–12 minutes until they soften. Raise the heat, push the vegetables to one side and add the pork, browning it on all sides. Add the bay leaves and peppercorns and season with salt.

2 Pour the hot milk into the casserole, cover and place in the centre of the oven. Cook for about 1½ hours, turning and basting the pork with the sauce about once every 20 minutes. Remove the cover for the last 20 minutes of cooking.

3 Remove the meat from the casserole and cut off the string. Place the meat on a warmed serving platter and cut into slices. Discard the bay leaves. Press about one-third of the carrots and all the liquids in the pan through a strainer. Arrange the remaining carrots around the meat.

4 Pour the sauce into a small pan, taste for seasoning and bring to the boil. If it seems too thin, boil it for a few minutes to reduce slightly. Serve the sliced meat with the carrots and pass the hot sauce separately.

PORK FILLET WITH CAPER SAUCE

The piquant caper sauce can be made in advance and reheated while the pork is sautéed, making it an ideal dish for an informal dinner party.

SERVES 4–5

INGREDIENTS
450g/1lb pork fillet, cut into thin slices
seasoned flour
25g/1oz/2 tbsp butter
30ml/2 tbsp olive oil

FOR THE CAPER SAUCE
30ml/2 tbsp olive oil
50g/2oz/¼ cup butter
½ small onion, very finely chopped
1 anchovy fillet, rinsed and chopped
15ml/1 tbsp flour
30ml/2 tbsp capers, rinsed
15ml/1 tbsp finely chopped fresh parsley
60ml/4 tbsp wine vinegar
60ml/4 tbsp water
60ml/4 tbsp balsamic vinegar

1 Make the sauce. Heat the oil and half the butter in a small pan and add the onion. Cook over a low heat for about 5 minutes until soft, stirring occasionally. Add the anchovy and mash it into the onion with a wooden spoon. Add the flour and stir to combine. Add the capers and parsley, then pour in the vinegar and water and cook over a low heat until thickened, stirring continuously.

2 Meanwhile, place the pork fillets between two sheets of clear film and pound with a rolling pin until thin. Spread out the seasoned flour in a shallow dish and dredge the meat, shaking off any excess.

3 Heat the butter and the oil in a large frying pan, then add the pork in a single layer. Cook for 5–6 minutes, turning the meat to brown both sides. Remove to a warmed dish and repeat with the remaining pork slices. Stir the remaining butter and the balsamic vinegar into the sauce and serve immediately with the pork.

PORK CHOPS WITH MUSHROOMS

The subtle flavours of pork and mushrooms make perfect partners. Adding dried porcini to the sauce gives the fresh cultivated mushrooms a richer flavour.

SERVES 4

INGREDIENTS
15g/½oz/3 tbsp dried porcini mushrooms
75g/3oz/6 tbsp butter
2 garlic cloves, peeled and crushed
300g/11oz fresh cultivated mushrooms, thinly sliced
15ml/1 tbsp olive oil
4 pork chops, trimmed of excess fat
2.5ml/½ tsp fresh thyme leaves, or 1.5ml/¼ tsp dried thyme
120ml/4fl oz/½ cup dry white wine
75ml/2½fl oz/⅓ cup single (light) cream
salt and ground black pepper

1 Place the porcini mushrooms in a small bowl and pour over 250ml/8fl oz/1 cup warm water. Leave to soak for 20 minutes, then drain, reserving the soaking water. Filter the mushroom soaking water and set aside.

2 Melt two-thirds of the butter in a large frying pan. Add the garlic. When the foam subsides, stir in all the mushrooms. Season and cook for about 10 minutes over a medium heat until the mushrooms give up their liquid.

3 Remove the mushrooms from the pan and set aside. Add the remaining butter and the oil to the frying pan. When hot, add the pork in one layer and sprinkle with thyme. Cook over a medium to high heat for about 3 minutes on each side, to seal. Reduce the heat and cook for a further 15–20 minutes. Remove the chops from the pan and place on a warmed plate.

4 Spoon off any fat in the pan. Pour in the wine and the mushroom soaking water. Cook over high heat until reduced by about half, stirring to scrape up the residues at the bottom of the pan. Add the mushrooms and the cream and cook for 4–5 minutes more. Pour the sauce over the chops and serve straight away.

Rabbit with Tomatoes & Garlic

Rabbit is very popular in Italy and is often eaten instead of chicken or veal. This hearty dish uses the robust flavours of garlic, pancetta and tomatoes but rabbit can be prepared in many different ways.

SERVES 4–5

INGREDIENTS

675g/1½lb boned rabbit, cut into chunks
2 garlic cloves, thinly sliced
115g/4oz/½ cup thinly sliced pancetta or bacon
675g/1½lb tomatoes, peeled, seeded and roughly chopped
45ml/3 tbsp chopped fresh basil
60ml/4 tbsp olive oil
salt and ground black pepper

1 Preheat the oven to 200°C/400°F/Gas 6. Pat the rabbit pieces dry with kitchen paper. Place a thin slice of garlic on each piece. Wrap a slice of pancetta or bacon around it, making sure the garlic is held in place.

2 Place the tomatoes in a non-stick pan and cook them for a few minutes until they give up some of their liquid and begin to dry out. Add the basil and season with salt and ground black pepper to taste. Spread the tomatoes in a layer in the bottom of a baking dish.

3 Arrange the pancetta- or bacon-wrapped rabbit pieces in the baking dish, on top of the tomatoes. Sprinkle with olive oil and roast, uncovered, for about 45 minutes. Baste the rabbit occasionally with any fat in the dish. After the rabbit has cooked for about 25 minutes the dish may be covered with foil if the sauce seems to be too dry.

VEGETABLES & PULSES

In Italy, vegetables are always eaten when they are fresh and young. They are imaginatively cooked and served as dishes in their own right, sometimes before, and sometimes after, the main course. Spinach and broccoli are often served at room temperature, dressed with a little olive oil and lemon juice. Other vegetables, such as artichokes, peppers and aubergines, are cooked in many different ways – sometimes lightly stewed in wine, drizzled with olive oil and grilled, baked in a creamy sauce as a gratin or stuffed with grains and other vegetables. Pulses, such as lentils and beans, are also very popular, particularly in northern Italy.

STEWED ARTICHOKES

Artichokes are a favourite vegetable throughout Italy and are prepared in many different ways. Here, they are are stewed lightly with garlic, parsley and white wine to create a wonderfully succulent and flavoursome dish.

SERVES 6

INGREDIENTS
1 lemon
4 large or 6 small globe artichokes
25g/1oz/2 tbsp butter
60ml/4 tbsp olive oil
2 garlic cloves, finely chopped
60ml/4 tbsp chopped fresh parsley
45ml/3 tbsp water
90ml/6 tbsp milk
90ml/6 tbsp white wine
salt and ground black pepper

1 Squeeze the lemon and put the juice and the squeezed halves in a large bowl of cold water. Wash the artichokes and prepare them one at a time. Cut off only the tip from the stem. Peel the stem with a small knife, pulling upwards towards the leaves. Pull off the small leaves around the stem and continue snapping off the upper part of the dark outer leaves until you reach the taller inner leaves.

2 Slice the topmost part of the leaves off. Cut the artichoke into 4 or 6 segments. Cut out the bristly "choke" from each segment. Place in the bowl of water and lemon juice to prevent the artichokes from darkening while you prepare the rest. Bring a large pan of water to a rapid boil and blanch the artichokes for about 4 minutes. Drain.

3 Heat the butter and olive oil in a large pan. Add the garlic and parsley and cook for 2–3 minutes. Stir in the artichokes. Season with salt and black pepper. Add the water and the milk and cook for about 10 minutes, or until the liquid has evaporated. Stir in the wine, cover and cook until the artichokes are tender. Serve hot or at room temperature.

GREEN BEANS WITH TOMATOES

This wonderful vegetable dish of fresh green beans cooked gently in a tomato sauce is particularly good when fresh tomatoes are used. However, canned ones make an acceptable substitute and will give good results.

SERVES 4–6

INGREDIENTS
450g/1lb fresh green beans
45ml/3 tbsp olive oil
1 onion, preferably red, very finely sliced
350g/12oz plum tomatoes, fresh or canned, peeled and finely chopped
120ml/4fl oz/½ cup water
5–6 fresh basil leaves, torn into pieces
salt and ground black pepper

1 Snap or cut the stem ends off the beans, and wash well in plenty of cold water. Drain and set aside.

2 Heat the oil in a large frying pan with a cover. Add the onion slices and cook for 5–6 minutes, until just soft. Add the tomatoes and cook over a medium heat for 6–8 minutes until they soften. Stir in the water. Season with salt and black pepper to taste, and add the torn basil.

3 Add the beans to the tomatoes, stirring to coat in the sauce. Cover the pan and cook over moderate heat for 15–20 minutes until tender. Stir occasionally, adding more water if the sauce dries out too much. Serve hot or cold.

BROCCOLI WITH OIL & GARLIC

This very simple vegetable dish transforms plain steamed or blanched broccoli into a succulent, aromatic treat. Lightly cooked broccoli is tossed in garlicky olive oil and can be eaten either hot or cold. Peeling the broccoli stalks allows for even cooking.

SERVES 6

INGREDIENTS
1kg/2¼lb fresh broccoli
90ml/6 tbsp extra virgin olive oil
2–3 garlic cloves, finely chopped
salt and ground black pepper

1 Wash the broccoli. Cut off any woody parts at the base of the stems, then use a small sharp knife to peel the thick skin away from the broccoli stems. Cut any very long or wide stalks in half.

2 Boil water in the bottom of a pan equipped with a steamer, or bring a large pan of water to the boil. If steaming the broccoli, put it in the steamer and cover tightly. Cook for 8–12 minutes, or until the stems are just tender when pierced with the point of a knife. Remove from the heat. If blanching, drop the broccoli into the pan of boiling water and blanch for 5–6 minutes until just tender. Drain.

3 In a frying pan large enough to hold all the broccoli pieces, gently heat the olive oil and add the finely chopped garlic. Cook gently for 2–3 minutes over a low heat until the garlic is light golden (do not let it brown or it will become bitter).

4 Add the broccoli to the pan and cook over a medium heat for 3–4 minutes, turning to coat with the garlicky oil. Season and serve hot or cold.

CARROTS WITH MARSALA

In this Sicilian dish, thinly sliced carrots are cooked slowly in Marsala to give a sweet and juicy result. If you can, buy fresh carrots in a bunch with the tops still on as they tend to have a much better flavour.

SERVES 4

INGREDIENTS
50g/2oz/¼ cup butter
450g/1lb carrots, thinly sliced
5ml/1 tsp sugar
2.5ml/½ tsp salt
50ml/2fl oz/¼ cup Marsala

1 Melt the butter in a medium pan, and add the carrots. Stir well to cover with the melted butter. Add the sugar and salt and mix well. Stir in the Marsala and simmer over a low heat for 4–5 minutes.

2 Pour enough water into the pan to barely cover the carrots. Cover and cook over low to medium heat for 8–10 minutes until the carrots are tender. Uncover and cook until the liquid reduces almost completely. Serve hot.

COOK'S TIP
Adding only a small amount of water to the carrots gives a very sweet and succulent result. Reducing the liquid at the end of cooking time allows the carrots to retain their delicious flavour, which can otherwise be lost in the cooking liquid.

ROASTED TOMATOES & GARLIC

These tomatoes are very quick and simple to prepare yet taste wonderful. Don't worry about the quantity of garlic as roasting softens its flavour. Use a large, shallow earthenware dish that will allow the tomatoes to sear and char in the oven.

SERVES 4

INGREDIENTS
8 tomatoes, halved
12 garlic cloves
60ml/4 tbsp extra virgin olive oil
3 bay leaves
salt and ground black pepper
45ml/3 tbsp fresh oregano leaves, to garnish

1 Preheat the oven to 230°C/450°F/Gas 8. Select an ovenproof dish that will hold all the tomatoes snugly in a single layer. Place the halved tomatoes in the dish and push the whole, unpeeled garlic cloves between them.

2 Brush the tomatoes with olive oil, add the bay leaves and sprinkle with black pepper. Bake for 45 minutes until the tomatoes have softened and are sizzling. They should be slightly charred around the edges. Season with salt and a little more black pepper. Garnish with oregano and serve either hot or at room temperature.

COOK'S TIPS
• Use ripe tomatoes for this recipe as they keep their shape and do not fall apart when roasted at such a high temperature. If possible, buy tomatoes ripened on the vine and leave the stalks on. Plum tomatoes will look very pretty and taste delicious.
• Leaving the tomatoes and garlic to stand for a few hours before serving at room temperature will allow the flavours to infuse and develop.

Courgettes with Sun-dried Tomatoes

Throughout southern Italy, tomatoes are dried and preserved in the sun, ready for winter. This wonderful dish combines the fresh, mild flavour of courgettes with the concentrated, sweet and tangy flavour of sun-dried tomatoes.

SERVES 6

INGREDIENTS
10 sun-dried tomatoes, dry or preserved in oil and drained
175ml/6fl oz/³⁄₄ cup warm water
75ml/5 tbsp olive oil
1 large onion, finely sliced
2 garlic cloves, finely chopped
1kg/2¼lb courgettes (zucchini), cut into thin strips
salt and ground black pepper

1 Using a sharp knife, slice the sun-dried tomatoes into thin strips. Place the tomato strips in a small bowl and pour over the warm water. Leave to stand for about 20 minutes.

2 Meanwhile, in a large frying pan, heat the olive oil, add the sliced onion and stir. Cook over a low to medium heat until the onion softens but does not brown. Add the garlic and the courgettes to the onions and stir. Cook for about 5 minutes, stirring frequently.

3 Add the sun-dried tomatoes and their soaking liquid to the pan. Season with salt and black pepper to taste. Raise the heat slightly and cook for 2–3 minutes more until the courgettes are just tender, stirring occasionally. Serve hot or cold.

Aromatic Stewed Mushrooms

This flavoursome mushroom dish comes from Piedmont in northern Italy. It combines both field and cultivated mushrooms, which gives a balanced but not overwhelming taste that is enhanced by the flavours of garlic and olive oil.

Serves 6

Ingredients
675g/1½lb firm fresh mushrooms, field and cultivated
90ml/6 tbsp olive oil
2 garlic cloves, finely chopped
45ml/3 tbsp finely chopped fresh parsley
salt and ground black pepper

1 Clean the mushrooms carefully by wiping them with a damp cloth or kitchen paper. Cut off the woody tips of the stems and discard. Slice the remaining stems and caps fairly thickly.

2 Heat the olive oil in a large frying pan. Stir in the garlic and cook for about 1 minute. Add the sliced mushrooms and cook for 8–10 minutes, stirring occasionally. Season with salt and black pepper and stir in the parsley. Cook for about 5 minutes more and serve at once.

SWEET & SOUR AUBERGINES

This delicious dish from the island of Sicily, combines deep-fried aubergines and lightly cooked celery in a piquant fresh tomato sauce flavoured with white wine vinegar, capers and green olives.

SERVES 4

INGREDIENTS

675g/1½lb aubergines (eggplant)
30ml/2 tbsp olive oil
1 onion, finely sliced
1 garlic clove, finely chopped
1 × 225g/8oz can plum tomatoes, peeled and finely chopped
120ml/4fl oz/½ cup white wine vinegar
30ml/2 tbsp sugar
tender central sticks of a head of celery (about 175g/6oz)
30ml/2 tbsp capers, rinsed
75g/3oz/½ cup green olives, stoned (pitted)
oil, for deep-frying
30ml/2 tbsp chopped fresh parsley
salt and ground black pepper

1 Wash the aubergines and pat dry with kitchen paper. Cut into small cubes, sprinkle with salt and leave to drain in a colander for about 1 hour.

2 Heat the olive oil in a large pan. Stir in the onion and cook for 5–10 minutes until soft. Stir in the garlic and tomatoes and fry over a medium heat for about 10 minutes. Stir in the vinegar and sugar and season with black pepper. Simmer for about 10 minutes more until the sauce reduces.

3 Meanwhile, blanch the celery stalks in a large pan of boiling water for 2–3 minutes until just tender. Drain, allow to cool slightly, then chop into 2cm/¾in pieces. Add to the sauce with the capers and olives.

4 Rinse the aubergine cubes and pat dry with kitchen paper. Heat the oil to 185°C/365°F, and deep-fry the aubergine in batches until golden. Drain on kitchen paper and add to the sauce. Stir gently and season. Stir in the parsley. Leave to stand for 30 minutes. Serve at room temperature.

Fried Spring Greens with Bacon

These can be served as a vegetable accompaniment or enjoyed simply on their own, with warm crusty bread. The salty flavour of smoked bacon complements the tender, juicy greens perfectly. Red cabbage can be cooked in the same way, but cook for about 10 minutes more as it tends to be tougher than spring greens.

SERVES 4

INGREDIENTS
30ml/2 tbsp olive oil
25g/1oz/2 tbsp butter
75g/3oz rindless smoked streaky (fatty), chopped
1 large onion, thinly sliced
2 garlic cloves, finely chopped
250ml/8fl oz/1 cup dry white wine
900g/2lb spring greens (collards), shredded
salt and ground black pepper

1 In a large frying pan, heat the olive oil and butter and add the chopped bacon. Fry for about 2 minutes, stirring occasionally. Add the sliced onions and fry for 3 minutes more until the onion begins to soften. Add the garlic and wine, stir, and simmer vigorously for about 2 minutes until reduced.

2 Lower the heat, add the spring greens to the pan and season with salt and black pepper. Cover and cook gently over a low heat for about 15 minutes until the greens are tender. Serve hot.

Grilled Radicchio & Courgette

In Italy, radicchio is often brushed with olive oil and grilled or barbecued. This dish is delicious and very quick to prepare. The mild, sweet taste of courgette goes very well with the slightly bitter flavour of radicchio.

SERVES 4

INGREDIENTS
2–3 radicchio heads, round or long type
4 courgettes (zucchini)
90ml/6 tbsp olive oil
salt and ground black pepper

1 Preheat the grill (broiler), or prepare a barbecue. Cut the radicchio in half through the root section or base. If necessary, wash in cold water. Drain. Cut the courgettes into 1cm/½in diagonal slices.

2 When the grill or barbecue is hot, brush the vegetables all over with olive oil, and sprinkle with salt and black pepper. Arrange the vegetables on the grill rack and cook for 4–5 minutes on each side. Serve on their own or as an accompaniment to grilled fish or meats.

Roasted Potatoes with Red Onions

These mouth-watering potatoes are a fine accompaniment to just about anything.
The key is to use small firm potatoes; the smaller they are, the quicker they will cook.

SERVES 4

INGREDIENTS
675g/1½lb small firm potatoes
25g/1oz/2 tbsp butter
30ml/2 tbsp olive oil
2 red onions, cut into chunks
8 garlic cloves, unpeeled
30ml/2 tbsp chopped fresh rosemary
salt and ground black pepper

1 Preheat the oven to 230°C/450°F/Gas 8. Peel and quarter the potatoes, rinse well and pat dry on kitchen paper. Place the butter and olive oil in a roasting pan and place in the oven to heat.

2 When the butter has melted and is foaming, add the potatoes, red onions, garlic and rosemary to the roasting pan. Toss well to coat evenly in the oil and butter, spread out in a single layer and roast for about 25 minutes until the potatoes are golden and tender, shaking the tin from time to time. Season with salt and ground black pepper and serve immediately.

COOK'S TIP
To ensure that the potatoes are crisp, make sure they are completely dry before cooking. Resist the urge to turn the potatoes and onions too often and allow them to brown on one side before turning. Do not salt until the end of cooking – salting beforehand encourages them to give up their liquid, making the potatoes soggy rather than crisp.

SAVOURY POTATO, PUMPKIN & RICOTTA PUDDING

This savoury pudding is flavoured with garlic, nutmeg and Parmesan. The addition of whisked egg whites gives a light and fluffy result. Serve with rich meat dishes.

SERVES 4

INGREDIENTS
45ml/3 tbsp olive oil
1 garlic clove, sliced
675g/1½lb pumpkin flesh, cut into 2cm/¾in chunks
350g/12oz potatoes
25g/1oz/2 tbsp butter
90g/3½oz/scant ½ cup ricotta cheese
50g/2oz/⅔ cup grated Parmesan cheese
a pinch of grated nutmeg
4 eggs, separated
salt and ground black pepper
chopped fresh parsley, to garnish

1 Preheat the oven to 200°C/400°F/Gas 6. Grease a 1.75 litre/3 pint/7½ cup, shallow, oval baking dish. Heat the oil in a large pan, add the garlic and pumpkin and cook for about 15 minutes until the pumpkin is tender.

2 Meanwhile, cook the potatoes in salted boiling water for about 15 minutes until tender. Drain, leave to cool slightly, then peel off the skins. Place the potatoes and pumpkin in a bowl and mash well with the butter.

3 In a small bowl, mash the ricotta until smooth, then stir into the potato and pumpkin mixture. Add the Parmesan, nutmeg and seasoning and mix until smooth and creamy. Stir in the egg yolks, one at a time, until thoroughly combined.

4 Whisk the egg whites until they form stiff peaks, then fold gently into the potato and pumpkin mixture. Spoon into the prepared baking dish and bake for 30 minutes until golden and firm. Serve hot, garnished with parsley.

Radicchio & Chicory Gratin with Sun-dried Tomatoes

Slightly bitter radicchio and chicory take on a different flavour when baked in the oven with a creamy sauce. The rich béchamel sauce and sweet Emmental cheese that are used in this recipe combine wonderfully with the bitter leaves.

SERVES 4

INGREDIENTS
2 radicchio heads, quartered lengthways
2 chicory (Belgian endive) heads, quartered lengthways
25g/1oz/½ cup drained sun-dried tomatoes in oil, chopped roughly
25g/1oz/2 tbsp butter
15g/½oz/1 tbsp plain (all-purpose) flour
250ml/8fl oz/1 cup milk
a pinch of grated nutmeg
50g/2oz/½ cup grated Emmental cheese
salt and ground black pepper
chopped fresh parsley, to garnish

1 Preheat the oven to 180°C/350°F/Gas 4. Grease a 1.2 litre/2 pint/5 cup baking dish. Trim the radicchio and chicory and discard any damaged or wilted leaves. Quarter them lengthways and arrange in the baking dish.

2 Scatter the sun-dried tomatoes over the radicchio and chicory and brush the leaves liberally with oil from the jar. Sprinkle with salt and black pepper and cover with foil. Bake for 15 minutes, then remove the foil and bake for a further 10 minutes until the vegetables are softened.

3 Make the sauce. Melt the butter in a small pan over a medium heat. When the butter is foaming, add the flour and cook for 1 minute, stirring. Remove from the heat and gradually whisk in the milk. Return to the heat and bring to the boil. Simmer for 2–3 minutes until thickened. Season, then stir in the nutmeg.

4 Pour the sauce over the vegetables and sprinkle with the Emmental. Bake for about 20 minutes until golden brown. Serve at once, garnished with parsley.

BAKED FENNEL
WITH PARMESAN CHEESE

Fennel is widely eaten throughout Italy, both raw and cooked. Cooking subdues its distinctive aniseed flavour and, in this recipe, it is complemented perfectly with the sharp flavour of Parmesan cheese.

SERVES 4–6

INGREDIENTS
1kg/2¼lb fennel bulbs, washed and cut in half
50g/2oz/¼ cup butter
40g/1½oz/⅓ cup freshly grated Parmesan cheese

1 Bring a large pan of water to the boil, add the halved fennel bulbs and cook for about 5 minutes until soft but not mushy. Drain well. Preheat the oven to 200°C/400°F/Gas 6 and butter a medium baking dish.

2 Cut the cooked fennel bulbs lengthwise into 4 or 6 pieces. Place them in the prepared baking dish. Dot with butter and sprinkle with the grated Parmesan cheese. Bake for about 20 minutes until the cheese is golden brown. Serve at once.

RED PEPPER GRATIN

Serve this simple but delicious gratin as a starter with a small mixed leaf salad and some crusty Italian bread to mop up the sweet juices. Grilling the peppers imparts a wonderful smoky flavour to the dish.

SERVES 4

INGREDIENTS
2 red (bell) peppers
30ml/2 tbsp extra virgin olive oil
60ml/4 tbsp fresh white breadcrumbs
1 garlic clove, finely chopped
5ml/1 tsp drained bottled capers
8 black olives, stoned (pitted) and roughly chopped
15ml/1 tbsp chopped fresh oregano
15ml/1 tbsp chopped fresh flat leaf parsley
salt and ground black pepper
fresh herbs, to garnish

1 Preheat the oven to 200°C/400°F/Gas 6. Place the peppers under a hot grill (broiler) and cook, turning occasionally, until blackened all over. Remove from the heat, place in a bowl and cover. Set aside to cool.

2 When the peppers are cool, peel off the blackened skins and discard. Cut the peppers in half, remove the seeds and cut the flesh into wide strips.

3 Use a little of the olive oil to grease a small baking dish. Arrange the pepper strips in the dish. Scatter the breadcrumbs, garlic, capers, olives and herbs over the top, drizzle with the remaining olive oil and season with salt and black pepper. Bake for about 20 minutes until the breadcrumbs have browned. Garnish with fresh herbs and serve immediately.

COOK'S TIP
Don't peel the peppers under a running tap as the running water will wash away the delicious smoky flavour that gives this dish its character.

Aubergine Parmigiana

This classic dish is a speciality of southern Italy and makes a good vegetarian lunch or supper. Slices of aubergine are layered with tomato sauce, mozzarella and Parmesan cheese, then baked until golden brown and bubbling.

SERVES 4–6

INGREDIENTS
1kg/2¼lb aubergines (eggplant)
flour, for coating
oil, for frying
25g/1½oz/⅓ cup freshly grated Parmesan cheese
400g/14oz/2 cups mozzarella cheese, very thinly sliced
salt and ground black pepper

FOR THE TOMATO SAUCE
60ml/4 tbsp olive oil
1 onion, very finely chopped
1 garlic clove, finely chopped
450g/1lb tomatoes, fresh or canned, chopped, with their juice
a few fresh basil leaves or sprigs parsley

1 Cut the aubergines into rounds about 1cm/½in wide, place in a colander, sprinkle with salt and leave to drain for about 1 hour. Meanwhile, make the tomato sauce. Heat the oil in a pan. Add the onion, and cook over a medium heat for 5–8 minutes until translucent. Stir in the garlic and the tomatoes. Season and add the basil or parsley. Cook for 20–30 minutes. Purée in food processor.

2 Pat dry the salted aubergine slices with kitchen paper and coat lightly in the flour. Heat the oil in a large frying pan. Cook the aubergine in batches, for a few minutes on each side.

3 Preheat the oven to 180°C/350°F/Gas 4. Grease a shallow baking dish. Spread a little tomato sauce in the bottom, cover with a layer of aubergine, sprinkle over a few teaspoons of Parmesan, season and cover with a layer of mozzarella. Repeat until all the ingredients are used up, ending with a layer of sauce and a sprinkling of Parmesan. Bake for about 45 minutes. Serve immediately.

STUFFED AUBERGINES

This Ligurian dish is flavoured with paprika and allspice, a legacy from the days when spices from the East came into northern Italy via the port of Genoa. It makes a good vegetarian main course, served with a green salad.

SERVES 4

INGREDIENTS
2 aubergines (eggplant), about 225g/8oz each, stalks removed
275g/10oz potatoes, peeled and diced
30ml/2 tbsp olive oil
1 small onion, finely chopped
1 garlic clove, finely chopped
good pinch of ground allspice and paprika
1 egg, beaten
40g/1½oz/½ cup grated Parmesan cheese
15ml/1 tbsp fresh white breadcrumbs
salt and ground black pepper
fresh mint sprigs, to garnish

1 Bring a large pan of lightly salted water to the boil. Add the whole aubergines and cook for 5 minutes, turning frequently. Remove with a slotted spoon and set aside. Add the potatoes to the pan and cook for 15 minutes until tender. Drain.

2 Meanwhile, halve the aubergines lengthways and scoop out the flesh with a spoon, leaving 5mm/¼in of the shell intact. Brush a large baking dish with oil. Put the aubergine shells in the dish and chop the aubergine flesh roughly.

3 Heat the oil in a frying pan, add the onion and cook gently for about 5 minutes until softened. Add the aubergine flesh and garlic. Cook for 6–8 minutes, stirring frequently. Tip into a bowl. Preheat the oven to 190°C/375°F/Gas 5.

4 Mash the potatoes. Add to the frying pan with the spices, beaten egg, half the Parmesan and salt and pepper. Spoon into the aubergine shells. Mix the breadcrumbs with the remaining cheese and sprinkle over the aubergines. Bake for 40–45 minutes until the topping is crisp. Garnish with mint and serve immediately.

TUSCAN BAKED BEANS

Beans, both dried and fresh, are particularly popular in Tuscany, where they are cooked in many different ways. In this dish, the beans are cooked slowly with tomatoes and are flavoured with fresh sage or parsley.

SERVES 6–8

INGREDIENTS

600g/1lb 6oz dried beans, such as cannellini
60ml/4 tbsp olive oil
2 garlic cloves, crushed
3 fresh sage leaves or 60ml/4 tbsp chopped fresh parsley
1 leek, finely sliced
1 × 400g/14oz can plum tomatoes, chopped, with their juice
salt and ground black pepper

1 Carefully pick over the dried beans, discarding any stones or other particles. Place in a large bowl and cover with cold water. Leave to soak for at least 6 hours, or overnight. Drain.

2 Preheat the oven to 180°C/350°F/Gas 4. In a small pan heat the olive oil and sauté the crushed garlic and sage or parsley for 3–4 minutes. Remove from the heat and set aside.

3 In a large deep baking dish combine the beans with the sliced leek and tomatoes. Stir in the oil with the garlic and herbs. Add enough fresh water to cover the beans by 2cm/¾in. Mix well. Cover the dish with a lid or foil and place in the centre of the oven. Bake for about 1¾ hours.

4 Remove the dish from the oven, stir the beans and season with plenty of salt and black pepper. Return the beans to the oven, uncovered, and cook for another 15 minutes, or until tender. Remove from the oven and allow to stand for 7–8 minutes before serving. Serve hot or at room temperature.

Broad Bean Purée with Ham

The subtle, slightly sweet flavour of broad beans goes well with the saltiness of prosciutto crudo in this Tuscan dish. They can sometimes have a tough outer skin; peeling them ensures they are tender and sweet.

SERVES 4

INGREDIENTS
*1kg/2¼lb fresh broad (fava) beans, shelled, or 400g/14oz shelled broad
  beans, thawed if frozen*
1 onion, finely chopped
2 small potatoes, peeled and diced
50g/2oz/¼ cup prosciutto crudo
45ml/3 tbsp extra virgin olive oil
salt and ground black pepper

1 Place the broad beans in a pan and cover with water. Bring to the boil and cook for 5 minutes. Drain and peel when they are cool enough to handle.

2 Place the peeled beans in a pan with the onion and potatoes. Pour over enough water just to cover, then bring to the boil. Lower the heat slightly, cover, and simmer for 15–20 minutes until the vegetables are very soft. Check occasionally, adding a little more water if necessary.

3 Chop the prosciutto into very small dice. Heat the oil in a small pan and sauté the prosciutto over a medium heat until just golden. Mash or purée the bean mixture. Return it to the pan. If it is very moist, cook it over moderate heat until reduced slightly. Stir in the oil and ham. Season with salt and black pepper and cook for 2 minutes. Serve immediately.

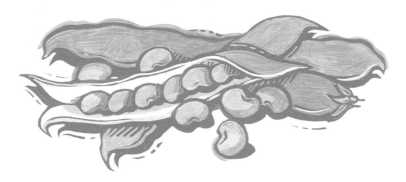

STEWED LENTILS

In Italy, lentils are grown in the area around Umbria. They are very often eaten as an accompaniment to duck and zampone or cotechino sausages, but this dish is very good eaten on its own.

SERVES 6

INGREDIENTS
450g/1lb/2 cups green or brown lentils
50g/2oz/¼ cup pancetta or salt pork
45ml/3 tbsp olive oil
1 onion, very finely chopped
1 celery stick, very finely sliced
1 carrot, very finely chopped
1 garlic clove
1 bay leaf
45ml/3 tbsp chopped fresh parsley
salt and ground black pepper

1 Carefully pick over the lentils, removing any stones or other particles. Place them in a large bowl and cover with cold water. Set aside and leave to soak for several hours. Drain.

2 Cut the pancetta or salt pork into small dice. In a large heavy pan heat the oil. Add the chopped ham or pork and cook for about 4 minutes. Stir in the onion and sauté over low heat for 5–10 minutes until soft. Add the celery and carrot and cook for 3–4 minutes more.

3 Add the lentils to the pan, stirring to coat them with the oil. Pour in enough boiling water to cover. Stir well, adding the garlic, bay leaf and parsley. Season with plenty of salt and pepper. Cook over a medium heat for about 1 hour until the lentils are tender. Check occasionally, adding more water if necessary. Remove the garlic and bay leaf and discard. Serve hot or at room temperature.

SALADS

Italian salads are very versatile and are eaten warm as well as cold. The colours and tastes of fresh Italian vegetables help to create some wonderful salads, such as Sweet and Sour Artichoke Salad, and Roasted Red Pepper and Tomato Salad with its rich blend of colours, flavours and textures. Vegetable salads, such as Sicilian Aubergine, Lemon and Caper Salad, can be eaten as an accompaniment to cold meats, with pasta, or on thier own with crusty bread. More substantial salads, such as Country Pasta Salad, and Chicken and Broccoli Salad, often include pasta, poultry, meat and fish or shellfish and can be eaten as a meal in themselves.

PANZANELLA

This classic tomato, pepper and bread salad is enjoyed all over Italy. Toasted ciabatta absorbs the tangy flavours of tomato juice, olive oil and red wine vinegar and combines wonderfully with roasted peppers, anchovies, capers and black olives.

SERVES 4–6

INGREDIENTS
225g/8oz/about ⅔ loaf ciabatta
150ml/¼ pint/⅔ cup olive oil
3 red (bell) peppers
3 yellow (bell) peppers
50g/2oz can anchovy fillets
675g/1½lb ripe plum tomatoes, peeled
4 garlic cloves, crushed
60ml/4 tbsp red wine vinegar
50g/2oz capers
115g/4oz/1 cup stoned (pitted) black olives
salt and ground black pepper
fresh basil leaves, to garnish

1 Preheat the oven to 200°C/400°F/Gas 6. Cut the ciabatta into 2cm/¾in chunks and drizzle with 50ml/2fl oz/¼ cup of the oil. Arrange the bread on a grill (broiler) rack and cook under a preheated grill until golden.

2 Put the peppers on a foil-lined baking sheet and bake for 45 minutes until the skins begins to char. Place the peppers in a large bowl and cover with a plate. When cool, peel off the skins, then cut into quarters, discarding the stalk ends and seeds. Drain, then roughly chop the anchovies. Set aside.

3 Halve the tomatoes, scoop the seeds into a strainer set over a bowl and press to extract the juice. Discard the seeds and stir the remaining oil, garlic, vinegar and seasoning into the juice. Layer the toasted bread, peppers, tomatoes, anchovies, capers and olives in a large bowl. Pour the tomato dressing over and leave to stand for 30 minutes, then serve garnished with plenty of basil leaves.

Radicchio & Jerusalem Artichoke Salad

The distinctive, earthy taste of Jerusalem artichokes makes a lovely contrast to the sharp freshness of radicchio and lemon in this salad. Serve warm or cold as an accompaniment to grilled steak or barbecued meats.

SERVES 4

INGREDIENTS
1 large radicchio head or 150g/5oz radicchio leaves
40g/1½oz/6 tbsp walnut pieces
45ml/3 tbsp walnut oil
500g/1¼lb Jerusalem artichokes
pared rind and juice of 1 lemon
coarse sea salt and ground black pepper
flat leaf parsley, to garnish (optional)

1 If using a whole radicchio, cut into 8–10 wedges. Put the radicchio wedges or leaves in a shallow flameproof dish. Scatter the walnuts over the top, then pour over the oil. Season. Place under a hot grill (broiler) and cook for 2–3 minutes.

2 Peel the artichokes and cut up any large ones so the pieces are all roughly the same size. Bring a pan of salted water to the boil, add the artichokes and half the lemon juice and cook for 5–7 minutes until tender. Drain.

3 Add the artichokes, remaining lemon juice and pared lemon rind to the radicchio and toss. Season with salt and pepper, then grill under high heat until beginning to brown. Serve at once, garnished with flat leaf parsley, if you like.

VARIATION
If you cannot find Jerusalem artichokes, use new potatoes instead. They do not have the same nutty flavour but still make a good partner for radicchio.

ROASTED RED PEPPER & TOMATO SALAD

This lovely cooked salad brings together perfectly the colours, flavours and textures of southern Italian food. To enjoy its rich, sweet flavours to the full, allow the salad to stand for a few hours and eat at room temperature.

SERVES 4

INGREDIENTS
3 red (bell) peppers
6 large plum tomatoes
2.5ml/½ tsp dried red chilli flakes
1 red onion, finely sliced
3 garlic cloves, finely chopped
grated rind and juice of 1 lemon
45ml/3 tbsp chopped fresh flat leaf parsley, plus extra to garnish
30ml/2 tbsp extra virgin olive oil
salt
black and green olives, to garnish

1 Preheat the oven to 220°C/425°F/Gas 7. Place the peppers on a baking sheet and roast, turning occasionally, for 10 minutes or until the skins are almost blackened. Add the tomatoes to the baking sheet and roast for 5 minutes more. Place the peppers in a bowl, cover and set aside, with the tomatoes, to cool.

2 When the peppers are cool enough to handle, carefully peel off the charred skin. Remove the seeds, then chop the peppers and tomatoes roughly and place in a large mixing bowl.

3 Add the chilli flakes, onion, garlic, lemon rind and juice to the tomatoes and peppers. Sprinkle over the chopped parsley. Mix well, then transfer to a serving dish. Sprinkle with a little salt, drizzle over the olive oil and scatter olives and extra parsley over the top. Serve at room temperature.

BABY SPINACH SALAD WITH ROAST GARLIC

Baby spinach leaves are sweet and tender and make great salads. Don't worry about the amount of garlic in this dish as it becomes sweet and subtle when roasted and loses its pungent taste.

SERVES 4

INGREDIENTS
12 garlic cloves, unpeeled
60ml/4 tbsp extra virgin olive oil
450g/1lb baby spinach leaves
50g/2oz/½ cup pine nuts, lightly toasted
juice of ½ lemon
salt and ground black pepper

1 Preheat the oven to 190°C/375°F/Gas 5. Place the unpeeled garlic cloves in a small ovenproof dish, toss in 30ml/2 tbsp of the olive oil and bake for about 15 minutes until slightly charred around the edges.

2 While still warm, tip the roasted garlic into a salad bowl. Add the spinach, toasted pine nuts, lemon juice, remaining olive oil and a little salt. Toss well and season with black pepper to taste. Serve immediately, inviting guests to squeeze the softened garlic purée out of the skin to eat.

Sweet & Sour Artichoke Salad

The sweet and sour dressing in this recipe really brings out the flavours of the young, tender vegetables. There is no better way to enjoy small globe artichokes, tiny sweet green peas and crisp broad beans.

SERVES 4

INGREDIENTS
6 small globe artichokes
juice 1 lemon
30ml/2 tbsp olive oil
2 onions, roughly chopped
175g/6oz/1 cup fresh or frozen shelled broad (fava) beans
175g/6oz/1½ cups fresh or frozen shelled peas
salt and ground black pepper
fresh mint leaves, to garnish

FOR THE SWEET AND SOUR DRESSING
120ml/4fl oz/½ cup white wine vinegar
15ml/1 tbsp caster (superfine) sugar
handful fresh mint leaves, roughly torn

1 Peel the outer leaves from the artichokes and discard. Cut the artichokes into quarters and place in a bowl of water with the lemon juice. Heat the oil in a large pan, add the onions and cook until golden. Add the beans and stir, then drain the artichokes and add to the pan. Pour in about 300ml/½ pint/1¼ cups of water and cook, covered, for 10–15 minutes.

2 Add the peas to the pan, season and cook for 5 minutes, stirring occasionally, until the vegetables are tender. Drain well, then place in a large bowl. Leave to cool, then cover and chill.

3 To make the dressing, mix all the ingredients in a small pan. Heat gently for 2–3 minutes until the sugar dissolves. Simmer gently for about 5 minutes, stirring occasionally. Leave to cool. To serve, drizzle the dressing over the vegetables and garnish with fresh mint leaves.

POTATO SALAD WITH GARLIC & LEMON DRESSING

There are many variations of potato salad. This one uses a very simple dressing of olive oil, garlic, lemon juice and fresh herbs, which is poured over the potatoes while they are still warm, helping the flavours to be fully absorbed.

SERVES 6

INGREDIENTS
1kg/2¼lb waxy potatoes

FOR THE DRESSING
90ml/6 tbsp extra virgin olive oil
juice of 1 lemon
1 garlic clove, very finely chopped
30ml/2 tbsp chopped fresh herbs, such as parsley, basil, thyme or oregano
salt and ground black pepper

1 Wash the potatoes, but do not peel them. Boil or steam them whole for about 15 minutes or until tender. Set aside to cool slightly. When they are cool enough to handle, peel and cut into dice.

2 Meanwhile, make the dressing. Place the olive oil, lemon juice, garlic, herbs and salt and pepper in a small bowl or jug (pitcher) and mix together. Pour the dressing over the potatoes while they are still warm and toss to combine. Serve at room temperature or cold.

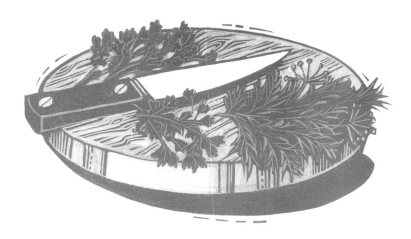

FENNEL, ORANGE & ROCKET SALAD

This light and refreshing salad is perfect served with spicy or rich foods. Raw fennel is crisp with a distinctive aniseed flavour and combines wonderfully with sweet, juicy oranges and peppery green rocket.

SERVES 4

INGREDIENTS
2 oranges
1 fennel bulb
115g/4oz rocket leaves
50g/2oz/⅓ cup black olives

FOR THE DRESSING
30ml/2 tbsp extra virgin olive oil
15ml/1 tbsp balsamic vinegar
1 small garlic clove, crushed
salt and ground black pepper

1 With a vegetable peeler, cut thin strips of rind from the oranges, leaving the white pith behind, and slice into thin julienne strips. Cook in boiling water for a few minutes, then drain. Peel the oranges, removing all the white pith. Slice them into thin rounds and discard any seeds.

2 Cut the fennel bulb in half lengthways and slice across the bulb as thinly as possible, preferably in a food processor fitted with a slicing disc or using a mandolin. Place the sliced oranges and fennel in a serving bowl and toss with the rocket leaves and toss to combine.

3 Make the dressing. Mix together the olive oil, vinegar, garlic and salt and black pepper in a small jug (pitcher) and pour over the salad. Toss together and leave to stand for a few minutes. Sprinkle with the black olives and the julienne strips of orange and serve immediately.

Aubergine, Lemon & Caper Salad

This moist and flavoursome salad is a classic Sicilian dish. For a perfect result, make sure the aubergine is cooked until meltingly soft. Serve on its own with plenty of crusty Italian bread or serve tossed with pasta or as an accompaniment to cold meat.

SERVES 4

INGREDIENTS
1 large aubergine (eggplant), about 675g/1½lb
60ml/4 tbsp olive oil
grated rind and juice of 1 lemon
30ml/2 tbsp capers, rinsed
12 stoned (pitted) green olives
30ml/2 tbsp chopped fresh flat leaf parsley
salt and ground black pepper

1 Cut the aubergine into 2.5cm/1in cubes. Heat the olive oil in a large frying pan and cook the cubes over a medium heat for about 10 minutes, tossing regularly, until soft and golden. You may need to do this in two batches. Drain on kitchen paper and sprinkle with a little salt.

2 Place the aubergine cubes in a large serving bowl, toss with the lemon rind and juice, capers, olives and chopped parsley and season well with salt and black pepper. Serve at room temperature.

COOK'S TIP
This will taste even better when made the day before and can be stored, covered in the refridgerator, for up to 4 days. To serve it on its own as a main course, add toasted pine nuts and shavings of Parmesan cheese. Serve with crusty bread.

CHICKPEA SALAD

This tasty, wholesome salad makes a good light meal, and is quickly assembled if canned chickpeas are used. Serve with crusty Italian bread, such as ciabatta.

SERVES 4–6

INGREDIENTS
2 × 400g/14oz cans chickpeas, or 450g/1lb/2 cups cooked chickpeas
6 spring onions (scallions), chopped
2 tomatoes, cut into cubes
1 small red onion, finely chopped
12 black olives, stoned (pitted) and cut in half
15ml/1 tbsp capers, drained
30ml/2 tbsp finely chopped fresh parsley or mint
4 hard-boiled (hard-cooked) eggs, cut into quarters, to garnish

FOR THE DRESSING
75ml/5 tbsp olive oil
45ml/3 tbsp wine vinegar
salt and ground black pepper

1 Place the chickpeas in a colander and rinse under cold water. Drain well and place in a large serving bowl. Add the spring onions, tomatoes, red onion, olives and capers and stir well to combine.

2 Mix the dressing ingredients together in a small bowl or jug (pitcher). Add the herbs to the salad and toss. Pour over the dressing and mix well. Taste for seasoning and add more salt and pepper if necessary. Allow to stand for at least 1 hour. Just before serving, decorate with egg wedges.

VARIATION
Use cooked cannellini beans or borlotti beans in place of the chickpeas and replace the chopped parsley or mint with 10ml/2 tsp chopped fresh sage.

STROZZAPRETTI WITH COURGETTE FLOWERS

This pretty, summery dish is strewn with courgette flowers, but you can make it
without the flowers, if you like. In Italy, bunches of courgette flowers are a common
sight on vegetable stalls in summer, and are used for stuffing and cooking.

SERVES 4

INGREDIENTS
50g/2oz/¼ cup butter
30ml/2 tbsp extra virgin olive oil
1 small onion, thinly sliced
200g/7oz small courgettes (zucchini), cut into thin julienne
1 garlic clove, crushed
10ml/2 tsp finely chopped fresh marjoram
350g/12oz/3 cups dried strozzapreti
1 large handful courgette flowers, thoroughly washed and dried
salt and ground black pepper
thin shavings of Parmesan cheese, to serve

1 Heat the butter and half the olive oil in a medium pan or skillet. Add the sliced
onion and cook gently, stirring frequently, for about 5 minutes, until softened.
Add the courgettes to the pan and sprinkle with the garlic and marjoram. Season
with salt and black pepper to taste. Cook for about 6 minutes until the courgettes
have softened but are not coloured, turning occasionally.

2 Meanwhile, cook the pasta in a pan of salted boiling water according to the
instructions on the packet. Set aside a few courgette flowers, then shred the rest
and add them to the courgette mixture. Stir and taste for seasoning.

3 Drain the pasta, tip it into a warmed serving bowl and add the remaining oil.
Toss, add the courgette mixture and toss again. Top with Parmesan shavings
and the reserved courgette flowers.

ROASTED CHERRY TOMATO & PASTA SALAD

This pasta salad is a great accompaniment to barbecued chicken, steaks or chops. Roasted cherry tomatoes are very juicy and have an intense, smoky-sweet flavour that is set off perfectly by the peppery taste of fresh rocket.

SERVES 4

INGREDIENTS
225g/8oz/2 cups dried chifferini or pipe
450g/1lb ripe baby Italian plum tomatoes, halved lengthways
75ml/5 tbsp extra virgin olive oil
2 garlic cloves, cut into thin slivers
30ml/2 tbsp balsamic vinegar
2 pieces sun-dried tomato in olive oil, drained and chopped
a large pinch of sugar, to taste
1 handful rocket, about 65g/2½oz
salt and ground black pepper

1 Preheat the oven to 190°C/375°F/Gas 5. Meanwhile, cook the pasta in a large pan of salted boiling water according to the instructions on the packet.

2 Arrange the halved tomatoes cut side up in a roasting tin, drizzle 30ml/2 tbsp of the oil over them and sprinkle with the slivers of garlic and salt and pepper. Roast in the oven for 20 minutes, turning once.

3 Put the remaining oil in a large bowl with the vinegar, sun-dried tomatoes, sugar and a little salt and pepper to taste. Stir well to mix. Drain the pasta, add it to the bowl of dressing and toss to combine.

4 Add the roasted tomatoes to the pasta and mix gently. Before serving, add the rocket, toss lightly and taste for seasoning, adding more if necessary. Serve either at room temperature or chilled.

COUNTRY PASTA SALAD

This salad is packed with vegetables and is ideal for a summer picnic. Use fresh Parmesan from the delicatessen, which is less mature and sold as a table cheese, rather than the hard, mature Parmesan used for grating.

SERVES 6

INGREDIENTS
300g/11oz/2¾ cups dried fusilli
150g/5oz green beans, topped and tailed and cut into 5cm/2in lengths
1 potato, about 150g/5oz, diced
200g/7oz baby tomatoes, hulled and halved
2 spring onions (scallions), finely chopped
90g/3½oz Parmesan cheese, diced or coarsely shaved
6–8 stoned (pitted) black olives, cut into rings
15–30ml/1–2 tbsp capers, to taste

FOR THE DRESSING
90ml/6 tbsp extra virgin olive oil
15ml/1 tbsp balsamic vinegar
15ml/1 tbsp chopped fresh flat leaf parsley
salt and ground black pepper

1 Cook the pasta according to the instructions on the packet. Drain and rinse under cold running water, then shake to remove as much water as possible. Leave to drain, shaking occasionally.

2 Cook the beans and diced potato in a pan of salted boiling water for about 5 minutes, or until tender. Drain and leave to cool. To make the dressing, put all the ingredients in a large bowl, season and whisk well to mix.

3 Add the tomatoes, spring onions, Parmesan, olives and capers to the dressing. Place the pasta, beans and potato in a large bowl and pour over the dressing. Toss well, cover and leave to stand for 30 minutes. Taste for seasoning and serve.

Chicken & Broccoli Salad

The strong, pungent flavour of Gorgonzola makes a wonderfully tangy dressing that goes well with both chicken and broccoli. Serve for lunch or supper, with plenty of crusty Italian bread, such as Ciabatta.

Serves 4

Ingredients
175g/6oz broccoli florets, divided into small sprigs
225g/8oz/2 cups dried farfalle
2 large cooked chicken breast portions

For the dressing
90g/3½oz Gorgonzola cheese
15ml/1 tbsp white wine vinegar
60ml/4 tbsp extra virgin olive oil
2.5–5ml/½–1 tsp finely chopped fresh sage, plus extra sage sprigs to garnish
salt and ground black pepper

1 Cook the broccoli florets in a large pan of salted boiling water for 3 minutes. Remove with a slotted spoon and rinse under cold running water, then spread out on kitchen paper to drain and dry.

2 Add the pasta to the broccoli cooking water, bring back to the boil and cook according to the instructions on the packet. Drain the pasta, rinse under cold running water, then leave to drain, shaking occasionally.

3 Remove the skin from the cooked chicken breasts and cut the meat into bite-size pieces. Set aside. To make the dressing, put the cheese in a large bowl and mash with a fork, then whisk in the vinegar followed by the oil, sage and seasoning.

4 Add the cooked pasta, chicken and broccoli florets to the bowl of dressing and toss well to combine. Season with salt and black pepper and serve, garnished with fresh sage sprigs.

PAN-FRIED CHICKEN LIVER SALAD

This classic salad comes from Florence. The dressing is made with vin santo, a sweet dessert wine from Tuscany, but this is not an essential ingredient and any dessert wine or sweet sherry will do.

SERVES 4

INGREDIENTS
75g/3oz baby spinach leaves
75g/3oz lollo rosso leaves
75ml/5 tbsp olive oil
15ml/1 tbsp butter
225g/8oz chicken livers, trimmed and thinly sliced
45ml/3 tbsp vin santo
50–75g/2–3oz fresh Parmesan cheese, shaved into curls
salt and ground black pepper

1 Wash the baby spinach and lollo rosso in cold water and gently pat dry with a clean dishtowel. Tear the leaves into a large bowl, season with salt and black pepper and toss gently to mix.

2 Heat 30ml/2 tbsp of the olive oil with the butter in a large, heavy frying pan. When foaming, add the chicken livers and toss over a medium to high heat for about 5 minutes, or until the livers are browned on the outside but still pink in the centre. Remove the pan from the heat.

3 Lift the livers from the pan with a slotted spoon, drain them on kitchen paper, then place on top of the torn spinach and lollo rosso leaves.

4 Return the pan to a medium heat, add the remaining olive oil and the vin santo and stir until sizzling. Pour the mixture over the salad leaves and chicken liver and toss to coat. Transfer to a serving bowl and sprinkle over the Parmesan shavings. Serve at once.

TUNA & BEAN SALAD

This is a substantial salad that makes an excellent light meal. It can be quickly assembled from canned ingredients so makes a great standby if you suddenly find yourself with unexpected lunch or supper guests.

SERVES 4–6

INGREDIENTS
2 × 400g/14oz cans cannellini or borlotti beans
2 × 200g/7oz cans tuna fish, drained
60ml/4 tbsp extra virgin olive oil
30ml/2 tbsp lemon juice
15ml/1 tbsp chopped fresh parsley
3 spring onions (scallions), thinly sliced
salt and ground black pepper

1 Pour the cannellini or borlotti beans into a large strainer and rinse under cold water. Drain well and place in a serving dish. Break the tuna into fairly large flakes with a fork and arrange over the beans.

2 In a small bowl or jug (pitcher), whisk together the olive oil and lemon juice. Season with salt and black pepper and add the chopped parsley. Mix well, then pour over the beans and tuna. Sprinkle the salad with the sliced spring onions and toss well before serving.

GENOESE SQUID SALAD

This garlicky salad combines slow-cooked squid in red wine with lightly cooked green beans and new potatoes. It is the perfect dish for summer, when new potatoes and green beans are at their best. Serve as a first course or light lunch.

SERVES 4–6

INGREDIENTS
450g/1lb prepared squid, cut into rings
4 garlic cloves, roughly chopped
300ml/½ pint/1¼ cups Italian red wine
450g/1lb waxy new potatoes, scrubbed clean
225g/8oz green beans, trimmed and cut into short lengths
2–3 drained sun-dried tomatoes in oil, thinly sliced lengthways
60ml/4 tbsp extra virgin olive oil
15ml/1 tbsp red wine vinegar
salt and ground black pepper

1 Preheat the oven to 180°C/350°F/Gas 4. Put the squid rings in an earthenware dish with half the garlic, the red wine and black pepper to taste. Cover and cook for about 45 minutes, or until the squid is tender.

2 Put the potatoes in a pan, cover with cold water and add a good pinch of salt. Bring to the boil, cover and simmer for 15–20 minutes, or until tender. Using a slotted spoon, lift out of the pan and set aside. Add the green beans to the boiling water and cook for 3 minutes. Drain.

3 When the potatoes are cool enough to handle, slice them thickly on the diagonal and place them in a bowl with the warm beans and sun-dried tomatoes. Whisk the oil, red wine vinegar and the remaining garlic in a small jug (pitcher) and season with salt and black pepper. Pour over the potato mixture.

4 Drain the squid and discard the wine and garlic. Add the squid to the potato mixture and turn very gently to combine. Arrange the salad on individual plates and grind pepper liberally all over. Serve warm.

Mixed Seafood Salad

All along Italy's coastline, versions of this salad appear. This one has a very simple dressing of olive oil, lemon juice and garlic, which works wonderfully with the subtle flavours of squid, prawns, mussels and clams.

Serves 6–8

Ingredients
350g/12oz small squid
1 small onion, cut into quarters
1 bay leaf
200g/7oz prawns (shrimp), in their shells
675g/1½lb fresh mussels, in their shells
450g/1lb fresh small clams, in their shells
175ml/6fl oz/¾ cup white wine
1 fennel bulb
75ml/5 tbsp extra virgin olive oil
45ml/3 tbsp fresh lemon juice
1 garlic clove, finely chopped
salt and ground black pepper

Cook's Tip
The cooking liquid from the squid and prawns can be strained and reserved for use in soup. It can be stored in the freezer for up to 3 months.

1 Clean the squid. Peel off the thin skin from the body section. Rinse well. Pull the head and tentacles away from the sac section. Some of the intestines will come away with the head. Remove and discard the translucent quill and any remaining insides from the sac. Sever the tentacles from the head. Discard the head and intestines. Remove the small hard beak from the base of the tentacles. Rinse the sac and tentacles under cold water. Drain well.

2 Bring a large pan of water to the boil. Add the onion and bay leaf. Drop in the squid and cook for about 10 minutes, or until tender. Remove the squid with a slotted spoon and allow to cool before slicing into rings 1cm/½in wide. Cut each tentacle section into 2 pieces, place in a large bowl and set aside.

3 Drop the prawns into the same pan of boiling water and cook for about 2 minutes until they turn pink. Remove with a slotted spoon and, when cool enough to handle, peel and devein. Place in the bowl with the squid.

4 Scrape off the beards from the mussels. Scrub and rinse the mussels and clams well in several changes of cold water, discarding any that do not close when sharply tapped with the back of a knife. Place in a large pan with the white wine. Cover, and steam until the shells have opened. Lift the clams and mussels out with a slotted spoon, discarding any that have not opened.

5 Remove the clams from their shells with a spoon and add to the bowl of squid and prawns. Remove all but 8 of the mussels from their shells and add to the bowl. Leave the remaining mussels in their half shells and set aside.

6 Cut the green, leafy part of the fennel away from the bulb, chop finely and set aside. Chop the bulb into bite-size pieces and add it to the serving bowl with the cooked seafood.

7 Make the dressing. Mix together the olive oil, lemon juice, garlic and chopped fennel leaves in a small bowl. Add salt and pepper to taste. Pour over the salad and toss well. Decorate with the remaining mussels in the half shell. Serve at room temperature or lightly chilled.

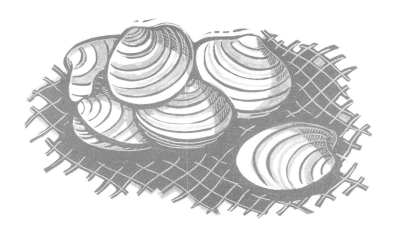

ICE CREAMS, CAKES
& DESSERTS

In Italy, family meals usually end with cheese or fresh fruit, so a dessert is a treat for a really special occasion. Rich and sumptuous confections, such as Zabaglione, Tiramisu and Ricotta Pudding, are popular choices, as are hot desserts, such as Stuffed Peaches. Pastries and cakes, such as Pine Nut Tart and Apple Cake, are often eaten with a cup of espresso coffee at other times of the day. The Italians were the pioneers of ice cream, and they still excel at making creamy Cassata and Tutti Frutti, as well as delicious fruit-flavoured water ices.

TUTTI FRUTTI ICE CREAM

This classic Italian ice cream takes its name from the expression meaning "all the fruits". Four fruits have been used here, but you can create your own combinations, including exotic fruits such as papaya or mango. For extra bite, steep the fruits in a little Kirsch before adding to the ice cream.

SERVES 4–6

INGREDIENTS
300ml/½ pint/1¼ cups semi-skimmed (low-fat) milk
1 vanilla pod
4 egg yolks
75g/3oz/6 tbsp caster (superfine) sugar
5ml/1 tsp cornflour (cornstarch)
300ml/½ pint/1¼ cups whipping cream
150g/5oz/²/3 cup multi-coloured glacé (candied) cherries
50g/2oz/¹/3 cup glacéed (candied) lime and orange peel
50g/2oz/¹/3 cup glacéed (candied) pineapple

> COOK'S TIP
> *If you have an ice cream maker, do not whip the cream in step 4: simply stir into the custard and churn in the ice cream maker until thick, then add the glacéed fruit and churn for 5–10 minutes more.*

1 Pour the milk into a heavy pan. Using a sharp knife slit the vanilla pod lengthways, add it to the milk and bring to the boil. Immediately remove the pan from the heat and leave to stand for about 15 minutes.

2 Lift out the vanilla pod from the pan. Scrape the small black seeds into the milk with a narrow bladed knife. Rinse the vanilla pod in cold water and set aside, for later re-use. Bring the milk back to the boil over a gentle heat.

3 Meanwhile, whisk the egg yolks, sugar and cornflour in a large bowl until thick and foamy. Gradually whisk in the hot milk, then pour back into the pan. Cook over a gentle heat, stirring constantly, until the custard thickens. Pour the mixture back into the bowl and cover. Set aside to cool, then chill.

4 Whip the cream until quite thickened – but still soft enough to fall from a spoon. Fold the cream into the chilled custard, then pour the mixture into a plastic tub or freezerproof container.

5 Freeze the mixture for 4 hours, beating once with a fork or electric beater to break up any ice crystals. Alternatively, scrape the mixture into a food processor and process briefly to break up the crystals, then return to the plastic tub or freezerproof container.

6 Meanwhile, finely chop the glacéed cherries, lime and orange peel and pineapple. Fold into the beaten ice cream and return the mixture to the freezer. Freeze for 2–3 hours until firm enough to scoop.

GINGERED SEMI-FREDDO

This ice cream is rather like the original soft-scoop ice cream. It is made with boiled sugar syrup rather than a traditional egg custard, and speckled with chopped stem ginger, which allows it to stay soft when frozen.

SERVES 6

INGREDIENTS
4 egg yolks
115g/4oz/generous ½ cup caster (superfine) sugar
120ml/4fl oz/½ cup cold water
300ml/½ pint/1¼ cups double (heavy) cream
115g/4oz/⅔ cup drained preserved stem ginger, finely chopped,
 plus extra slices, to decorate

1 Put the egg yolks in a large heatproof bowl and whisk until frothy. Bring a pan of water to the boil, reduce the heat and simmer gently.

2 Put the sugar and cold water in a separate pan and heat gently, stirring, until the sugar has dissolved. Increase the heat and boil for 4–5 minutes until the syrup reaches 115°C/239°F on a sugar thermometer. Alternatively, test by dropping a little of the syrup into a cup of cold water. When you pour the water away, you should be able to mould the syrup into a ball.

3 Put the bowl of egg yolks over the pan of simmering water and whisk in the sugar syrup. Continue whisking until the mixture is very thick. Remove from the heat and whisk until cool.

4 Whip the cream and fold into the yolk mixture, with the stem ginger. Pour into a freezerproof container and freeze for 1 hour. Stir to bring any ginger that has sunk to the bottom of the tub to the top, then return to the freezer for 5–6 hours until firm. Scoop into dishes or chocolate cases. Decorate with slices of ginger.

RASPBERRY GRANITA

Granitas are the classic Italian water ice. This vibrant bright red granita is an excellent dessert for anyone on a low-fat diet but, for something a little more indulgent, serve with whole berries and crème fraîche or clotted cream.

SERVES 6

INGREDIENTS
115g/4oz/½ cup caster (superfine) sugar
300ml/½ pint/1¼ cups water
500g/1¼lb/3½ cups raspberries, hulled, plus extra, to decorate
juice of 1 lemon
sifted icing (confectioners') sugar, for dusting (optional)

1 Put the sugar and water into a large pan and bring to the boil, stirring occasionally, until the sugar has dissolved. Pour the sugar syrup into a large bowl, leave to cool, then chill.

2 Place the raspberries in a food processor or blender and process to a smooth purée. Spoon the purée into a fine sieve set over a large bowl. Press through the sieve with the back of a wooden spoon and discard the seeds.

3 Scrape the purée into a large measuring jug (pitcher), stir in the sugar syrup and lemon juice and top up to 1 litre/1¾ pints/4 cups with cold water. Pour the mixture into a large plastic container so that the depth is no more than 2.5cm/1in. Cover and freeze for 2 hours until the mixture is mushy around the sides.

4 Using a fork, break up the ice crystals and mash finely. Return to the freezer for 2 hours, beating every 30 minutes until the ice forms fine, even crystals. Spoon into tall glass dishes and decorate with extra raspberries dusted with a little sifted icing sugar, if you wish.

CASSATA

This pretty Italian ice cream terrine is usually made of three different layers of ice cream, frozen in a bombe mould. This version combines the complementary flavours and colours of pistachio, vanilla and tutti frutti.

SERVES 8

INGREDIENTS
6 egg yolks
225g/8oz/generous 1 cup caster (superfine) sugar
15ml/1 tbsp cornflour (cornstarch)
600ml/1 pint/2½ cups milk
600ml/1 pint/2½ cups double (heavy) cream
75g/3oz/¾ cup pistachios
2.5ml/½ tsp almond essence (extract)
dash each of green and red food colouring
40g/1½oz/¼ cup candied peel, finely chopped
50g/2oz/¼ cup glacé (candied) cherries, washed, dried and finely chopped
5ml/1 tsp vanilla essence (extract)
amaretti, to serve (optional)

> COOK'S TIP
> *If using an ice cream maker, freeze the three ice creams separately. Churn the pistachio ice cream in an ice cream maker and spread into the prepared tin. Level the surface and place in the freezer while preparing the remaining ice creams in the same way.*

1 In a large mixing bowl, whisk together the egg yolks, sugar, cornflour and a little of the milk until pale and creamy. Place the remaining milk and the cream in a large, heavy pan and bring to the boil.

2 Pour the hot milk and cream into the egg yolk mixture in a steady stream, whisking constantly. Pour the mixture back into the pan and cook gently over a very low heat, stirring continuously, until thickened. Do not let the mixture boil. Remove the pan from the heat and divide the custard equally among three bowls. Cover each with clear film and leave to cool.

3 Meanwhile, put the pistachios in a bowl. Pour over boiling water to cover and leave to stand for 1 minute. Drain the nuts and spread between several thicknesses of kitchen paper. Rub between the paper to loosen the skins.

4 Pick out the nuts, rubbing off any remaining skins. Roughly chop and add to one bowl of cooled custard with the almond essence and a drop of green food colouring. Stir well until thoroughly combined.

5 Stir the candied peel, glacé cherries and a drop of red food colouring into the second bowl of custard and stir the vanilla essence into the third. Line a dampened 900g/2lb terrine or loaf tin with non-stick baking parchment.

6 Pour each of the mixtures into a separate plastic tub or freezerproof container and freeze for 2–3 hours until thickened, beating twice with a fork or a food processor to break up the ice crystals. Put the frozen pistachio ice cream into the prepared tin and spread out into an even layer. Layer the vanilla ice cream on top and then the tutti frutti. Freeze overnight until firm.

7 To serve, dip the terrine or loaf tin in very hot water for 2–3 seconds, then place a long serving plate upside down on top of it. Holding the two together, turn them over. Lift off the container and peel away the lining paper. Serve the cassata in slices with amaretti, if you like.

ZUCCOTTO

There are many versions of this classic frozen chocolate and nut bombe. This one has a rich ricotta, fruit, chocolate and nut filling, which is encased in a moist, chocolate and liqueur-flavoured sponge.

SERVES 8

INGREDIENTS

3 eggs
75g/3oz/6 tbsp caster (superfine) sugar
75g/3oz/⅔ cup plain (all-purpose) flour
25g/1oz/¼ cup cocoa powder (unsweetened)
90ml/6 tbsp kirsch
250g/9oz/generous 1 cup ricotta cheese
50g/2oz/½ cup icing (confectioners') sugar
50g/2oz plain (semisweet) chocolate, finely chopped
50g/2oz/½ cup blanched almonds, chopped and toasted
75g/3oz/scant ½ cup natural glacé (candied) cherries, quartered
2 pieces preserved stem ginger, finely chopped
150ml/¼ pint/⅔ cup double (heavy) cream
cocoa powder (unsweetened), for dusting

1 Preheat the oven to 180°C/350°F/Gas 4. Grease and line a 23cm/9in cake tin (pan). Whisk the eggs and sugar in a heatproof bowl over a pan of simmering water until the whisk leaves a trail. Remove the bowl from the heat and continue to whisk the mixture for 2 minutes.

2 Sift the flour and cocoa powder into the egg mixture and fold it in with a large metal spoon. Spoon the mixture into the prepared tin and bake for about 20 minutes until just firm. Leave to cool.

3 When the cake is completely cool, carefully cut into three thin layers. Drizzle 60ml/4 tbsp of the kirsch over the layers and set aside.

4 Beat the ricotta in a bowl until softened, then beat in the icing sugar, chocolate, almonds, cherries, ginger and remaining kirsch. Pour the cream into a separate bowl and whip it lightly until it forms soft peaks. Using a large metal spoon, fold the cream into the ricotta mixture. Chill.

5 Cut a 20cm/8in circle from one sponge layer, using a plate as a guide, and set it aside. Use the remaining sponge to make the case for the zuccotto. Cut the cake to fit the bottom of a 2.8–3.4 litre/5–6 pint/12½–15 cup freezerproof mixing bowl. Cut more sponge for the sides of the bowl, fitting the pieces together and taking them about one third of the way up.

6 Spoon the ricotta mixture into the bowl up to the height of the sponge and level the surface. Fit the reserved circle of sponge on top of the filling. Trim off the excess sponge around the edges. Cover and freeze overnight.

7 Transfer the zuccotto to the fridge 45 minutes before serving, so that the filling softens slightly. Place a serving plate upside down over the bowl and, holding the two together, turn them over. Peel away the clear film from the zuccotta and dust with cocoa powder. Serve at once, in slices.

COOK'S TIPS
• In Italy, there are special dome-shaped moulds for making this dessert, the name of which comes from the Italian word zucca, meaning pumpkin.
• Any kind of nut is good in this ice cream dessert. Substitute the almonds for other blanched, toasted nuts, such as hazelnuts or walnuts.

ZABAGLIONE

This light and foamy dessert is flavoured with sweet, musky Marsala. It is very quick to make but must be served at once. For a dinner party, assemble all the ingredients and equipment ahead of time so that you mix everything together at the last minute.

SERVES 6

INGREDIENTS
4 egg yolks
65g/2½oz/⅓ cup caster (superfine) sugar
120ml/4fl oz/½ cup dry Marsala
savoiardi (Italian sponge fingers), to serve

1 Half fill a pan with water and bring to simmering point. Put the egg yolks and sugar in a large heatproof bowl and beat with a hand-held electric mixer until very pale and creamy.

2 Put the bowl of beaten egg yolks over the pan of simmering water and gradually pour in the Marsala, whisking continuously until it is very thick and glossy and has increased in volume.

3 Remove the bowl from the water and pour the zabaglione into six heatproof, long-stemmed glasses. Serve at once, with sponge fingers.

COOK'S TIPS
• *When whisking the egg yolks over boiling water, make sure that the bottom of the bowl does not touch the water or the egg yolks will scramble.*
• *If you do not have Marsala to hand, sherry makes a good substitute.*

STUFFED PEACHES

These wonderful baked peaches are stuffed with crushed amaretti and flavoured with amaretto liqueur. The intense almond flavour of the cookies and liqueur is the perfect partner for sweet, juicy peaches.

SERVES 4

INGREDIENTS
4 ripe but firm peaches
50g/2oz amaretti
25g/1oz/2 tbsp butter, softened
25g/1oz/2 tbsp caster (superfine) sugar
1 egg yolk
60ml/4 tbsp amaretto liqueur
250ml/8fl oz/1 cup dry white wine
8 tiny basil sprigs, to decorate
ice cream or pouring cream, to serve

1 Preheat the oven to 180°C/350°F/Gas 4. Following the natural indentation line on each peach, cut in half around the stone (pit). Twist the halves in opposite directions to separate. Remove the peach stones, then cut away a little of the central flesh to make a larger hole for the stuffing. Chop this flesh finely and set aside.

2 Put the amaretti in a bowl and crush finely with the end of a rolling pin. In another bowl, cream the butter and sugar together. Stir in the chopped peach flesh, egg yolk and half the amaretto with the amaretti crumbs. Lightly butter a baking dish that is just large enough to hold the peach halves in a single layer.

3 Spoon the stuffing into the peaches, then stand in the dish. Mix the remaining liqueur with the wine, pour over the peaches and bake for about 25 minutes until tender. Decorate with basil and serve at once, with ice cream or cream.

TIRAMISU

The name of this popular dessert translates as "pick me up", which is said to be because it is so good that it literally makes you swoon when you eat it. There are many, many versions, and the recipe can be adapted to suit your own taste.

SERVES 6–8

INGREDIENTS
3 eggs, separated
450g/1lb/2 cups mascarpone cheese, at room temperature
1 sachet of vanilla sugar
175ml/6fl oz/¾ cup cold, very strong, black coffee
120ml/4fl oz/½ cup Kahlúa or other coffee-flavoured liqueur
18 savoiardi (Italian sponge fingers)
sifted cocoa powder and grated dark (bittersweet) chocolate, to decorate

1 Put the egg whites in a grease-free mixing bowl and whisk with an electric mixer until they form peaks. In another bowl, mix together the mascarpone, sugar and egg yolks. Whisk with the electric mixer until evenly combined. Fold in the egg whites, then put a few spoonfuls of the mixture in the bottom of a large serving bowl and spread it out evenly.

2 Pour the coffee and liqueur into a shallow dish and stir to combine. Dip a sponge finger into the mixture, turn it quickly so that it becomes saturated but does not disintegrate, and place it on top of the mascarpone in the bowl. Add five more dipped sponge fingers, placing them side by side.

3 Spoon in one-third of the remaining mixture and spread it out. Make more layers in the same way, ending with mascarpone. Level the surface, then sift cocoa powder over the top. Cover and chill overnight. Before serving, sprinkle with more cocoa and grated chocolate.

RICOTTA PUDDING

This creamy dessert from Sicily is a classic combination of mild ricotta cheese and sweet candied fruits. It is very easy to make and, as it can be made up to 24 hours ahead, is ideal for a dinner party.

SERVES 4–6

INGREDIENTS
225g/8oz/1 cup ricotta cheese
50g/2oz/⅓ cup glacéed (candied) fruits
60ml/4 tbsp sweet Marsala
250ml/8fl oz/1 cup double (heavy) cream
50g/2oz/¼ cup caster (superfine) sugar, plus extra to serve
finely grated rind of 1 orange
350g/12oz/2 cups fresh raspberries
strips of thinly pared orange rind, to decorate

1 Press the ricotta through a sieve into a large bowl. Finely chop the glacéed fruits and stir into the ricotta with half of the Marsala. Put the cream, sugar and orange rind in another bowl and whip until the cream is standing in soft peaks.

2 Fold the whipped cream into the ricotta mixture. Spoon into individual glass serving bowls and top with the raspberries. Chill. To serve, sprinkle with the remaining Marsala and dust the top of each bowl liberally with caster sugar. Decorate with the orange rind.

COOK'S TIP
For this recipe, try to buy glacéed fruits in large pieces from a good delicatessen as tubs of chopped candied peel tend to be too tough to eat raw.

PINE NUT TART

This traditional tart is an Italian version of the English Bakewell tart. The pastry case is first spread with raspberry jam, then filled with a light almond and pine nut filling.

SERVES 8

INGREDIENTS
115g/4oz/½ cup butter, softened
115g/4oz/generous ½ cup caster (superfine) sugar
1 egg
2 egg yolks
150g/5oz/1¼ cups ground almonds
115g/4oz/1 cup pine nuts
60ml/4 tbsp seedless raspberry jam (jelly)
icing (confectioners') sugar, to decorate
whipped cream, to serve (optional)

FOR THE PASTRY
175g/6oz/1½ cups plain (all-purpose) flour
65g/2½oz/⅓ cup caster (superfine) sugar
1.5ml/¼ tsp baking powder
a pinch of salt
115g/4oz/½ cup chilled butter, diced
1 egg yolk

1 Make the pastry. Sift the flour, sugar, baking powder and salt on to a cold work surface and make a well in the centre. Put the butter and egg yolk in the well and gradually work in the flour, using your fingertips. Gather the dough together. Press into a 23cm/9in fluted tart tin (pan) with a removable base. Chill for 30 minutes.

2 Meanwhile, make the filling. Cream the butter and sugar together with an electric mixer until light and fluffy, then beat in the egg and egg yolks a little at a time, alternating them with the ground almonds. Beat in the pine nuts.

3 Preheat the oven to 160°C/325°F/Gas 3. Spread the jam over the pastry base, then spoon in the filling. Bake for 30–35 minutes. Transfer to a wire rack and leave to cool. Dust with icing sugar and serve with whipped cream, if you like.

CHOCOLATE SALAMI

This after-dinner sweetmeat resembles a salami in shape, hence its curious name. It is very rich so slice it very thinly and serve with espresso coffee and amaretto liqueur.

SERVES 8–12

INGREDIENTS
24 petit beurre biscuits (cookies), broken
350g/12oz dark (bittersweet) or plain (semisweet) chocolate, broken into squares
225g/8oz/1 cup unsalted (sweet) butter, softened
60ml/4 tbsp amaretto liqueur
2 egg yolks
50g/2oz/½ cup flaked (sliced) almonds, lightly toasted and
   thinly shredded lengthways
25g/1oz/¼ cup ground almonds

1 Crush the biscuits in a food processor. Place the chocolate in a large heatproof bowl over a pan of barely simmering water. Add a small chunk of the butter and all the liqueur and heat until the chocolate melts, stirring occasionally.

2 Remove the bowl from the heat, cool slightly, then stir in the egg yolks followed by the remaining butter, a little at a time. Tip in most of the crushed biscuits and stir well to mix. Stir in the shredded almonds. Leave the mixture in a cold place for about 1 hour until it begins to stiffen.

3 Process the remaining crushed biscuits until they are very finely ground. Tip into a bowl and mix with the ground almonds. Cover and set aside.

4 Turn the chocolate and biscuit mixture on to a sheet of lightly oiled greaseproof (waxed) paper, then shape into a 35cm/14in sausage with a metal spatula, tapering the ends slightly so that the roll looks like a salami. Wrap in the paper and freeze for at least 4 hours until solid.

5 To serve, unwrap the "salami". Spread the ground biscuits and almonds out on a clean sheet of greaseproof paper and roll the salami in them until evenly coated. Transfer to a board and leave to stand for about 1 hour before serving.

RICOTTA CHEESECAKE

Low-fat ricotta cheese is excellent for cheesecake fillings because it has a good, firm texture. Here it is enriched with eggs and cream and enlivened with tangy orange and lemon rind to make a Sicilian-style dessert.

SERVES 8

INGREDIENTS
450g/1lb/2 cups low-fat ricotta cheese
120ml/4fl oz/½ cup double (heavy) cream
2 eggs, plus 1 egg yolk
75g/3oz/⅓ cup caster (superfine) sugar
finely grated rind of 1 orange
finely grated rind of 1 lemon

FOR THE PASTRY
175g/6oz/1½ cups plain (all-purpose) flour
45ml/3 tbsp caster (superfine) sugar
a pinch of salt
115g/4oz/½ cup chilled butter, diced
1 egg yolk

VARIATIONS
- Add 50–115g/2–4oz/⅓–⅔ cup finely chopped candied peel to the filling in step 3, or 50g/2oz/⅓ cup plain chocolate chips.
- For a really rich dessert, you can add both candied peel and some grated plain chocolate.

1 To make the pastry, sift the flour, sugar and salt on to a cold work surface and make a shallow well in the centre. Put the diced butter and egg yolk in the well and gradually work in the flour, using your fingertips.

2 Gather the dough together, reserve about a quarter for the lattice, then press the rest into a 23cm/9in fluted tart tin (pan) with a removable base. Chill the pastry case for about 30 minutes.

3 Meanwhile, preheat the oven to 190°C/375°F/Gas 5 and make the filling. Put all the ricotta, cream, eggs, egg yolk, sugar and orange and lemon rinds in a large bowl and beat together until evenly mixed.

4 Prick the bottom of the pastry case, then line with foil and fill with baking beans. Bake blind for 15 minutes, then transfer to a wire rack, remove the foil and beans and allow the tart shell to cool in the tin.

5 Spoon the ricotta mixture into the pastry case and level the surface. Roll out the reserved dough and cut into strips. Arrange the strips on the top of the filling in a lattice pattern, sticking them in place with water.

6 Bake the cheesecake for 30–35 minutes until golden and set. Transfer to a wire rack and leave to cool. When it is completely cooled, remove the side of the tin, leaving the cheesecake on the base and serve cold or chilled.

WALNUT & RICOTTA CAKE

This nutty whisked egg sponge contains creamy ricotta and is flavoured with orange.
Don't worry if the cake sinks slightly – it gives it an authentic appearance.

MAKES 10 SLICES

INGREDIENTS
115g/4oz/1 cup walnut pieces
150g/5oz/10 tbsp unsalted (sweet) butter, softened
150g/5oz/³⁄4 cup caster (superfine) sugar
5 eggs, separated
finely grated rind of 1 orange
150g/5oz/²⁄3 cup ricotta cheese
40g/1¹⁄2oz/6 tbsp plain (all-purpose) flour
60ml/4 tbsp apricot jam (jelly)
30ml/2 tbsp brandy
50g/2oz plain (bittersweet) chocolate, coarsely grated

1 Preheat the oven to 190°C/375°F/Gas 5. Grease and line the base of a deep 23cm/9in round, loose-based cake tin (pan). Chop the walnut pieces and toast under a preheated grill (broiler) for 1–2 minutes.

2 In a large bowl, cream together the butter and 115g/4oz/½ cup of the sugar until light and fluffy. Add the egg yolks, orange rind, ricotta cheese, flour and walnuts. Whisk the egg whites in a separate bowl until stiff, then gradually whisk in the remaining sugar. Using a large metal spoon, fold a quarter of the whisked whites into the ricotta mixture. Carefully fold in the rest of the whisked whites.

3 Tip the mixture into the prepared tin and carefully level the surface. Bake for about 30 minutes, or until risen and firm. Leave the cake to cool in the tin, then transfer to a serving plate. Heat the apricot jam in a small pan with 15ml/1 tbsp water. Press through a sieve and stir in the brandy. Use to coat the top and sides of the cake. Scatter the cake generously with grated chocolate.

APPLE CAKE

This lovely, moist cake, which is best served warm, comes from Genoa, home of the whisked sponge. When whipping the cream, add a little grated lemon rind – it tastes delicious.

SERVES 6

INGREDIENTS

115g/4oz/½ cup butter, melted and cooled, plus extra for greasing
675g/1½lb golden delicious apples
juice and finely grated rind of 1 large lemon
4 eggs
150g/5oz/¾ cup caster (superfine) sugar
150g/5oz/1¼ cups plain (all-purpose) flour
5ml/1 tsp baking powder
a pinch of salt
1 sachet of vanilla sugar and finely pared strips of citrus rind, to decorate
whipped cream, to serve

1 Preheat the oven to 180°C/350°F/Gas 4. Brush a 23cm/9in springform tin (pan) with melted butter and line the base with baking parchment. Quarter, core and peel the apples, then slice thinly. Put in a bowl and pour over the lemon juice.

2 Put the eggs, sugar and lemon rind in a bowl and whisk with an electric mixer until thick and mousse-like. The whisks should leave a trail. Sift half the flour, all the baking powder and the salt over the egg mousse, then fold in gently.

3 Slowly drizzle the melted butter into the side of the bowl and fold it in gently. Sift over the remaining flour, fold it in gently, then fold in the the apples.

4 Spoon into the prepared tin and level the surface. Bake for 40 minutes, or until a skewer comes out clean. Leave in the tin for about 10 minutes, then invert on a wire rack. Turn the cake the right way up and sprinkle the vanilla sugar over the top and decorate with the citrus rind. Serve warm, with whipped cream.

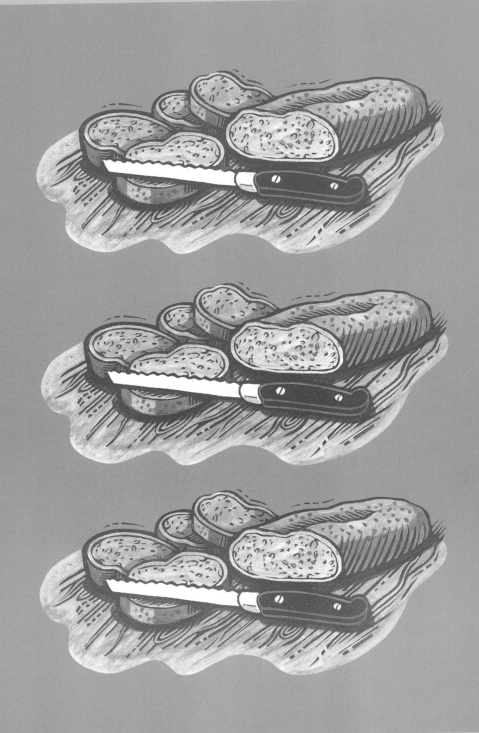

BAKING

S weet biscuits (cookies), such as amaretti and biscotti, are traditionally served at the end of a formal meal, with the coffee, or sometimes dipped in the sweet dessert wine, Vin Santo. They are often flavoured with vanilla and contain almonds or hazelnuts. Traditional breads, such as ciabatta and focaccia, are now readily available outside Italy, but the less well-known breads, such as schiacciata and pane toscano, are equally delicious. There are also sweet breads, such as panettone, which can be found everywhere in Italy around Christmas time. The Italians also use polenta and semolina in their loaves, which give a lovely nutty flavour.

AMARETTI

These sugar-encrusted macaroons are made from ground almonds, sugar and egg whites. They gain their distinctive flavour from the addition of bitter almonds. If bitter almonds are not available, make up the weight with sweet almonds.

MAKES ABOUT 36

INGREDIENTS
150g/5oz/1¼ cups almonds
50g/2oz/½ cup bitter almonds
225g/8oz/1 cup caster (superfine) sugar
2 egg whites
2.5ml/½ tsp almond essence (extract) or 5ml/1 tsp vanilla essence (extract)
flour and icing (confectioners') sugar, for dusting

1 Preheat the oven to 160°C/325°F/Gas 3. Drop the almonds into a pan of boiling water and leave to stand for 1–2 minutes. Drain, then tip onto a clean dishtowel and rub to remove the skins.

2 Place the almonds on a baking tray and let them dry out in the oven for about 10 minutes without browning. Remove from the oven and allow to cool. Tip into a food processor with half the sugar and process until finely ground.

3 Whisk the egg whites until they form soft peaks. Sprinkle in half the remaining sugar and continue beating until stiff peaks form. Gently fold in the remaining sugar and the almond or vanilla essence. Line a flat baking sheet with baking parchment and dust with flour.

4 Spoon the almond mixture into a pastry bag with a smooth nozzle. Pipe out the mixture in rounds the size of a walnut. Sprinkle lightly with the icing sugar, and allow to stand for 2 hours.

5 Near the end of standing time, preheat the oven to 180°C/350°F/Gas 4. Bake the amaretti for 15 minutes, or until pale gold. Remove from the oven and leave to cool on a rack.

BISCOTTI

These Italian almond cookies are part-baked, sliced to reveal a feast of mixed nuts, then baked again until crisp and golden. They are traditionally served with a glass of Vin Santo, into which they should be dipped.

MAKES 24

INGREDIENTS
50g/2oz/¼ cup unsalted butter, softened
115g/4oz/½ cup caster (superfine) sugar
175g/6oz/1½ cups self-raising (self-rising) flour
1.5ml/¼ tsp salt
10ml/2 tsp baking powder
5ml/1 tsp ground coriander
finely grated rind of 1 lemon
50g/2oz/½ cup polenta
1 egg, lightly beaten
10ml/2 tsp brandy or orange-flavoured liqueur
50g/2oz/½ cup unblanched almonds
50g/2oz/½ cup shelled pistachio nuts

1 Preheat the oven to 160°C/325°F/Gas 3. Lightly grease a baking sheet. Cream together the butter and sugar using a wooden spoon until smooth. Sift together the flour, salt, baking powder and ground coriander into the bowl. Add the lemon rind, polenta, egg and brandy or liqueur and mix together to make a soft dough.

2 Add the nuts to the dough and mix until evenly combined. Halve the mixture. Shape each half into a flat sausage about 23cm/9in long and 6cm/2½in wide. Place on the greased baking sheet and bake for about 30 minutes until risen and just firm. Remove from the oven and set aside to cool.

3 When cool, cut each sausage diagonally into 12 slices. Return to the baking sheet and cook for 10 minutes more until crisp. Transfer to a wire rack to cool completely. The cookies may be stored in an airtight container for up to 1 week.

HAZELNUT BITES

These little cookies are delicious served as petits fours with after-dinner coffee. They are wonderfully hard when cooled but will be soft when first removed from the oven.

MAKES ABOUT 26

INGREDIENTS
115g/4oz/½ cup butter, softened
75g/3oz/¾ cup icing (confectioners') sugar, sifted
115g/4oz/1 cup plain (all-purpose) flour, sifted
75g/3oz/¾ cup ground hazelnuts
1 egg yolk
blanched whole hazelnuts and icing (confectioners') sugar, to decorate

1 Preheat the oven to 180°C/350°F/Gas 4. Line 3–4 baking sheets with baking parchment. Place the butter and sugar in a large mixing bowl and cream together with an electric mixer until light and fluffy. Beat in the sifted flour, ground hazelnuts and egg yolk until evenly mixed.

2 Take a teaspoonful of the mixture at a time and shape it into a round with your fingers. Place the rounds well apart on the baking parchment and press a whole hazelnut into the centre of each one.

3 Bake the cookies, one tray at a time, for about 10 minutes or until golden brown, then transfer to a wire rack and sift over icing sugar. Leave to cool and harden and store in an airtight container.

> VARIATION
> *To make almond bites, use ground almonds in place of the ground hazelnuts and decorate each cookie with a blanched whole almond.*

LADIES' KISSES

These old-fashioned almond cookies from Piedmont are sandwiched together with chocolate and make great petits fours, served in frilly paper cases.

MAKES 20

INGREDIENTS

150g/5oz/10 tbsp butter, softened
115g/4oz/½ cup caster (superfine) sugar
1 egg yolk
2.5ml/½ tsp almond essence (extract)
115g/4oz/1 cup ground almonds
175g/6oz/1½ cups plain (all-purpose) flour
50g/2oz plain (semisweet) chocolate

1   Place the butter and sugar in a bowl and cream together with an electric mixer until light and fluffy, then beat in the egg yolk, almond essence, ground almonds and flour until evenly mixed. Chill for about 2 hours, until firm.

2   Preheat the oven to 160°C/325°F/Gas 3. Line 3–4 baking sheets with baking parchment. Break off small pieces of dough and roll into balls with your hands, making 40 altogether. Place the balls on the baking sheets, spacing them out as they will spread in the oven.

3   Bake the cookies for 20 minutes, or until golden. Remove the baking sheets from the oven, lift off the paper with the cookies on, then place on wire racks. Leave the cookies to cool on the paper. Repeat with the remaining mixture.

4   When the cookies are cold, lift them off the paper. Melt the chocolate in a bowl over a pan of hot water. Sandwich the cookies in pairs, with the melted chocolate. Leave to cool and set before serving.

PANETTONE

In Italy, this classic spiced yeast bread is a traditional gift at Christmas time. Even though it is rich with butter, eggs and dried fruit, it has a surprisingly light, almost dry, texture. This is often attributed to its traditional shape – a squat cylinder that has billowed out into a golden crust.

MAKES 1 LOAF

INGREDIENTS
150g/5oz/10 tbsp butter, softened, plus extra for greasing
400g/14oz/3½ cups unbleached white bread flour
2.5ml/½ tsp salt
15g/½oz fresh yeast
120ml/4fl oz/½ cup lukewarm milk
2 eggs, plus 2 egg yolks
75g/3oz/6 tbsp caster (superfine) sugar
115g/4oz/⅔ cup mixed chopped (candied) peel
75g/3oz/½ cup raisins
melted butter, for brushing

1 Using a double layer of greaseproof (waxed) paper, line and butter a 15cm/6in deep cake tin (pan) or soufflé dish. Leave the paper to protrude about 7.5cm/3in above the top of the tin.

2 Sift most of the flour and salt together into a large mixing bowl. Make a well in the centre. Put the yeast in a small bowl and cream with 60ml/4 tbsp of the milk before mixing in the remainder.

3 Pour the yeast mixture into the well in the flour, add the whole eggs and mix in sufficient flour to make a thick batter. Sprinkle a little of the remaining flour over the top and leave in a warm place, for 30 minutes.

4 Add the egg yolks and sugar and mix to a soft dough. Work in the softened butter, then turn out on to a lightly floured surface and knead for 5 minutes until smooth and elastic. Place in a lightly oiled bowl, cover with lightly oiled clear film and leave to rise, in a warm place, for 1½–2 hours, or until doubled in bulk.

5 Knock back the dough and turn out on to a lightly floured surface. Gently knead in the chopped peel and raisins. Shape into a ball and place in the prepared cake tin or soufflé dish. Cover with lightly oiled clear film and leave to rise, in a slightly warm place, for about 1 hour, or until doubled in bulk.

6 Meanwhile, preheat the oven to 190°C/375°F/Gas 5. Brush the surface of the loaf with melted butter and cut a cross in the top using a sharp knife. Bake for 20 minutes, then reduce the oven temperature to 180°C/350°F/Gas 4.

7 Brush the top with more melted butter and bake for 25–30 minutes, or until golden brown. Cool in the tin for 5–10 minutes, then turn out on to a wire rack to cool. Serve cut into wedges.

COOK'S TIPS
- *Once the dough has been enriched with butter at step 4, do not prove in too warm a place or the loaf will become greasy.*
- *Panettone can be stored in an airtight container for up to a week.*

FOCACCIA

This simple, dimple-topped Italian flat bread is the original Italian hearth bread. It is punctuated with olive oil and the aromatic flavours of fresh sage and garlic to produce a truly succulent loaf.

MAKES 2 ROUND LOAVES

INGREDIENTS
20g/³⁄₄oz fresh yeast
325–350ml/11–12fl oz/1⅓–1½ cups lukewarm water
45ml/3 tbsp extra virgin olive oil
500g/1¼lb/5 cups unbleached white bread flour
10ml/2 tsp salt
15ml/1 tbsp chopped fresh sage

FOR THE TOPPING
60ml/4 tbsp extra virgin olive oil
4 garlic cloves, chopped
12 fresh sage leaves

> ### VARIATIONS
> *Try making small rolls, focaccette, from the focaccia dough. Sprinkle with coarse sea salt and onions, or prosciutto, rather than garlic and sage and bake for 15–20 minutes or until golden.*

1 Oil 2 × 25cm/10in shallow round cake or pizza tins (pans). In a small bowl, cream the yeast with 60ml/4 tbsp of the water, then stir in the remaining water. Stir in the olive oil and mix well.

2 Sift the flour and salt together into a large bowl and make a well in the centre. Pour the yeast mixture into the well and mix to a soft dough.

3 Turn out the dough on to a lightly floured surface and knead for 8–10 minutes until smooth and elastic. Place in a lightly oiled bowl, cover with lightly oiled clear film or a large, lightly oiled polythene bag, and leave to rise, in a warm place, for about 1–1½ hours, or until the dough has doubled in bulk.

4 Knock back the dough and turn out on to a lightly floured surface. Gently knead in the chopped sage. Divide the dough into 2 equal pieces. Shape each into a ball, roll out into 25cm/10in circles and place in the prepared tins.

5 Cover with lightly oiled clear film and leave to rise in a warm place for about 30 minutes. Uncover and, using your fingertips, poke the dough to make deep dimples over the entire surface. Replace the clear film cover and leave to rise until doubled in bulk.

6 Meanwhile, preheat the oven to 200°C/400°F/Gas 6. Drizzle over the olive oil for the topping and sprinkle each focaccia evenly with chopped garlic. Dot the sage leaves over the surface.

7 Bake for 25–30 minutes, or until both loaves are golden. Immediately remove the focaccia from the tins and transfer them to a wire rack to cool slightly. These loaves are best served warm.

CIABATTA

This classic Italian bread is flavoured with olive oil and has a wonderfully chewy crust and a light, holey crumb that makes it a perfect accompaniment for soups or tomato salads as it mops up the juices beautifully. Ciabatta obtains its name from its irregular shape, which is thought to look like an old shoe or slipper.

MAKES 3 LOAVES

INGREDIENTS

FOR THE *BIGA* STARTER
7g/¼oz fresh yeast
175–200ml/6–7fl oz/¾–scant 1 cup lukewarm water
350g/12oz/3 cups unbleached plain (all-purpose) flour, plus extra
  for dusting

FOR THE DOUGH
500g/1¼lb/5 cups unbleached white bread flour, plus extra for dusting
15g/½oz fresh yeast
400ml/14fl oz/1⅔ cups lukewarm water
60ml/4 tbsp lukewarm milk
10ml/2 tsp salt
45ml/3 tbsp extra virgin olive oil

1 To make the *biga* starter, cream the fresh yeast with a little of the water in a small bowl. Sift the plain flour into a large mixing bowl. Gradually mix in the creamed yeast mixture and add enough of the remaining lukewarm water to form a firm dough.

2 Turn out the *biga* starter dough on to a lightly floured surface and knead for about 5 minutes until smooth and elastic. Return the dough to the mixing bowl, cover with lightly oiled clear film and leave in a warm place for 12–15 hours, or until the dough has risen and is starting to collapse.

3 Sprinkle 3 baking sheets with flour. In a small bowl, mix the yeast for the dough with a little of the lukewarm water until creamy, then stir in the remaining water. Add the yeast mixture to the *biga* starter dough and gradually mix in until thoroughly combined.

4 Mix the warm milk into the dough, beating with a wooden spoon until thoroughly combined. Using your hand, gradually beat in the flour, lifting the dough as you mix. Mixing the dough will take 15 minutes or more and form a very wet mix that is impossible to knead on a work surface.

5 Beat the salt and olive oil into the dough. Cover with lightly oiled clear film and leave to rise, in a warm place, for 1½–2 hours, or until doubled in bulk.

6 Using a spoon, carefully tip one-third of the dough on to a prepared baking sheet, trying to avoid knocking back the dough in the process. Divide the remaining dough between the other two baking sheets in the same way.

7 Using floured hands, shape into rough oblong loaf shapes, about 2.5cm/1in thick. Flatten slightly with splayed fingers. Sprinkle with flour and leave to rise in a warm place for 30 minutes.

8 Meanwhile, preheat the oven to 220°C/425°F/Gas 7. Bake for 25–30 minutes, or until golden brown and sounding hollow when tapped on the base. Transfer to a wire rack to cool.

VARIATIONS
- To make olive ciabatta, add 115g/4oz/1 cup halved and stoned (pitted) black or green olives with the olive oil in step 5.
- To make tomato-flavoured ciabatta, add 115g/4oz/1 cup chopped, drained sun-dried tomatoes in olive oil with the olive oil in step 5.
- To add a little spice to tomato or olive ciabatta, add 5ml/1 tsp very finely chopped fresh red chilli.

SCHIACCIATA

This Tuscan version of Italian pizza-style flat bread can be rolled out to varying thicknesses, which will give either a crisp or soft, bread-like finish.

MAKES 1 LARGE LOAF

INGREDIENTS
60ml/4 tbsp extra virgin olive oil, plus extra for greasing
350g/12oz/3 cups unbleached white bread flour, plus extra for dusting
2.5ml/½ tsp salt
15g/½oz fresh yeast
200ml/7fl oz/scant 1 cup lukewarm water

FOR THE TOPPING
30ml/2 tbsp extra virgin olive oil, for brushing
30ml/2 tbsp fresh rosemary leaves
coarse sea salt, for sprinkling

1 Lightly oil a baking sheet. Sift the flour and salt into a large bowl and make a well in the centre. Cream the yeast with half the water. Add to the centre of the flour with the remaining water and olive oil and mix to a soft dough.

2 Turn out on to a lightly floured surface and knead for 10 minutes until smooth and elastic. Place in a lightly oiled bowl, cover with lightly oiled clear film and leave to rise, in a warm place, for about 1 hour, or until doubled in bulk.

3 Knock back the dough, turn out on to a lightly floured surface and knead gently. Roll to a 30 × 20cm/12 × 8in rectangle and place on the prepared baking sheet. Brush lightly with some of the olive oil for the topping and cover with lightly oiled clear film.

4 Leave to rise, in a warm place, for about 20 minutes, then brush with the remaining oil, prick all over with a fork and sprinkle with rosemary and sea salt. Leave to rise again in a warm place for 15 minutes. Meanwhile, preheat the oven to 200°C/400°F/Gas 6. Bake for 30 minutes, or until light golden. Transfer to a wire rack to cool slightly. Serve warm.

PANE TOSCANO

This bread from Tuscany is made without salt and probably originates from the days when salt was heavily taxed. It is usually served with salty foods, such as anchovies.

MAKES 1 LOAF

INGREDIENTS
500g/1¼lb/5 cups unbleached white bread flour
350ml/12fl oz/1½ cups boiling water
15g/½oz fresh yeast
60ml/4 tbsp lukewarm water

1 First make the starter. Sift 175g/6oz/1½ cups of the flour into a large bowl. Pour over the boiling water, leave for a couple of minutes, then mix well. Cover the bowl with a damp dish towel and leave for 10 hours.

2 Lightly flour a baking sheet. In a small bowl, cream the yeast with the lukewarm water. Stir into the starter. Gradually add the remaining flour and mix to form a dough.

3 Turn out on to a lightly floured surface and knead for about 6 minutes until smooth and elastic. Place in a lightly oiled bowl, cover with oiled clear film and leave to rise, in a warm place, for 1–1½ hours until doubled in bulk.

4 Turn out the dough on to a lightly floured surface, knock back, and shape into a round. Fold the sides of the round into the centre and seal. Place seam side up on the prepared baking sheet. Cover with lightly oiled clear film and leave to rise, in a warm place, for 30–45 minutes, or until doubled in size.

5 Flatten the loaf to about half its risen height and flip over. Cover with a large upturned bowl and leave to rise, in a warm place, for 30 minutes.

6 Meanwhile, preheat the oven to 220°C/425°F/Gas 7. Slash the top of the loaf, using a sharp knife, if you like. Bake for 30–35 minutes, or until golden. Transfer to a wire rack to cool.

POLENTA BREAD

For centuries, polenta has been a staple food in the north of Italy and it is widely used in Italian cooking. Here it is combined with pine nuts to make a truly Italian bread with a fantastic flavour and glorious colour.

MAKES 1 LOAF

INGREDIENTS
25g/1oz/2 tbsp butter, plus extra for greasing
50g/2oz/½ cup polenta
300ml/½ pint/1¼ cups lukewarm water
15g/½oz fresh yeast
2.5ml/½ tsp clear honey
225g/8oz/2 cups unbleached white bread flour
45ml/3 tbsp pine nuts
7.5ml/1½ tsp salt

FOR THE TOPPING
1 egg yolk
15ml/1 tbsp water
pine nuts, for sprinkling

COOK'S TIP
Salt controls the action of yeast in bread so the leavening action is more noticeable. Don't let this unsalted bread over-rise or it may collapse.

---

1 Lightly grease a baking sheet. Mix the polenta and 250ml/8fl oz/1 cup of the water together in a pan and slowly bring to the boil, stirring continuously with a large wooden spoon. Reduce the heat and simmer for 2–3 minutes, stirring occasionally. Set aside to cool for 10 minutes, or until just warm.

2 In a small bowl, mix the yeast with the remaining water and honey until creamy. Sift 115g/4oz/1 cup of the flour into a large bowl. Gradually beat in the yeast mixture, then gradually stir in the polenta mixture to combine. Turn out on to a lightly floured surface and knead for 5 minutes until smooth and elastic.

3 Cover the bowl with lightly oiled clear film or a lightly oiled polythene bag. Leave the dough to rise, in a warm place, for about 2 hours, or until it has doubled in bulk.

4 Meanwhile, melt the butter in a small pan, add the pine nuts and cook over a medium heat, stirring, until pale golden. Set aside to cool.

5 Add the remaining flour and the salt to the polenta dough and mix to a soft dough. Knead in the pine nuts. Turn out on to a lightly floured surface and knead for 5 minutes until smooth and elastic.

6 Place in a lightly oiled bowl, cover with lightly oiled clear film and leave to rise, in a warm place, for 1 hour, or until doubled in bulk.

7 Knock back the dough and turn it out on to a lightly floured surface. Cut the dough into 2 equal pieces and roll each piece into a fat sausage about 38cm/15in long. Plait together and place on the prepared baking sheet. Cover with lightly oiled clear film and leave to rise, in a warm place, for 45 minutes. Meanwhile, preheat the oven to 200°C/400°F/Gas 6.

8 Mix the egg yolk and water and brush over the loaf. Sprinkle with pine nuts and bake for 30 minutes, or until golden and sounding hollow when tapped on the base. Cool on a wire rack.

SICILIAN SCROLL

This pale yellow, crusty-topped loaf has a delicious nutty flavour, which is obtained from the sesame seed topping. It is perfect for serving with cheese.

MAKES 1 LOAF

INGREDIENTS
oil, for greasing
450g/1lb/4 cups finely ground semolina
115g/4oz/1 cup unbleached white bread flour, plus extra for dusting
10ml/2 tsp salt
20g/³⁄₄oz fresh yeast
350ml/12½fl oz/1½ cups lukewarm water
30ml/2 tbsp extra virgin olive oil
sesame seeds, for sprinkling

1 Lightly grease a baking sheet. Mix the semolina, flour and salt together in a large bowl and make a well in the centre. In a jug (pitcher), cream the yeast with half the water, then stir in the remainder. Pour into the centre of semolina and flour with the oil. Gradually incorporate the semolina and flour to form a firm dough.

2 Turn out on to a lightly floured surface and knead for 8–10 minutes until smooth and elastic. Place in a lightly oiled bowl, cover with lightly oiled clear film and leave to rise, in a warm place, for 1–1½ hours, or until doubled in bulk.

3 Turn the dough out on to a lightly floured surface and knock back. Knead gently, then shape into a fat roll about 50cm/20in long. Form into an "S" shape. Transfer on to the prepared baking sheet, cover with lightly oiled clear film and leave to rise, in a warm place, for 30–45 minutes, or until doubled in size.

4 Meanwhile, preheat the oven to 220°C/425°F/Gas 7. Brush the scroll with water and sprinkle with sesame seeds. Bake for 10 minutes, spraying the inside of the oven with water twice. Reduce the oven temperature to 200°C/400°F/Gas 6 and bake for 25–30 minutes more, or until golden. Transfer to a wire rack to cool.

SESAME-STUDDED GRISSINI

These crisp, pencil-like breadsticks are easy to make and far more delicious than the commercially manufactured grissini. Once you start to nibble one, it will be difficult to stop eating the whole lot.

MAKES 20 GRISSINI

INGREDIENTS
30ml/2 tbsp extra virgin olive oil, plus extra for brushing
225g/8oz/2 cups unbleached white bread flour, plus extra for dusting
7.5ml/1½ tsp salt
15g/½oz fresh yeast
135ml/4½fl oz/scant ⅔ cup lukewarm water
sesame seeds, for coating

1 Lightly oil 2 baking sheets. Sift the white bread flour and salt together into a large mixing bowl and make a well in the centre. In a jug (pitcher), cream the yeast with the water. Pour into the centre of the flour with the olive oil and mix to a soft dough. Turn out on to a lightly floured surface and knead for 8–10 minutes, until smooth and elastic.

2 Roll the dough into a rectangle about 15 × 20cm/6 × 8in. Brush with olive oil, cover with lightly oiled clear film and leave to rise, in a warm place, for about 1 hour, or until doubled in bulk.

3 Preheat the oven to 200°C/400°F/Gas 6. Spread out the sesame seeds. Cut the dough into two 7.5 × 10cm/3 × 4in rectangles. Cut each piece into ten 7.5cm/ 3in strips. Stretch each strip gently until it is about 30cm/12in long.

4 Roll each strip of dough in the sesame seeds, as it is made. Place the grissini on the prepared baking sheets, spaced well apart. Lightly brush with olive oil. Leave to rise, in a warm place, for 10 minutes, then bake for 15–20 minutes. Transfer to a wire rack to cool.

INDEX

spaghetti with, 120
melon, 47
Milanese veal
    chops, 220
milk: pork braised in milk
    with carrots, 226
minestrone: Genoese
    minestrone, 94–5
    rich minestrone, 92–3
monkfish: monkfish
    medallions with tomatoes
    and thyme, 187
    monkfish with tomato
    sauce, 191
Morello cherries, 48
mortadella, 26
mozzarella, 23
    fried mozzarella, 78
    mozzarella, tomato
    and basil salad, 69
mullet see red mullet
mushrooms, 44–5
    aromatic stewed
    mushrooms, 238
    hunter's chicken, 201
    marinated vegetable
    antipasto, 70–1
    porcini and Parmesan
    risotto, 146–7
    pork chops
    with, 228
    prosciutto, mushroom
    and artichoke
    pizza, 172
    pumpkin gnocchi with
    a chanterelle parsley
    cream, 140–1
    wild mushroom
    soup, 104
mussels, 34

sautéed mussels with
    garlic, 85
stewed mussels and
    clams, 194
stuffed mussels, 84
mustard fruit
    chutney, 59

N

navy beans see
    haricot beans
nectarines, 48
Nocino, 65
nuts, 50–1
see also individual types
    of nut

O

octopus, 34
offal, 27, 29
olive oil, 56
    olive paste, 57
olives, 58
    marinated vegetable
    antipasto, 70–1
    monkfish medallions
    with tomatoes and
    thyme, 187
    pizza with onions and
    black olives, 164
    trout baked in paper
    with, 188
    turkey cutlets with, 205
onions, 38
    pizza with black
    olives and, 164
    roasted potatoes with
    red onions, 242

orange, 49
    fennel, orange and
    rocket salad, 260
orecchiette with anchovies
    and broccoli, 117
oregano, 52–3
osso buco, 222–3
oxtail, 29

P

paglia e fieno with walnuts
    and Gorgonzola, 118
pancetta, 25
    broad bean
    risotto, 151
pane Toscano, 305
panettone, 62, 298–9
panforte, 62
pansotti with herbs and
    cheese, 126–7
panzanella, 254
Parmesan, 19
parcels, grilled
    aubergine, 74–5
Parma ham, 24
    chicken with Parma ham
    and cheese, 202
    saffron risotto with
    chicken and, 153
parsley, 53
    pumpkin gnocchi with a
    chanterelle and parsley
    cream, 141
passata, 57
pasta, 10–12, 106–35
    cappelletti in broth, 90
    country pasta salad, 265
    pasta and chickpea
    soup, 100

US$14.95

THE ITALIAN COOKBOOK

Contemporary and classic recipes from every corner of Italy, with an essential cook's guide to ingredients

The essence of Italian cooking is its simplicity, relying on the delicious tastes and textures of freshly grown ingredients.

Gabriella Rossi guides you through the wonderful array of local ingredients, from the plump, sun-ripened tomatoes of the south, to the fish and shellfish of the coast, and creamy cheeses of the dairy-farming north.

A comprehensive collection of recipes includes all the classic dishes from antipasti, pastas and pizzas to fish, shellfish and meats, and from ices and desserts to cakes and breads.

Create your own taste of Italy with this mouthwatering selection, choosing from such dishes as Grilled Aubergine Parcels, Pansotti with Herbs and Cheese, Spinach and Ricotta Gnocchi, Gingered Semi-freddo, and Tiramisu.

An indispensable handbook for anyone who wants to explore the wonders of authentic Italian cooking.

ISBN 0-7548-0806-8

9 780754 808060

Jacket printed in Singapore